ALSO BY DARRELL BRICKER
AND JOHN IBBITSON

The Big Shift (2013)

ALSO BY JOHN IBBITSON

Stephen Harper (2015)
Open & Shut (2009)
The Polite Revolution (2005)
Loyal No More (2001)
Promised Land (1997)

ALSO BY DARRELL BRICKER

Canuckology (2010)
We Know What You're Thinking (2009)
What Canadians Think About Almost Everything,
    co-authored by John Wright (2005)
Searching for Certainty, co-authored by Ed Greenspon (2001)

DARRELL BRICKER AND JOHN IBBITSON

E M P T Y

P L A N E T

THE SHOCK OF GLOBAL POPULATION DECLINE

CROWN
NEW YORK

Published in the United States by Crown,
an imprint of the Crown Publishing Group,
a division of Penguin Random House LLC, New York.
crownpublishing.com

CROWN and the Crown colophon are registered trademarks
of Penguin Random House LLC.

Library of Congress Cataloging-in-Publication Data
Names: Bricker, Darrell Jay, 1961– author. | Ibbitson, John, author.
Title: Empty planet: the shock of global population decline /
    Darrell Bricker and John Ibbitson.
Description: New York: Crown Publishers, 2019 | Includes
    bibliographical references and index.
Identifiers: LCCN 2018029016 (print) | LCCN 2018031644 (ebook) |
    ISBN 9781984823236 (ebook) | ISBN 9781984823212 (hardcover) |
    ISBN 9781984823229 (pbk.)
Subjects: LCSH: Demographic transition. | Population—Social
    aspects. | Population—Economic aspects.
Classification: LCC HB887 (ebook) | LCC HB887 .B75 2019 (print) |
    DDC 304.6/2—dc23
LC record available at https://lccn.loc.gov/2018029016.

ISBN 978-1-9848-2321-2
Ebook ISBN 978-1-9848-2323-6

Printed in the United States of America

Jacket design by Taylor Boudreaux

10   9   8   7   6   5   4   3   2   1

First Edition

To Nina and Emily. Without you, there is no me.
DARRELL BRICKER

○

In memory of Barry Bartmann, mentor and dearest friend.
JOHN IBBITSON

CONTENTS

PREFACE

I t was a girl.

On Sunday, October 30, 2011, just before midnight, Danica May Camacho entered the world in a crowded Manila hospital, bringing the human population of our planet to seven billion. Actually, the scales could have tipped a few hours later, in a village in Uttar Pradesh, India, with the arrival of Nargis Kumar. Or it might have been a boy, Pyotr Nikolayeva, born in Kaliningrad, Russia.[1]

Of course, it was none of them. The birth that took us to seven billion people was attended by no cameras and ceremonial speeches because we can never know where or when the event occurred. We can only know that, according to the United Nations' best estimates, we reached seven billion sometime around October 31 of that year. Different countries designated certain births to symbolize this landmark in history, and Danica, Nargis, and Pyotr were among those chosen.

For many, there was no reason to celebrate. Indian health minister Ghulam Nabi Azad declared that a global population of seven billion was "not a matter of great joy, but a great worry. . . . For us a matter of joy will be when the population stabilizes."[2] Many share Azad's gloom. They warn of a global population crisis. *Homo sapiens* is reproducing unchecked, straining our ability to feed, house, and clothe the 130 million or more new babies that UNICEF estimates arrive each year. As humans crowd the planet, forests disappear, species become extinct, the atmosphere warms.

Unless humankind defuses this population bomb, these prophets proclaim, we face a future of increasing poverty, food shortages, conflict, and environmental degradation. As one modern Malthus put it, "Barring a dramatic decline in population growth, a rapid decrease in greenhouse gas emissions, or a global outbreak of vegetarianism—all of which are trending in the opposite direction at the moment— we're facing nothing less than the end of plenty for the majority of the earth's people."[3]

All of this is completely, utterly wrong.

The great defining event of the twenty-first century—one of the great defining events in human history—will occur in three decades, give or take, when the global population starts to decline. Once that decline begins, it will never end. We do not face the challenge of a population bomb but of a population bust—a relentless, generation-after-generation culling of the human herd. Nothing like this has ever happened before.

If you find this news shocking, that's not surprising. The United Nations forecasts that our population will grow from seven billion to eleven billion in this century before leveling off after 2100. But an increasing number of demographers around the world believe the UN estimates are far too high. More likely, they say, the planet's population will peak at around nine billion sometime between 2040 and 2060, and then start to decline, perhaps prompting the UN to designate a symbolic death to mark the occasion. By the end of this century, we could be back to where we are right now, and steadily growing fewer.

Populations are already declining in about two dozen states around the world; by 2050 the number will have climbed to three dozen. Some of the richest places on earth are shedding people every year: Japan, Korea, Spain, Italy, much of Eastern Europe. "We are a dying country," Italy's health minister, Beatrice Lorenzin, lamented in 2015.[4]

But this isn't the big news. The big news is that the largest developing nations are also about to grow smaller, as their own fertility rates come down. China will begin losing people in a few years. By the middle of this century, Brazil and Indonesia will follow suit. Even India, soon to become the most populous nation on earth, will see its numbers stabilize in about a generation and then start to decline. Fertility rates remain sky-high in sub-Saharan Africa and parts of the Middle East. Even here, though, things are changing as young women obtain access to education and birth control. Africa is likely to end its unchecked baby boom much sooner than the UN's demographers think.

Some of the indications of an accelerating decline in fertility can be found in scholarly research and government reports; others can only be found by talking to people on the street. And so we did. To gather research for this book, we traveled to cities on six continents: to Brussels and Seoul, Nairobi and São Paulo, Mumbai and Beijing, Palm Springs and Canberra and Vienna. There were other stops as well. We talked to academics and public officials, but more important, we talked to young people: on university campuses and at research institutes and in favelas and slums. We wanted to know what they were thinking about the most important decision they will ever make: whether and when to have a baby.

Population decline isn't a good thing or a bad thing. But it is a big thing. A child born today will reach middle age in a world in which conditions and expectations are very different from our own. She will find the planet more urban, with less crime, environmentally health-ier but with many more old people. She won't have trouble finding a job, but she may struggle to make ends meet, as taxes to pay for health care and pensions for all those seniors eat into her salary. There won't be as many schools, because there won't be as many children.

But we won't have to wait thirty or forty years to feel the impact of population decline. We're feeling it today, in developed nations from Japan to Bulgaria that struggle to grow their economies even as the cohort of young workers and consumers diminishes, making it harder to provide social services or sell refrigerators. We see it in urbanizing Latin America and even Africa, where women are increas-ingly taking charge of their own destinies. We see it in every house-hold where the children take longer to move out because they're in no rush to settle down and haven't the slightest intention of having a baby before they're thirty. And we're seeing it, tragically, in roiling Mediterranean seas, where refugees from wretched places press against the borders of a Europe that is already starting to empty out.

We may see it, very soon, influencing the global contest for power. Population decline will shape the nature of war and peace in the decades ahead, as some nations grapple with the fallout of their shrink-ing, aging societies while others remain able to sustain themselves. The defining geopolitical challenge in the coming decades could involve accommodating and containing an angry, frightened China as it con-fronts the consequences of its disastrous one-child policy.

Some of those who fear the fallout of a diminishing population advocate government policies to increase the number of children couples have. But the evidence suggests this is futile. The "low-fertility trap" ensures that, once having one of two children becomes the norm, it stays the norm. Couples no longer see having children as a duty they must perform to satisfy their obligation to their families or their god. Rather, they choose to raise a child as an act of personal fulfillment. And they are quickly fulfilled.

One solution to the challenge of a declining population is to import replacements. That's why two Canadians wrote this book. For decades now, Canada has brought in more people, on a per capita basis, than any other major developed nation, with little of the ethnic tensions, ghettos, and fierce debate that other countries face. That's because the country views immigration as an economic policy—under the merit-based points system, immigrants to Canada are typically better educated, on average, than the native-born—and because it embraces multiculturalism: the shared right to celebrate your native culture within the Canadian mosaic, which has produced a peaceful, prosperous, polyglot society, among the most fortunate on earth.

Not every country is able to accept waves of newcomers with Canada's aplomb. Many Koreans, Swedes, and Chileans have a very strong sense of what it means to be Korean, Swedish, or Chilean. France insists its immigrants embrace the idea of being French, even as many of the old stock deny such a thing is possible, leaving immigrant communities isolated in their *banlieues*, separate and not equal. The population of the United Kingdom is projected to continue growing, to about 82 million at the end of the century, from 66 million today, but only if the British continue to welcome robust levels of immigration. As the Brexit referendum revealed, many Brits want to turn the English Channel into a moat. To combat depopulation, nations must embrace both immigration *and* multiculturalism. The first is hard. The second, for some, may prove impossible.

Among great powers, the coming population decline uniquely advantages the United States. For centuries, America has welcomed new arrivals, first from across the Atlantic, then the Pacific as well, and today from across the Rio Grande. Millions have happily plunged into the melting pot—America's version of multiculturalism—enriching both its economy and culture. Immigration made the twentieth century the American century, and continued immigration will define the twenty-first as American as well.

Unless. The suspicious, nativist, America First groundswell of recent years threatens to choke off the immigration tap that made America great by walling up the border between the United States and everywhere else. Under President Donald Trump, the federal government not only cracked down on illegal immigrants, it reduced legal admissions for skilled workers, a suicidal policy for the U.S. economy. If this change is permanent, if Americans out of senseless fear reject their immigrant tradition, turning their backs on the world, then the United States too will decline, in numbers and power and influence and wealth. This is the choice that every American must make: to support an open, inclusive, welcoming society, or to shut the door and wither in isolation.

The human herd has been culled in the past by famine or plague. This time, we are culling ourselves; we are choosing to become fewer. Will our choice be permanent? The answer is: probably yes. Though governments have sometimes been able to increase the number of children couples are willing to have through generous child care payments and other supports, they have never managed to bring fertility back up to the replacement level of, on average, 2.1 children per woman needed to sustain a population. Besides, such programs are extremely expensive and tend to be cut back during economic downturns. And it is arguably unethical for a government to try to convince a couple to have a child that they would otherwise not have had.

As we settle into a world growing smaller, will we celebrate or mourn our diminishing numbers? Will we struggle to preserve growth, or accept with grace a world in which people both thrive and strive less? We don't know. But it may be a poet who observes that, for the first time in the history of our race, humanity feels old.

ONE

A BRIEF HISTORY OF POPULATION

W e came so close to not being at all.

There were only a few thousand humans left, maybe fewer, clinging to the shores of southern Africa, on the brink of oblivion.[5] The catastrophic eruption of Mount Toba in Sumatra 70,000-odd years ago—there's been nothing its equal since—spewed 2,800 cubic kilometers of ash into the atmosphere, spreading from the Arabian Sea in the west to the South China Sea in the east, and giving the earth the equivalent of six years of nuclear winter. Toba "is considered by some scientists to be the most catastrophic event the human species has ever endured."[6] *Homo sapiens* was already in trouble; although we had mastered tools and fire during our 130,000-year history to that point, the earth was in a cooling cycle that had wiped out much of the food supply. Now Toba made things much, much worse. We foraged for tubers and harvested shellfish in the last inhabitable African enclaves. One more bit of bad news, and that might have been the end of us.

This, at least, is one theory held by anthropologists and archeologists; there are others who suggest humans had already migrated out of Africa by this time and that the impact of Toba is exaggerated.[7] But it's hard to abandon the thought of a bedraggled humanity on the cusp of extinction struggling to nourish its few remaining young in a hardscrabble world, before the skies cleared, the earth wobbled, and the sun once again warmed the land.

But we moved slowly. The bravest humans in history might have crossed the straits between Southeast Asia and Australia some fifty thousand years ago. (Though there is new evidence suggesting they might have gotten there earlier.)[8] Some might have been swept there by accident, but others must have set out with purpose onto a sea with an unbroken horizon, simply because of what they had heard from those who had made it back alive.[9] What is now China was also being settled, and about fifteen thousand years ago humans crossed the land bridge that then connected Siberia to Alaska, beginning their long trek down the Americas. (Again, all these dates are contested.)[10]

Around twelve thousand years ago, first in the Middle East and then, independently, elsewhere around the world, the most important of all human discoveries extended our lives and increased our numbers. People started to notice that seeds dropped from grasses produced new grasses the next year. Instead of wandering from place to place, herding and hunting animals and gathering fruits and grains, it made more sense to stay put, planting and harvesting the crops and tending the livestock. But not everyone was needed in the fields, so labor began to specialize, which made things complicated, which led to government and an organized economy. The hunter-gatherers retreated slowly—a few are with us to this day in isolated settings—but civilization emerged. Sumer, Egypt, the Xia Dynasty, the Indus Valley, the Mayans.

Progress was uncertain. The rise and fall of empires signaled waning-and-waxing stress: the planet warming or cooling and wreaking havoc with harvests; the arrival of the latest viral or bacterial scourge. Knowledge was lost that had to be painfully relearned. At first the East lagged behind the West, because it had been settled later, but by the time of Christ, the Roman and Han empires were roughly equivalent—so equivalent that each might have brought about the downfall of the other. "Each evolved their own unique combination of deadly diseases," writes Ian Morris, ". . . and until 200 BCE these developed almost as if they were on different planets. But as more and more merchants and nomads moved along the chains linking the cores, the disease pools began to merge, setting loose horrors for everyone."[11]

From the dawn of civilization in Mesopotamia and Egypt around 3200 BCE through to the dawn of the Renaissance in 1300 CE, the story was the same: some combination of geography, leadership, and technological advance conferred advantage on this tribe or that people, who conquered all before them. In the peace that followed, roads were built, plows improved, laws passed, taxes gathered. Then something happened: bad harvests, contagion, far-off tumult that sent warriors fleeing or raiding from the periphery to the center, which could not hold. Collapse. Rebuild. Repeat.

Yet not all progress was lost, and as East or West or South declined, things got better elsewhere. Islam preserved knowledge lost to the West with the fall of Rome, even as India discovered the zero, which made so much possible. The latest plague produced the latest antibodies to resist it. In Eurasia, at least, immunity became a powerful tool of progress.

The planet's population grew from those few thousands in the wake of the Toba eruption to between five and ten million during the first agricultural revolution. At 1 CE there were perhaps three hundred million. By 1300 CE, with China united, enlightened, and advanced under the Song Dynasty, Islam stretching from India to Spain, and Europe finally emerging from its post-Roman Dark Age, the global population had peaked at around four hundred million.[12] And then the most terrible thing happened.

Yersinia pestis, the bacterium that causes the bubonic plague, has long been with us. One theory holds that the lands between the Black Sea and China are a "plague reservoir," where the bacillus has long been, and is still, present. (There are occasional cases in the region even today.)[13] It is not a disease that primarily infects humans; rather it is "a disease of rats in which humans participate."[14] Rats are infected by fleas that carry the bacterium; after the rat dies the flea looks for a new host, and if a human is nearby, that's it for the human. But it takes from three to five days from the time a person is bitten until they become ill, giving someone plenty of time to infect others, because plague can be transmitted between humans by airborne droplets.[15]

There had been reports of outbreaks throughout ancient times; the first fully documented episode, the Plague of Justinian, broke out in 541 CE, crippling that Byzantine emperor's hopes of recapturing the lost territories of the Roman Empire.[16] But nothing compared to the Black Death, as it was later named. Most likely a highly virulent strain of bubonic plague, it traveled either from China or the Steppes to Crimea, arriving in 1346. According to one narrative, during the siege of Caffa, on the Black Sea, Mongol soldiers hurled infected corpses over the walls, in what was perhaps the first instance of biological warfare.[17] In any event, the disease was carried by ship from Crimean to Mediterranean ports.

Europe was uniquely vulnerable. A period of global cooling had depleted harvests, leaving people hungry and with their immune systems weakened. War was also stressing local populations. But despite all the bad news, the economy and population of medieval Europe were rapidly expanding after Dark Age centuries, with unprecedented growth in travel and trade between cities and regions. For all these reasons, the disease was able to spread rapidly—two kilometers a day along major routes, with ships allowing the fleas to hopscotch into northern Europe almost immediately. Within three years, the entire continent was gripped by plague.

Eighty percent of the time the infected person died, usually within a week of the first symptoms. The progress of the disease is described in a nursery rhyme:

> *Ring around the rosie*: buboes—a swelling of the lymph node in the groin, armpit, or neck—were ring-like and rose-colored in the center, and a sure sign of the disease.
> *A pocket full of posies*: As the disease progressed, the body would begin to rot from within. The smell was so awful the living would carry around packets of flowers as air fresheners.
> *Atch-chew! Atch-chew!* (or regional variations): Victims also suffered from headaches, dark rashes, vomiting, fever—and laboured breathing or sneezes.
> *We all fall down*: Death.[18]

While there is much debate based on little evidence as to how much China and India were affected,[19] at least a third of Europe was extinguished in the space of a few years—some estimates place the figure as high as 60 percent.[20] "All the citizens did little else except to carry dead bodies to be buried," wrote one chronicler in Florence, where more than half of the population was wiped out in the space

of a few months. The dead were thrown into pits, which were sometimes too shallow, and dogs would unearth and chew on the corpses.[21]
The plague shattered governments, undermined the authority of the
Catholic Church, stoked inflation because of shortages caused by
the disruption to trade, and encouraged hedonistic excess among
the survivors, because why not? It took hundreds of years, in some
regions, for the population to return to its former level.[22]

But though it seems hard to credit, some of the consequences
of the *magna pestilencia* were beneficial. Labor shortages weakened
the bond between serf and lord, increasing labor mobility and
workers' rights, and spurring productivity. Overall, wages rose faster
than inflation. Feudalism ultimately collapsed, with owners con-
tracting the services of laborers instead. Europeans had shunned
long sea voyages because of the high mortality rate. But now that
mortality rates on land were also so high, the risk seemed more
worthwhile. The plague might actually have helped launch the
European era of exploration and colonization.[23]

However, that colonization led, tragically, to even more horrific
loss of life in the New World, as European explorers, pillagers, and
then settlers introduced their diseases to the defenseless indigenous
populations of Central, South, and North America. Again, the actual
loss of life is hard to calculate, but at least half the American population perished in the wake of contact with Europeans,[24] making it "possibly the greatest demographic disaster in the history of the world."[25]
Some estimates of population loss reach beyond 90 percent.[26]
Smallpox was particularly virulent and lethal.

Pestilence, famine, and war combined to keep the human population in check throughout the middle centuries of the last millennium. If there were, perhaps, four hundred million people on earth
in 1300, there were not many more than six hundred million in 1700.[27]
The world was locked in Stage One of the Demographic Transition

Model, developed in 1929 by the American demographer Warren Thompson. In Stage One, which encompassed all of humanity from the dawn of the species until the eighteenth century, both birth rates and death rates are high, and population growth is slow and fluctuating. Hunger and disease are part of the problem: in medieval Europe, a typical Stage One society, about one third of all children died before the age of five, and if you did manage to grow up, chronic malnutrition meant that disease would probably carry you off in your fifties.

If, that is, you weren't killed. War and crime were constant threats in pre-industrial societies. And prehistory was even more violent. As Steven Pinker has observed, almost all prehistoric human specimens that have been preserved in bogs, ice fields, and the like show evidence of having died violently. "What is it about the ancients that they couldn't leave us an interesting corpse without resorting to foul play?" he wondered.[28] Hardly surprising, then, that from our first days until the Enlightenment, whether in China or the Americas or Europe or anywhere else, the population grew slowly if it grew at all.

But in eighteenth-century Europe, the curve began to bend upward. By 1800, the global population had passed one billion. The earth had added more people in a single century than in the previous four centuries combined. Europe had progressed from Stage One in the Demographic Transition Model to Stage Two: a high birth rate, but a gradually declining death rate. So why were people living longer?

Well, for one thing, the gaps between plague outbreaks were getting longer and longer, and the severity less and less, thanks to improvements in agricultural productivity that bolstered the local diet and made people more resistant to disease. (We'll talk more about this further on.) With the end of the traumatic Thirty Years War in 1648, Europe entered a period of relative calm that would last for more than a century. Peace brought new investments in infrastructure, such as canals, that increased trade and raised living standards. Corn, potatoes, and tomatoes, imported from the New World, fortified the European diet. "The coming together of the continents was a prerequisite for the population explosion of the past two centuries, and certainly played a role in the Industrial Revolution," argues historian Alfred Crosby.[29] But of course, the real cause of increasing lifespans was the Industrial Revolution itself: the acceleration in scientific and industrial knowledge that bequeathed the world we inhabit today. James Watt's steam engine went into commercial use in the remarkable year of 1776. (Also in that year, Adam Smith wrote *The Wealth of Nations* and the United States declared its independence from Great Britain.) Mechanized production accelerated productivity—the factory, the railway, the telegraph, electric light, the internal combustion engine. Those last three inventions were American; the United States was growing in wealth and power and confidence in the wake of its civil war.

Thanks to the industrial and agricultural revolutions, people started living longer. Now that famine and pestilence were on the wane, couples married earlier and had more children. And those children were more likely to survive, thanks to improved sanitation and the introduction of the smallpox vaccine, another scientific leap. The Victorian era was the first in human history to witness rapid and sustained population growth, as Europe and the United States raced to catch up with Great Britain. This is what any society looks like as it enters Stage Two. The most miserable places in the world today remain locked in it: people living longer, people having many babies, growth benefiting the few more than the many, poverty still rampant.

Industrial-revolutionary life in the nineteenth century was certainly miserable for most. People worked impossible hours in dreary, dangerous factories and lived in horrid, overcrowded slums that were disease incubators. Europe was ripe for a few bad harvests, increasing hunger, and another plague. But this time the march of science outpaced the march of germs. The story of the Broad Street pump best explains why.

Trade and the Raj brought the bacterium *vibrio cholerae* from its ancient home in the Ganges Delta to Europe via Russia, reaching Britain in 1831. Even today, cholera kills upward of 120,000 people a year in the poorest parts of the world; in the nineteenth century, the impact on Europe was devastating. When cholera arrived at Sunderland, its port of entry in England, 215 people perished.[30] As the disease marched up the island, tens of thousands died as doctors looked on helplessly. This was something they'd never seen before. (Not that their treatments for known ailments helped much anyway.) The disease accompanied the Industrial Revolution: industrialization and urbanization had swollen cities enormously— London in 1860 was the largest city in the world, with a population of 3.2 million—creating equally enormous health risks, with people living in appallingly unsanitary conditions. There were two hundred thousand private cesspools in the city at the time of the outbreak; waste and refuse filled the ditches and lined the alleys.[31] But the revolution was also transforming the sciences, especially medicine, with received wisdom forced to give way to empirical inquiry.

Cholera was believed to be inhaled through miasma, or tainted air. Doctors treated the stricken with opiates and leaches. Combating infection by draining blood from the victim was still a popular remedy, despite centuries of evidence that the treatment was useless or harmful. At least the opiates eased the agony.

One obscure physician, John Snow, was personally convinced that cholera was waterborne rather than airborne. An outbreak of the disease that began on August 31, 1854, in the London district of Soho, gave Snow a chance to prove his theory. Within ten days, five hundred were dead, with the survivors fleeing the area. But Snow didn't flee. Instead, he visited the homes of the victims, interviewing the families, retracing the steps of those who had fallen ill, and plotting deaths on a map of the neighborhood. He quickly realized that nearly all the victims shared one thing in common: they lived near, or had drawn water from, the pump on Broad Street. Drawing water himself from the pump and examining it under a microscope, Snow discovered what he called "white, flocculent particles." These, he correctly deduced, were the source of the disease.

Though his theory flew in the face of received wisdom, Snow managed to convince skeptical civic officials to remove the handle from the Broad Street pump, forcing residents to look elsewhere for water. The outbreak ended instantly.[32] Though it took years to overcome conservative resistance, the stubborn truth of Snow's observation prompted planners to begin work on the first modern urban sewage system. Opened in 1870, the tunnels of the London sewers were so well built that they remain in good working order to this day.

Though still largely unheralded, John Snow's contribution to human well-being was extraordinary: within the field, he is known as "the father of epidemiology."[33] He advanced human understanding of disease generally and advanced as well the importance of public health as a government priority. While cholera continued to ravage the rest of Europe, it disappeared from London, which the rest of Europe noticed. Before long, protecting the water supply became crucial to urban planners and politicians in every advanced nation. Medicine, too, was leaping ahead, especially in the areas of anesthetics and disinfectants. The infant mortality rate plunged, even as life expectancy increased and the fertility rate remained high. In 1750, the population of England and Wales was just under six million, about where it had been when the Black Death struck. By 1851, it was almost eighteen million; by 1900 it was thirty-three million.[34] Humanity was off to the races.

We think of the first half of the twentieth century as a time of unparalleled killing: more than sixteen million military and civilian deaths in the First World War; more than fifty-five million in the Second. The period also witnessed the last great pandemic: a vicious influenza known as the Spanish flu at the end of the First World War that killed between twenty million and forty million people. The pandemic was so terrible that it killed more Americans than died in the war. Nonetheless, population growth continued apace, decade after decade. In parts of the world, the growth would be so strong that it became alarming. In other, more advanced, parts of the world, population growth was more modest. In fact, in places like the United States, population growth slowed to the point where it almost ceased. To understand the twentieth century, we must understand two things: why death rates continued to fall, and why in some places birth rates started to fall as well—Stage Three of the Demographic Transition Model. Looking at Sweden helps us understand both trends.

The Swedes love to keep records. By 1749, they had established a statistical office, providing us with some of the first reliable data on population characteristics. The data contains fascinating insights into what was happening there—and, presumably, elsewhere in Europe and in North America. Until about 1800 the birth rate was only slightly higher than the death rate in Sweden. Infant mortality was heartbreakingly high, with 20 percent of all babies dying before their first birthday, and 20 percent of those who remained dying before their tenth.[35] Sweden, in other words, was a typical Stage One society, with both high birth and death rates. But not long after the nineteenth century arrived, Stage Two kicked in: the birth rate remained high, but the death rate began to slowly decrease, thanks to improved sanitation and nutrition. By 1820, Sweden's population was starting to grow rapidly; it had already climbed from 1.7 million in 1750 to two million. By 1900 it had exceeded five million. It would have grown even higher, had Sweden not entered Stage Three: a slowly declining death rate but also a declining birth rate.

Why was the fertility rate declining? Indisputably, the most important factor is urbanization. There is overwhelming evidence that as societies become more economically developed, they become more urban, and once a society urbanizes, fertility rates start to decline. But why, exactly?

In the Middle Ages, 90 percent of Europeans lived on farms. But the factories that accompanied the Industrial Revolution concentrated workers in cities. On a farm, a child is an investment—an extra pair of hands to milk the cow, or shoulders to work the fields. But in a city a child is a liability, just another mouth to feed. That trend continues to this day. In a 2008 study on urbanization and fertility in Ghana, the authors concluded that "urbanization reduces fertility because urban residence would likely increase the costs of raising children. Urban housing is more expensive, and children are probably less valuable in household production."[36] It may seem selfish, but parents who live in cities are only acting in their own economic interest by reducing the size of the litter.

Another factor was—and in the developing world still is—in play, a factor that we consider as important as urbanization itself. Cities have schools and libraries and other cultural institutions. In the nineteenth century, for the first time, mass media existed, in the form of newspapers. In the 1800s, a woman living in Chicago would have a better chance of learning about methods of birth control than a woman living on a farm downstate. Moving to cities, women started to become better educated, and as they became better educated, their subjugation at the hands of men became not the natural order of things but a wrong that needed to be made right. First, women campaigned for equality under the law in areas such as property and pensions. Then they campaigned for the vote. Then they campaigned for the right to work, and for equal pay with men. And as women won more rights and greater power, they stopped having so many children.

After all, babies are not always good news for women. In the nineteenth century, they posed a serious health risk, especially for women who had large numbers of children. Even today, with advanced maternal and neo-natal care, children are a burden to feed and raise. They also limit a woman's ability to work outside the home—work that can lead not only to more income but to more autonomy. As one researcher at the World Bank noted, "the higher the level of a woman's educational attainment, the fewer children she is likely to bear."[37]

In 1845, a new law granted Swedish women equal inheritance rights. By the 1860s, the fertility rate in Sweden had started to decline. By 1921, women had the vote. By 1930, the fertility rate in Sweden was once again only slightly higher than the death rate, but now both rates were much, much lower—less than half what they had been a century before. Sweden was entering Stage Four of the Demographic Transition Model, in which the birth rate is at or near the level needed to sustain the population, even as the death rate continues to decline. Stage Four is a Goldilocks-like stage: at this point a healthy, long-lived society produces just enough babies to keep the population stable or slowly growing.

The United Kingdom, France, Australia—most of the countries of the developed world more or less matched the Swedish model, as the Industrial Revolution of the nineteenth century and the knowledge revolution of the twentieth century transformed societies.

Meanwhile, a comparison with Chile, Mauritius, and China shows all three countries—part of what used to be called the Third World—growing more slowly, with both birth and death rates much higher than in the developed world.

While it took until the 1860s for the fertility rate to start declining in Sweden, in some advanced countries it began to come down earlier. In the United States and Britain, the arc began to bend downward in the early 1800s. Women still had lots of children; they just didn't have as many as before. In the U.S., for example, white women (there is no available data on African American or Native American women) gave birth to, on average, seven children in the early 1800s. By 1850, the average was 5.4. By 1900, it was 3.6. Over the course of the nineteenth century, the fertility rate in the United States fell by nearly half. By 1940, on the eve of America's entry into the Second World War, it was down to 2.2, barely above the level of 2.1 babies per woman needed to sustain a population.[38]

The popular conception of fertility decline is that it began in the 1970s, after the baby boom. But no. Prior to the baby boom, birth rates in advanced economies had been declining, in some cases, for a century and a half.

A quick aside: The term *fertility rate* has a crude, even offensive, baby-producing-machine sound to some ears. It is a term used by demographers to describe the number of children a woman is expected to produce, on average, in her lifetime. Although the terms *fertility rate* and *birth rate* have different meanings to demographers, we use them here interchangeably to avoid repetition. And in case you're wondering why the replacement rate is 2.1 and not 2.0, the 0.1 is needed to counteract childhood mortality and the premature deaths of some women.

———

We've seen why the fertility rate fell through the nineteenth and early twentieth centuries. But why did the death rate continue to decline, despite the horrors of the world wars and the depredations of the Spanish flu? Most people would point to advances in medicine: new treatments and vaccines for diseases, improvements in surgery and internal medicine, the wonder drugs that knocked down once-lethal infections, progress in fighting heart disease and cancer. But an even more important development still gets relatively little press. The first years of the twentieth century witnessed a revolution in public health—a revolution led by someone as important as John Snow and even less heralded. His name was John Leal.

Thanks to Dr. Snow, by the dawn of the twentieth century, improved sewers in advanced countries had reduced the danger of waterborne contamination. But sewers couldn't eliminate the risk, because the sewage ended up in the water eventually, and people drank the water. How could the water itself be purified?

The Swedish chemist Carl Wilhelm Scheele had discovered chlorine in 1774, and a century later German and English researchers had started using it to decontaminate pipes after a disease outbreak. There had even been a few crude, temporary efforts at chlorinating water in England and Germany. But the big breakthrough came in Jersey City, N.J., in 1908. The city's water supply had been a problem for decades, leading to regular outbreaks of typhoid fever and other diseases. In 1899, the city contracted with the Jersey City Water Supply Company to fix the problem. The company, in turn, hired John Leal, a local doctor with a strong interest in public health, to identify and remove sources of contamination.

The son of a small-town physician, Leal had watched his father suffer and die from dysentery, giving him a lifelong obsession with combating infectious disease.[39] He knew about the European experiments in chlorination and decided the real solution lay in permanently chlorinating Jersey City's water supply, even though public sentiment and many scientists condemned the idea. Willful, even reckless, Leal decided to act, hiring contractors who, in only ninety-nine days, constructed the first functioning water chlorination system. On September 26, 1908, without bothering to get anyone's permission, Leal began chlorinating the water in the Jersey City reservoir. Thank God, he got the concentration right; had he been wrong, Leal could have poisoned an entire city. The next year, when the city for the second time sued the Jersey City Water Supply Company, claiming the city's water was still unacceptably contaminated, the judge noted the amazing decline in infectious diseases that had resulted from chlorination, and found for the defendant. Leal's system worked.

Word spread as swiftly as infection. Within six years, half of all Americans served by municipal water supplies were drinking chlorinated water. Authorities in North America and Europe moved as quickly as their budgets permitted to introduce chlorination. The effect on public health was staggering. In 1908, when Leal first added chlorine to Jersey City's water supply, typhoid fever killed twenty out of every one hundred thousand Americans annually. By 1920, just twelve years later, it was down to eight per one hundred thousand. By 1940, a scourge as ancient as the race had effectively been eradicated in the developed world.

Chlorination was one of the great advances in the war against disease. But medicine is sexier than public health. Anyone who knows anything about medical history knows that Frederick Banting and Charles Best led the team of Canadian researchers that discovered the role insulin plays in diabetes and a method for manufacturing it. But who has heard of John Leal?[40]

By the middle of the twentieth century, breakthroughs in combating disease and in public health had hugely expanded life expectancy. A girl born in Australia in 1890 could expect to live fifty-one years. A girl born in Australia in 1940 could expect to live well into her sixties.[41] But even as the death rate declined, so too did the fertility rate, thanks to increasing urbanization and the growing empowerment of women. In 1931, when Australia began keeping such statistics, the fertility rate was already down to 2.4 babies per woman, just above the replacement rate of 2.1.[42] For the whole developed world, the first half of the twentieth century was a period of improved life expectancy but reduced fertility, leading to smaller and smaller families and less and less growth in population—a classic Stage Four population model. Meanwhile, the great majority of the planet's population suffered through the age-old misery of Stage One: a very high death rate and a very high birth rate, despite the so-called blessings of imperial rule by Britain, France, the United States or, God help you, Belgium.

And then, at the end of the last world war, all the patterns exploded, with both the developed and developing worlds flinging themselves into gyrations of fertility that we still live with today.

By the middle of 1943, it was clear to the leadership on both sides that the United Nations, as the Allies called themselves, would win the war against the Axis powers of Germany, Italy, and Japan. But what would come next? Planners in Washington knew what happened after the First World War. As governments wound down their war machines and the boys came home, unemployment rose, made worse by government moves to ward off inflation through increased interest rates, which brought on a sharp recession. The euphoric interlude of the Roaring Twenties ended on October 29, 1929, Black Tuesday, when the New York stock market crashed, bringing with it a decade of depression the likes of which the modern world had never seen. The aftermath of the First World

War helped create the conditions for the Second. Would history repeat itself? Would the end of war bring recession and unemployment and maybe even another depression? Harry Colmery was determined to prevent that.

Another man whose name was nearly lost to history, Colmery grew up in Braddock, Pennsylvania, working in his father's grocery store, holding down a paper route and also working part-time for the Union Pacific Railroad. That kind of industriousness got him to Oberlin College and then the University of Pittsburgh, where he earned a law degree. Before he could start to practice, however, the First World War arrived. Harry enlisted, training pilots stateside. After being discharged in 1919, he married and moved to Topeka, Kansas, where he lived and practiced law the rest of his life. Kind, compassionate, modest, Colmery was much loved in his adopted home town. But if Colmery lacked ego, he didn't lack conviction. He was appalled by the war veterans he saw in Topeka—"maimed and diseased; some grope with blinded eyes; some hobble on canes"[43]—who had been left to fend for themselves by an indifferent federal government.

Colmery became involved in the new American Legion, serving as its president in 1936–37. When the Second World War arrived, he worked as a planner within the Legion, advising the federal government. Democrats and Republicans, politicians and bureaucrats, civilians and generals fiercely debated whether and how to help veterans once the war was over. Colmery was convinced he had the answer. Shutting himself up in a room in Washington's Mayflower Hotel, he wrote out his proposal for reintegrating servicemen back into American life after the war.[44] Of all the plans for postwar reconstruction, his was the one that Franklin Delano Roosevelt and his advisers seized on, using Colmery's handwritten sheets as the basis for the Servicemen's Readjustment Act of 1944, better known as the

G.I. Bill. It didn't hurt that the Legion fought to get the bill through Congress, which ultimately passed it unanimously. Colmery stood beside the president as he signed the bill into law.

The G.I. Bill created the modern middle class. Thanks to its offer of free tuition and other education assistance, eight million veterans obtained a degree, diploma, or on-the-job training. Thanks to low-interest mortgages and other forms of housing support, 4.3 million veterans bought homes.[45] The G.I. Bill, coupled with the technological advances of the war, created the suburbs—and the freeways that linked those suburbs to each other and the city core. Almost everyone could afford a car and a modest home, complete with a newfangled television that Mom and Dad would watch in the evening with the kids. Lots and lots of kids.

Birth rates, which had been declining for decades, through boom and bust and peace and war, exploded. The Depression and the war had probably suppressed the birth rate below where it naturally would have been; postwar affluence certainly convinced many couples to marry younger and have more children. In any case, a fertility rate that had been declining since 1800 reversed itself, reaching 3.7 by the mid-fifties, back near where it had been at the turn of the century. It that sense, *Leave It to Beaver*, the popular 1950s comedy, was an anomaly. The Cleavers should have had 1.7 more children. Wally and the Beaver needed a sister.

In their own way, the Cleavers were inadvertent icons of propaganda. The family, everyone believed, consisted of a husband and wife and the children they produced. Though the image seemed eternal, in fact it had never before existed. Prior to the twentieth century, families were more extended and more fluid. A young married couple might live with one of their parents, until they got established or the overcrowding became intolerable. With mortality rates so high, it was anything but surprising if children lost a parent. The widow or widower would remarry, often creating two sets of siblings in a single household. Children might be sent to live with uncles or aunts or whatever arrangement seemed best—or least worst. Families were contingent. Had there been television in Victorian times, the hit show would have been *The Brady Bunch*.

Only after the war, with rising affluence and the arrival of modern medicine and advanced public health, could a couple reasonably expect to live on their own soon after marriage, and parents reasonably expect to live into their seventh or eighth decade and produce children who were almost certain to do the same. Christian and familial conventions, which had always condemned both bastardy and divorce, pushed for early marriage and large families, the surest way to tame the young, especially young men. The "baby boom," as it became known, was an experiment, as much as anything, in creating the nuclear family as the social and moral anchor of society. *Leave It to Beaver* was an idealized depiction of the suburban, nuclear, middle-class family to which everyone was supposed to aspire. The reaction against the experiment of the baby boom, and its accompanying propaganda, we called the sixties. Canada and Europe matched the United States in both policies and fertility, though the boom started later in West Germany, which needed a decade to rebuild and to see its own economic miracle, the *Wirtschaftswunder*, take hold. Throughout the developed world, mothers had a lot more children in the late 1940s and throughout the 1950s, until the curve began to bend in the 1960s back toward the close-to-replacement rate that it had reached at the outbreak of the war.

The baby boom is best seen as an anomaly. The affluence and exuberance that arrived with peacetime produced a temporary, one-generation blip, before the historical trend reasserted itself. The boom was a fluke, and one that certainly can't explain the massive growth in the global population that marked the second half of the twentieth century. For that, we must look elsewhere.

The developed nations of Europe and North America passed through Stage Two—in which the fertility rate remains high but the mortality rate starts to decline—over the course of the nineteenth and early twentieth centuries. The rest of the planet experienced it all at once, just as all the old flags started coming down and the maps were redrawn, then redrawn again.

At the end of the Second World War, the Allies dominated the planet, either as colonial powers or as victors in war. With victory came guilt: how could the Allies have been fighting for freedom while at the same time oppressing millions of colonial subjects? With victory came also the United Nations, the organization created by the winning powers to represent all the nations of the earth, with a mandate to ameliorate poverty and preserve the peace. As a peace-keeper, the UN proved to be a flawed chalice, but over the past half century it has succeeded in bringing food and at least the fundamentals of Western medicine and public health to the poorest of the earth, through its agencies of many acronyms—the WHO, WFP, UNESCO, UNICEF,[46] and others. Other forms of aid arrived directly, from former colonial powers or other developed nations who were just trying to do good—and maybe do well by having their businesses provide the aid and enter the local market as a result. A vast amount of this aid was squandered through corruption or poor planning. In some places, especially Africa, postcolonial life deteriorated. But in much of the world, year over year, things got better.

Yellow fever, dengue, malaria, Ebola. Through treatment, vaccination, and improvements in public health, such as clean drinking water and sewage treatment, foreign aid and economic development are rolling back the scourge of disease. Improved nutrition has also helped, thanks to the Green Revolution that we'll be looking at in the next chapter. Across the planet, even the poorest of the poor are living longer. In Ethiopia, which has often been wracked by famine and civil war, life expectancy improved from thirty-four years of age in 1950 to fifty-nine years in 2009; in Haiti, the poorest country in the Western Hemisphere, it went from thirty-eight to sixty-one over the same period.[47] Overall, the global average life expectancy has doubled to seventy years since 1900. As life expectancy improved in the developing world, and fertility rates remained high, the global population took off, from one billion around 1800, as we've already seen, to two billion by around 1927, to three billion by 1959, to four billion by 1974, to five billion by 1987, to six billion at the turn of the millennium, to seven billion today.[48]

Overall, foreign aid has been a blessing for the developing world. These days, the total reaches about $150 billion a year, one fifth of which is provided by the United States. That kind of money can help; in recent years, as donor countries have absorbed lessons learned from the past, foreign aid has done an especially good job at protecting maternal health. As we will see in a later chapter, economic growth in India and China also helped reduce global poverty and increase life expectancy.

The decades in which the developing world remained locked in Stage Two of population growth—with life expectancy increasing even as fertility rates remained high—account for the explosion of population since the Second World War. But look at those global population numbers again. It took about 125 years to double the planetary population from one billion to two billion. It took only three decades to get it to three billion, and fifteen years to get it to four billion, thirteen years to get it to five billion, and another thirteen years to get it to six billion. About the same amount of time got us to seven billion, and it will take, yes, around thirteen years to get us to eight billion.

The rate of increase has stabilized and begun to slow. And in the coming decades it will slow even more, stop, and then reverse. That's because much of the developing world has entered Stage Three: a declining mortality rate but a falling birth rate as well. Other developing countries have reached the Goldilocks stage of Stage Four: a stable birth rate along with increasing life expectancy. The real surprise is that most developed and many developing societies have passed into a new stage.

Remember what causes fertility to decline: urbanization. It removes the need for young brawn to work the farm and makes children, instead, an economic liability, and it empowers women, who invariably choose to have fewer children once they have control over their own bodies. Those two factors became entrenched in the developed world in the nineteenth and twentieth centuries. But now these forces are at work in developing societies as well. In 2007, the UN declared that on May 23, the world had become, for the first time in human history, more urban than rural.[49] (The UN just loves picking arbitrary symbolic dates.) Urbanization and the empowerment of women are having the same effect on developing countries that they had on developed countries, only everything is happening much, much faster. Across the planet, birth rates are plunging. That plunge is everything. That plunge is why the UN forecasts are wrong. That plunge is why the world is going to start getting smaller, much sooner than most people think.

TWO

MALTHUS AND SONS

"Soylent Green is people!" a horrified New York detective, played by Charlton Heston, shouts in warning. A global population of eighty billion has ravaged the environment, leaving only a plankton-based food produced by the Soylent Corporation to sustain humanity. At least everyone *thought* it was plankton.[50]

Soylent Green, released in 1973, was set in the year 2022. It is one in a long list of films, books, documentaries, and other entertainments based on the notion that overpopulation is destroying the planet's environment and outstripping the food supply, which must inevitably lead to an apocalypse. One of the most recent is *Inferno*, a simply awful film starring Tom Hanks, in which a billionaire scientist, Bertrand Zobrist, concludes that the earth is on the brink of a catastrophic population explosion—"It's one minute to midnight," he warns—and the only solution is to unleash a virus he has concocted that will kill half the people on earth.[51] Only Hanks, our hero, can stop him. No one in the film questions Zobrist's premise; they just don't like his solution.

All this is rot. The earth's population won't be eighty billion in 2022; it will be on its way to eight billion, though that's more than enough. Although the current population is straining the environment, contributing to species extinction and global warming, nothing apocalyptic is on the horizon. And a growing body of demographers are convinced that, far from continuing to expand, the earth's population will stabilize and then start to decline somewhere around the middle of the century.

Before we debunk the myth of a population explosion, let's look at how it came about. Then we'll try to explain why conventional wisdom really isn't very wise at all.

Thomas Robert Malthus (1766–1834) was a good man. His highly enlightened father, who had his son home-schooled, was a friend of the philosopher David Hume and a fan of the revolutionary French philosopher Jean-Jacques Rousseau. Gentle of disposition, Thomas did well at Cambridge and took holy orders, but his lack of clerical ambition and a cleft palette that hampered his oratorical abilities landed him in a small parish in Surrey, where he was distressed by the poverty and malnutrition that surrounded him. Later in life, he became an academic—the first person in Britain to be called a professor of political economy. When he was young, he advocated state support for the poor (though he later changed his mind), and his theories about the need for increased public spending during economic downturns anticipated John Maynard Keynes.[52] But he is remembered for none of this. Instead, he spawned an adjective: *Malthusian*, one of the darker words in the English language.

In 1798, Malthus published *An Essay on the Principle of Population as It Affects the Future Improvement of Society*, which started out as a pamphlet and ended, several decades and editions later, as a large tome. In the essay, Malthus asked the fundamental question that obsessed those engaged in the infant social sciences: "Whether man shall henceforth start forwards with accelerated velocity towards illimitable, and hitherto unconceived improvement; or be condemned to a perpetual oscillation between happiness and misery."[53] For Malthus, the answer was oscillation. He observed that, although humankind had progressed in industry and art and thought, "towards the extinction of the passion between the sexes, no progress whatever has hitherto been made."[54] Because people liked sex so much, they had many babies, and as a result the population, unhindered, would always grow at a geometric rate, while improvements in agriculture and food production only occurred at an arithmetic rate. "A slight acquaintance with numbers will shew the immensity of the first power in comparison of the second."[55] Therefore, just as rabbit or deer or other animal populations explode and collapse, so too must that of *Homo sapiens.*

In some ways, Malthus is misunderstood. In his writing, he shows genuine concern for the poor, whose misery is hidden because "the histories of mankind that we possess, are histories only of the higher classes."[56] It was the lower orders that suffered the most through the endless and grim oscillations, Malthus declared. A temporary increase in affluence, perhaps as a result of good harvests, new land brought under cultivation, or improvements in agricultural practices, would cause members of what we call the working class to breed with abandon. But inevitably, they would overreproduce. Overpopulation caused the price of labor to fall and the price of food to rise. People starved. Ultimately parents stopped having children they knew they couldn't feed, population declined, stability returned. In such circumstances, Malthus concluded, offering relief to the poor only worsened their already miserable situation by postponing the inevitable.

"This natural inequality of the two powers of population, and of production in the earth . . . form the great difficulty that to me appears insurmountable," he wrote. ". . . No fancied equality, no agrarian regulations in their utmost extent, could remove the pressure of it . . . and it appears, therefore, to be decisive against the possible existence of a society, all the members of which, should live in ease, happiness, and comparative leisure."[57] The poor, in other words, will always be with us, in numbers that rise and fall depending on circumstance, but with sustained population growth and sustained increased prosperity impossibly at odds with each other.

Malthus's prophesy was grim, implacable, and wrong. For at the very time that he was working out his theories, the population of the earth had reached, for the first time in human history, one billion people. A century later it would be two billion. Today it is seven billion. And yet almost all of us today live longer, healthier, happier lives than the poor of England in the time of Malthus.

This pioneer political economist, who lived much of his life among the green fields of Hertfordshire, literally stood in the middle of the explanation for why his theory was hopelessly flawed. By 1798, the British agricultural revolution was already a century old. It began with the enclosures, in which powerful men banished peasant farmers from communally owned fields. To this day, poets lament the theft, but farmers who controlled their fields could innovate so as to maximize yields and profits. New experiments in selective breeding took the average weight of a cow carcass from 370 pounds in 1710 to 550 pounds in 1795.[58] People like Viscount Charles "Turnip" Townsend experimented with turnips, clover, and other crops to improve soil quality and reduce the need for fallow fields.[59] And then there were the inventions: Jethro Tull's seed drill, the threshing machine, the reaping machine, the all-iron plow. When he first wrote his essay, Malthus had no access to a census (the British conducted their first in 1801), but we estimate today that the population of England and Wales in 1700 was about 5.5 million. By the time Malthus wrote his treatise, it was over 9 million.[60] Britain was at the leading edge of a global revolution in agriculture and industry, accompanied by a population explosion that never went into reverse because the former easily sustained the latter.

That hasn't, however, dimmed the determination of some writers who were convinced that Malthus was simply premature. The most popular and doom-laden prediction of overpopulation leading to population collapse came a century and a half later. Published in 1968, *The Population Bomb* was a big bestseller by Stanford University biologist Paul Ehrlich. The book begins with a single, simple, dramatic assertion: "The battle to feed humanity is over. In the 1970s and 1980s hundreds of millions of people will starve to death in spite of any crash programs embarked on now."[61]

The problem, as Ehrlich and the demographers from which he drew his conclusions saw it, was simple: modern medicine and the Green Revolution—an astronomical increase in food productivity that followed the Second World War—had greatly reduced the death rate in what Ehrlich called underdeveloped countries, while doing nothing to reduce the birth rate. "Overdeveloped" countries such as the United States were bringing their birth rate down, but were still growing in population and had already maxed out their agricultural capacity, at tremendous environmental cost, making them vulnerable to any sudden or sustained decline in food output. In any case, the overdeveloped countries lacked the means and the will to distribute any food surpluses to people in underdeveloped countries, who were now on the brink of mass starvation.

"There are two kinds of solution to the population problem," Ehrlich concluded. "One is the 'birth rate solution' in which we find ways to lower the birth rate. The other is the 'death rate solution,' in which ways to raise the death rate—war, famine, pestilence—*find us*."[62] Governments in both underdeveloped and overdeveloped nations, Ehrlich argued, must undertake systemic, universal, even authoritarian programs to lower their birth rates, "hopefully by changes in our value system, but by compulsion if voluntary methods fail."[63] But that would only improve things down the road, he warned. Nothing, including the taxes on diapers and even forced sterilizations that Ehrlich advocated, could prevent the famine to come. "There is not enough food today. How much there will be tomorrow is open to debate," he wrote. "If the optimists are correct, today's level of misery will be perpetuated perhaps two decades into the future. If the pessimists are correct, massive famines will occur soon, possibly in the 1970s, certainly in the early 1980s. So far, most of the evidence seems to be on the side of the pessimists."[64]

And yet fifty years later, even though the planet hosts some 7.5 billion of us, famine has been virtually eradicated. Those who have died in large numbers in recent decades for lack of food perished through the incompetence or depravity of their own government and/or the wasteland of war: Somalia, North Korea, Sudan, Yemen. In the decades since Ehrlich wrote his book, many developing (as we call them today) nations have become developed: South Korea, Taiwan, Singapore, Chile. Between 1990 and 2015, the number of people living in extreme poverty, defined by the United Nations as subsisting on an income of $1.25 per day or less, was cut by more than half, from 1.9 billion to 836 million. The number of children who died each year fell from 6 million in 1990 to 2.7 million today. Maternal mortality was also halved.[65]

So what went right? Several things. Ehrlich predicted that water and air pollution from overpopulation would contaminate the environment to the point of collapse. But although global warming is a major concern today, the developed world, at least, has done a good job of improving air and water quality, both of which are in far better shape than they were fifty years ago. In the United States, for example, nitrogen dioxide and sulfur dioxide (NOX and SOX), which are major sources of smog, are down about 60 percent and 80 percent respectively from 1980 levels.[66] The health of the Great Lakes has improved dramatically since Canada and the United States signed a treaty in 1972 that committed both countries to restoring those vital inland seas.[67]

An even bigger factor has been the Green Revolution. Ehrlich was aware that dramatic improvements in agricultural productivity were underway, but he hugely underestimated their consequences. Chemical fertilizers, synthetic herbicides and pesticides, multiple cropping, genetic modification, and other landmark (if controversial) measures led to a massive increase in agricultural productivity that was more than sufficient to meet demand. Although the human population more than doubled between 1950 and 2010, food production tripled, despite only a 30 percent increase in land under cultivation. "Dire predictions of a Malthusian famine were belied, and much of the developing world was able to overcome its chronic food deficits."[68]

The most important factor of all, however, has been the rise of China and India, the greatest advance in human well-being ever witnessed. These two countries alone account for just under 40 percent of humanity. The British, bankrupted by the Second World War and unable to control an increasingly restive population, granted independence to India in 1947. Two years later, Communist leader Mao Zedong completed his consolidation of power in China, excluding Taiwan and Hong Kong. Initially, neither nation grew much in wealth, thanks to tragically unsound economic thinking. India tried to jump-start its economy by throwing up protective tariffs that instead held the country back; Mao's Great Leap Forward aimed to bring on rapid industrialization but instead produced the Great Chinese Famine of the late 1950s, which killed upward of forty-five million people—"the greatest manmade disaster in history"[69]—a catastrophic slaughter even by twentieth-century standards.

But with the passing of Mao and the arrival of Deng Xiaoping, China finally took off. The economy doubled between 1980 and 1990, tripled between 1990 and 2000, and more than tripled between 2000 and 2010. Let's put it another way. In 1980, the wealth created by a Chinese citizen in one year was $205 (in constant dollars based on purchasing power parity). In 2016, it was $8,523.00. Over the past forty years, wealth creation in China has lifted a fifth of humanity out of dire poverty.[70]

India grew more slowly, thanks to the foolish policies of the government in New Delhi. But despite protectionism, internal corruption, and regional rivalries, India's economy too has experienced rapid growth, though nothing like China's. In the 1980s, the federal government increasingly embraced private capitalism over public ownership, and then in the 1990s it began to slowly liberalize the economy. The average GDP in 1960 was $304, well above the level in China. In 2016, it was just under $1,860—well below Chinese standards but still impressive.[71]

As China and India grew and urbanized, their birth rates declined. India's happened naturally—that country was forecast to reach the Goldilocks level of a 2.1 replacement rate by around now. China's birth rate has already dropped precipitously, to an official level of 1.6, thanks to the "one child" policy imposed by the Chinese government in 1979. Intended to curb the country's rapidly expanding population, the draconian rule may be one of history's greatest examples of unintended consequences. We'll look at those consequences further on. What matters here is that the combined economic growth of China and India has hugely reduced global poverty, even as these countries' declining birth rates have lessened the dangers of planetary overpopulation.

If you look at any respectable graph of global poverty levels,[72] you will notice two trends. The first starts in the early 1800s. At that time, about 85 percent of the world's population lived in what we would today call extreme poverty, the level at which just keeping yourself and your family fed is a daily challenge. But then, very slowly, things start to improve for people living in Europe and North America. By 1950, after a century and a half of development, extreme poverty as a share of the global population has declined to about 55 percent. Then the second trend kicks in. The line no longer drifts gently down—it plummets. Today, the searching-for-the-next-meal poor account for about 14 percent of the global population. Think about that. It took 150 years to reduce the extreme poverty level from 85 percent of the population to about one half, but less than half that time to bring it from one half to one sixth. Just as an aside, isn't it remarkable that, while we continue to rightly worry about those still living in extreme poverty, we don't even bother to celebrate what we have achieved—the near-elimination of extreme poverty around the world in our lifetime?

China and India are the largest of the developing countries that have grown impressively in the latter part of the twentieth century. Along with countries that transitioned from developing to developed—South Korea, Taiwan, Singapore, Chile—are the Asian "tigers" Indonesia, Malaysia, and Thailand. But what really impresses is not that the wealth of the average citizen has increased around the world since the end of the Second World War. What really impresses is that this massive expansion of wealth occurred while the global population was also growing massively in size.

Ehrlich was unrepentant. "One of the things that people don't understand is that timing to an ecologist is very different from timing to an average person," he said in a 2015 documentary on his book. Yes, he overstated the case, he acknowledged, but only because he was trying "to get something done." Population growth remains catastrophically out of control, and the day of reckoning approaches. "I do not think my language was too apocalyptic in *The Population Bomb*," he insisted. "My language would be even more apocalyptic today. The idea that every woman should have as many babies as she wants is to me exactly the same kind of idea as everybody ought to be permitted to throw as much of their garbage into their neighbor's backyard as they want."[73]

The predictive failure of Ehrlich, and of Malthus before him, have proved no disincentive for those who, generation after generation, insist The End Is Nigh. The next big doomsaying blockbuster was *The Limits to Growth*, published in 1972 by the Club of Rome, a newly created think tank that sought to tie disparate trends together to create a comprehensive global analysis. Using a computer model developed at the Massachusetts Institute of Technology, analysts concluded, "If the present growth trends in world population, industrialization, pollution, food production, and resource depletion continue unchanged, the limits to growth on this planet will be reached sometime within the next one hundred years. The most probable result will be a rather sudden and uncontrollable decline in both population and industrial capacity."[74] Malthusian growth in population and resource extraction would bring on a decline in per capita output in the 2010s, a scarcity-induced rise in the death rate in the 2020s, and global population decline around 2030, along with a general collapse of civilization as we know it. The authors called for immediate and drastic curbs to population and capital growth, to prevent this collapse. "Taking no action to solve these problems is equivalent to taking strong action," the authors warned. "Every day of continued exponential growth brings the world system closer to the ultimate limits to that growth. A decision to do nothing is a decision to increase the risk of collapse."[75]

Obviously, none of this has happened. Nonetheless, periodic updates assure us that humankind continues along its path to perdition. In 2014, researchers at the University of Melbourne declared that the MIT predictions were on track, with the financial downturn of 2008–09 a harbinger of things to come. "*Limits to Growth* was Right: New research shows we're nearing collapse," the headline warned, and the authors concluded, "It may be too late to convince the world's politicians and wealthy elites to chart a different course. So to the rest of us, maybe it's time to think about how we protect ourselves as we head into an uncertain future."[76]

More recently we've had *Stuffed and Starved: The Hidden Battle for the World Food System*, by Raj Patel, author and professor at the University of Texas at Austin, and *The Reproach of Hunger: Food, Justice, and Money in the Twenty-First Century*, by David Rieff, author and son of the feminist pioneer Susan Sontag. The smartest of the lot may be *The End of Plenty*, by agronomist and journalist Joel Bourne, published in 2015. Bourne fully acknowledged that previous purveyors of doom had been proved wrong through agricultural innovation. But this time, he insisted, things are different. Rising food prices in recent years reflect the maxing out of the productive capacity of the earth. Forests and oceans are being depleted and thousands of species rendered extinct, intensive farming is damaging the soil and water, and all of these activities contribute to the specter of global warming, which itself floods farmland, damages crops and reduces yields. "If we continue at this pace, one day the next species we extinguish may be our-selves," Bourne warned.[77]

But the biggest neo-Malthusian of them all is an institution, and a highly respected one at that. The United Nations Population Division, a critical component of the UN's Department of Economic and Social Affairs, is almost as old as the UN itself, having existed in one form or another since 1946. Its principal goal is to develop statistical models that will accurately project the growth of the global population. The demographers and statisticians who work there are good at their jobs. In 1958, the division predicted that the global population would reach 6.28 billion by 2000. In fact, it was a bit lower, at 6.06 billion, about 200 million out—a difference small enough not to count.[78] This was remarkably impressive, given that demographers at that time had highly inadequate data for Africa and China. So most people take the division's prediction for how this century will play out very seriously, especially as the quality of data for developing countries has improved and the modeling become more sophisticated.

So, what is the UN saying? On the face, it looks pretty grim: In 2017, the UN put the planetary population at 7.6 billion. It will add more than another billion by 2030, bringing the total to 8.6 billion. After another twenty years, in 2050, the number will reach 9.8 billion—so 10 billion, give or take. And as our descendants ring in the new century, the planetary population of 2100 will sit at 11.2 billion, at which point our numbers will stabilize and eventually start to decline.[79]

But that is only one scenario that the UN has put forward. This medium variant, as it is called, is the one UN demographers consider most likely to prove correct, the one that has proved correct in the past. It is based on best guesses for how the fertility rate in each country will play out over the rest of this century. But those same demographers acknowledge that their predictions could be off. If the global fertility rate over the century is 0.5 higher than the medium variant—that is, if women overall produce, on average, half a baby more than predicted, then catastrophe looms. This high-variant scenario would see the global population at almost 17 billion by 2100 and still growing strong, with no stabilization in sight. How on earth would we feed all those people? How would we cope with the impact on the environment? Where would we put everybody? Even the most optimistic projections for increased agricultural productivity would surely fall short of the need to feed 17 billion souls. Malthus and his heirs might finally be proven right.

But there's another scenario, known as the low variant. In that scenario, women produce half a baby *less* than predicted. Fertility rates crash, not only in the developed world but in the developing and the least-developed worlds as well. In that scenario, the planet's population would peak at 8.5 million sometime around 2050, and then would start to decline, rapidly. So rapidly that by the end of the century the planetary population would be back down to around 7 billion, where it is right now. Instead of growing, the global population would be shrinking.

You might think this would be cause for celebration. The planet's lungs would surely breathe easier without the press of so many billions of humans; famine and poverty would surely wane with fewer mouths to feed and families to house. And you would be right— partly. The economic and geopolitical impact, however, would be more mixed. We'll be looking at the consequences of a sustained population decline in chapters to come. The real question is, which variant is the likely variant? By 2100, will we be 17 billion and growing fast, 11 billion and leveling off, or 7 billion and in decline? It would be good to know the answer to that question. It doesn't take a clever economist or political scientist to figure out that a world of 17 billion people would likely be a tumultuous and unhappy place. Even 11 billion could be hard to manage. But 7 billion? We're chugging along with that number right now.

John Wilmoth, who has been the director of the United Nations Population Division (UNPD) since 2013, is confident the medium variant, or something very close to it, shall come to pass. "For the world as a whole, after about thirty years or so, [the high or low variant] becomes really implausible," he said in an interview with the authors. While the UN forecasts for this country may be too high or for that country too low, the differences tend to cancel each other out, he says. The UN's method of calculating population trends has proved sound in the past, and Wilmoth is convinced it remains sound. What is that method? Simply put: the UNPD assumes the fertility rate in a given country or region will match other countries or regions that have had similar experiences but that are further down the road. Let's say Country A has lowered its fertility rate from six to four over the space of thirty years. Country B once had a fertility rate of six, and it also took thirty years to reduce its fertility rate to four. Country B then lowered its fertility rate from four to two in the space of forty years. The UNPD predicts that the fertility rate of Country A will also decline from four to two over forty years. "Following that historical experience, we imagine that countries that currently have higher levels of fertility and lower levels of life expectancy will make progress in the future in a similar manner, at a similar speed, to what was experienced by countries in the past," he believes. "It's all grounded in past experience."

Wilmoth also has an explanation for why some countries with low fertility rates are experiencing a minor rebound—though nothing close to replacement rate. In some societies, he believes, couples have concluded that they want more children than couples were able to have in the recent past, as women become more equal and child care becomes more affordable and available. His department believes that uptick will be a permanent feature in future decades, and will contribute to population growth.

The UNPD's projections rest on the assumption that the rate of fertility decline is constant between countries and regions, that Country A will always mimic country B. Psychologists and financial analysts call this assumption "recency bias," the belief that, because things have gone a certain way in the past, they are bound to go the same way in the future. Recency bias is why so many stock brokers ignore the warning signs of an approaching bear market.

Past is usually prologue, but with statistical projections, some-times it isn't. Things change. What was important in the past may not matter as much in the future, and what was insignificant before can become a big deal. For example, what happens if a trend that took a certain amount of time before, such as declining fertility brought on by urbanization and the empowerment of women, begins to accelerate? What if something that once took forty years now only takes twenty?

Still, the United Nations medium variant has always proved to be accurate. Common sense suggests that variant will prove accurate once again. But this time, we think common sense is wrong. And we're not alone.

We are in the bright, white, almost antiseptic office of Wolfgang Lutz, at the Vienna University of Economics and Business, where he teaches. Tall, balding, gray-haired, with an almost stereotypical goatee, Lutz is a classic boomer, born in 1956. What is not typical is his pair of Ph.D.s, one from the University of Pennsylvania, the other from the University of Vienna, both involving demographics and statistics. Courteous, focused, exuding a sort of nervous energy as he unfolds his beloved population charts, Lutz wants the visitor to understand why the United Nations population projections are wrong. The reason, in a word, is education.

"The brain is the most important reproductive organ," he asserts. Once a woman receives enough information and autonomy to make an informed and self-directed choice about when to have children, and how many to have, she immediately has fewer of them, and has them later. "Once a woman is socialized to have an education and a career, she is socialized to have a smaller family," he explains. "There's no going back."[80] Lutz and his fellow demographers at Vienna's International Institute for Applied System Analysis believe that advancing education in developing countries, brought about by increasing urbanization, should be factored into future population projections, which the UN doesn't do. The IIASA, using those factors, predicts a stabilizing population by mid-century, followed by a decline. Lutz believes that the human population will be shrinking as early as 2060.

His is hardly a lone voice. Jørgen Randers is a Norwegian academic who co-authored *The Limits to Growth*. But since then he has changed his mind. "The world population will never reach nine billion people," he now believes. "It will peak at eight billion in 2040, and then decline."[81] He attributes the unexpected drop to women in developing countries moving into urban slums. "And in an urban slum it does not make sense to have a large family."

The Economist is also skeptical of the UN estimates: previous projections, it observed in a 2014 analysis, failed to forecast "the spectacular declines in fertility in Bangladesh or Iran since 1980 (in both countries, from roughly six children per woman to about two now). At the moment, Africa is the source of much new population growth and the authors assume that fertility rates will continue to fall more slowly there than they did in Asia and Latin America. But no one can be sure."[82]

The Swedish statistician Hans Rosling founded the Gapminder Institute to spread knowledge of great demographic shifts underway using language the general public can understand. In one popular video, "Don't Panic," he tells the audience that "mankind already is doing better than many of you think."[83] He talks about the convergence of birth rates and life expectancy between developed and developing countries, noting, "We no longer live in a divided world." He points out that his granddaughter, who was born in 2000, arrived in the year of "peak child." There were two billion children at the turn of this century, and there will be two billion at its end. Rosling believes that, even if the planet does reach eleven billion, thanks to increased life expectancy, that stable cohort of the young, along with improved education and health care, will easily sustain a population that steadily grows more prosperous. Other analyses fall into the same ballpark. A Deutsche Bank report, for example, has the planetary population peaking at 8.7 billion in 2055 and then declining to 8 billion by century's end.[84]

So who is right: the demographers at the UN or their critics in Europe and elsewhere? One way to begin to answer that question is to look around the world to see at what stage of the demographic transition various countries and regions of the world find themselves.

When the Demographic Transition Model was first developed, back in 1929, it contained only four stages. Stage Four, the final stage, envisioned a world in which life expectancy was high and the fertility rate was low, around the level needed to sustain the population: 2.1 babies per mother. But as it turned out, there is a fifth stage: one in which life expectancy continues to slowly increase, even as fertility rates continue to decline *below* the replacement rate, leading eventually to a declining population. Just about the entire developed world is in Stage Five.

In the 1970s, the fertility rate began to drop below 2.1 in the most advanced economies, and began dropping in developing countries as well, a phenomenon that has been described as "one of history's most astounding global shifts."[85] In hindsight, it shouldn't have been a surprise at all. The more a society urbanizes, and the more control women exert over their bodies, the fewer babies they choose to have. In most Western nations, such as the United States and Canada, 80 percent of the population live in cities today. And women have something close to total control over their reproductive choices, thanks in part to a chance encounter in 1951.

Margaret Sanger coined the term *birth control* and opened the first birth control clinic. Sanger was determined, when she moved to New York as a young woman in 1910, to avoid the traps of married domesticity. Her work as a nurse among impoverished women in the Lower East Side, including the literally thousands of brothels found there, revealed to her the terrible risks that women trying to end a pregnancy faced. She was even arrested for promoting contraception, maintaining that each woman should be "the absolute mistress of her own body,"[86] and borrowing from anarchist Emma Goldman the slogan: "No Gods, No Masters." She won the right for doctors to prescribe contraception. She opened clinics, published magazines, and spread the good word. And in 1951, after meeting the endocrinologist Gregory Pincus at a dinner party, she convinced him to devote his research to developing a birth control pill. She also secured the funding. By 1954, human trials were underway. By 1957, the pill was approved for women with severe menstrual disorders, which produced a sudden upsurge in women complaining of severe menstrual disorders. In 1960, the Food and Drug Administration approved the pill for contraceptive use.

The pill revolutionized sexuality. Women and men could have sex for fun, without fear of unwanted babies. If a woman did become pregnant, abortion became a legal option when, thirteen years after the pill went on the market, the United States Supreme Court in *Roe v. Wade* ruled that women were constitutionally entitled to access to an abortion, as part of their right to privacy. By the end of the 1970s, access to the pill and to a safe, legal abortion was common throughout the developed world. And fertility rates continued to plunge.

Let's take Spain as an example. The former imperial giant is firmly in Stage Five of population growth. It has a very low fertility rate— at 1.3 births per woman, far below the rate of reproduction. It also has a very high life expectancy: 82.5 years, the fourth highest in the world (behind Japan, Iceland, and Switzerland).[87] But even with all those old people, in 2012 Spain's population started to decline, because in some regions, two people die for every baby that is born.[88] Thus far, the drop has been gradual, shaving 400,000 souls off the 2011 population of 46.8 million. But the trend is about to accelerate. Madrid estimates that a million people will disappear from the country within a decade, and 5.6 million by 2080.[89] The government is so eager to reverse, or at least slow, this trend that it appointed a "sex tzar," charged with developing a national strategy to address Spain's demographic imbalances.[90]

Most European countries, especially those that limit immigration, are like Spain. But Europe is not alone. Japan's population is expected to decline by 25 percent over the next thirty-five years, taking it from 127 million to 95 million. The numbers are similar for South Korea and Singapore, two other fully developed Asian societies. The prospects are more encouraging for the United States and Canada, but only because both countries embrace robust (though very different) immigration policies. We'll come back to these two exceptions later in the book.

But fertility declines aren't unique to the developed world. Urbanization and the empowerment of women are global phenomena. We know that China and India are at or below the 2.1 replacement rate. But so are other developing countries: Brazil (1.8), Mexico (2.3), Malaysia (2.1), Thailand (1.5). Birth rates are still very high in Africa (Niger: 7.4; Malawi: 4.9; Ghana: 4.2) and parts of the Middle East (Afghanistan: 5.3; Iraq 4.6; Egypt: 3.4). But these high-fertility countries share one thing in common with their low-fertility counterparts: everywhere, virtually without exception, birth rates are coming down. Nowhere are they going up.

We know that urbanization changes the economic calculus of having children and leads to the empowerment of women through education. Recent research has shown that other factors are in play as well. One of them is the decline in the ability of kin to influence kin. If you live in a more rural, less developed society, your social environment most likely revolves around the family, in which the elders endlessly nag the young to get married and have kids, thus fulfilling the ancient evolutionary impulse to reproduce. But as societies become more modern and urban, friends and co-workers replace siblings, parents, and uncles and aunts. In your own family, we're willing to bet that your parents and grandparents at one time exerted pressure, however subtle, on you to find a life partner, settle down, and have children. But did any of your friends press you to have kids? Do your co-workers care one way or another? "Family members now constitute a smaller part of people's social interactions than at any time in our evolutionary history," writes psychologist Ilan Shrira of Chicago's Loyola University. "This change is the critical factor in decreasing birth rates *because family members encourage each other to have children,* whereas non-kin don't."[91]

Another factor is the declining power of religion in most parts of the world. We don't need to get into the various reasons that have been put forward for why faith is weakening in many societies, though it's worth pointing out that the same forces that reduce fertility—rising affluence,[92] improved education, the emancipation of women,[93] the weakening influence of kin—also weaken the power of organized religion to limit personal autonomy. But there is no question that societies in which religion wields considerable influence over individual decisions have higher fertility rates than societies in which religious influence is minimal. Three WIN/Gallup polls, taken in 2008, 2009, and 2015, asked respondents whether they felt religious or not. In Malawi and Niger—which, as we've seen, have among the highest fertility rates in the world—99 percent of those polled answered yes. Only 39 percent said yes in Spain, which is now considered one of the least religious countries in the world.[94] (Interesting correlation: societies where the power of the Catholic Church rapidly collapsed, such as Spain, Quebec, and Ireland, tend to go from having relatively high to relatively low fertility rates especially quickly.)

We must also point out that the rising power of women to control their own reproductive fate is, in many ways, a zero-sum game: fertility has declined despite, until quite recently, the stern but futile opposition of men. Men didn't grant women property rights, voting rights—even, eventually, something approaching full equality— willingly. They did it kicking and screaming, against their will. Through most of history, men controlled women, including their bodies, in fact and in law, and they only gave up that control when forced to by women—urbanized, educated, and autonomous women. Yes, men and women have loved each other and lived together in love since the dawn of the race, but only on men's terms, and those terms could be harsh. To pick just one from many millennia of examples: We mentioned that Margaret Sanger went to jail for promoting contraception. That's because she violated the United States' Comstock Laws, first passed in 1873, which not only banned the use of all pornography, erotica, and contraceptives, but also made it illegal to promote contraception or inform the public about how to practice it. Versions of the Comstock Law in the U.S. and other countries remained on the books into the 1970s. Even in that decade, condoms were generally sold only in pharmacies and were kept behind the counters, so that the customer had to specifically ask for them—a terror to teenage males. This fight is not over. Today, politicians and preachers, most of them male, try to limit a woman's right to an abortion in the United States and elsewhere. In the autumn of 2017, cascading revelations of powerful men sexually abusing women galvanized the #MeToo campaign. The legacy of men owning the bodies of women haunts us still.

As a society urbanizes, and women gain more power, the ties of kin, the power of organized religion, and the dominance of men declines, along with the fertility rate. For one example that wraps all of these forces together, let's take a look at the Philippines: a large, poor, archipelagic country in the Western Pacific. In 1960, the rural population of the Philippines (nineteen million) was more than twice that of the urban population (eight million). Today the population is evenly split between rural and urban, and by 2030 the Philippines is projected to be 65 percent urban.[95]

As the Philippines urbanizes, the rights of women in Filipino society grow stronger. In 2010 the government passed what it called "the Magna Carta for Women," a comprehensive series of laws banning discrimination of any kind against women and affording them increased legal protection from violence. Today, the Philippines ranks seventh (Iceland comes in first) in the World Economic Forum's *Global Gender Gap Report*.[96] In 1965, the Filipino fertility rate was seven. Today it's three, and falling at a rate of about half a baby every five years. Half a baby every five years! The Philippines offers further proof that, while fertility rates declined in the developed world over more than a century, they are collapsing in the developing world in the space of a few decades.

But how can the Filipino fertility rate be falling so quickly? The Catholic Church is a powerful force in that country, and, as it happens, the Church itself provides the answer. "Church attendance in Philippines declines," reports the UCA *News*, which promotes itself as "Asia's most trusted independent Catholic news service."[97] As it turns out, only four in ten Filipinos now attend church regularly. "The failure of families to sustain values formation among young people is one of the factors that has led to a decline of church attendance in the predominantly Catholic Philippines," the author laments.

The Church is still powerful in the Philippines. Abortion is illegal and there is no divorce law. Whatever that magna carta may say, women still face discrimination and are at risk of violence at home and harassment on the street. "The fight for women's rights in the Philippines [is] a battle that never really ends, and requires continual vigilance in the fight for equality and its requisite protection— however fragile the wins may be," one recent assessment concluded.[98] Nonetheless, progress only goes in one direction. The Philippines population is expected to increase from its current level of 101 million to 142 million by 2045, and will then probably start to decline.[99] This story is repeated throughout the world. Urbanization, the empowerment of women, and declining fertility are universal phenomena, though each proceeds at a different pace, depending on characteristics of the local culture.

If you talk to some demographers off the record, you will hear them wonder whether the UN is keeping its population projections high, despite all the evidence to the contrary, to maximize a sense of crisis, thus justifying interventions to limit economic growth (there are few ardent laissez-faire capitalists at the UN) while ensuring the continued need for UN-based aid programs. But there is no need to indulge in conspiracy theories to conclude that the UN is employing a faulty model based on assumptions that worked in the past but that may not apply to the future.

We believe the UN's low-variant scenario, or something like it, will come to pass. Most people reading this book will live to see the day when the earth's population starts to decline. Mount Toba, the Black Death, the ravages of colonization, and other calamities have caused populations to crash in the past. This time, it will be different. This time, it will be slow and deliberate. As a result of our own choices, there will be fewer of us each year than there were the year before, year after year after year. Most of us understand this, have woven it into our lives. It's just that we don't notice, until someone points it out. Say, at a dinner party in Brussels.

THREE

THE GRAYING OF EUROPE

There are fifteen to dinner, crowded around a long wooden table in the large room that is most of Judith and Nathaniel's flat. The six couples are in their twenties and thirties and consider themselves very enlightened. Two children—Roman is six and Tilda is four months—complete the scene. Most of the men are students or artists, while the women work and pay the rent. After dinner, the men smoke on the balcony while the women clean up. (Well, maybe not *that* enlightened.)

Judith and Nathaniel live in Schaerbeek, one of the nineteen self-governing communes in Brussels. Belgium must surely win the dubious prize of having more governments than any other place on earth. Carved from the Netherlands in 1830 when some hotheaded young men started a riot after an opera, this tiny country crammed with 11.3 million people consists of Flanders, where people speak Flemish, a form of Dutch, and Wallonia, whose residents speak French. There is also a German-speaking enclave to the east and

Brussels, more or less in the middle, the only part of the country that is bilingual in Flemish and French, though everyone knows that English is an unofficial official language. Belgians are fiercely attached to the principle of local autonomy—hence the nineteen communes of Brussels.

If you work on the assumption that all European city centers are charming to North Americans, whose cities generally lack either preserved historic cores or good urban planning, then the commune of Schaerbeek is certainly charming, with its streets of three- and four-story brick row houses, mostly dating from the nineteenth century, narrow in width but graced with large windows to let in light. The shops are small and locally owned, the parks and other public spaces neat and trim. It's only when you look closer that you realize many of the row houses need paint, and some a lot more than paint. Rules and regulations in Brussels are so many and complex as to make them unenforceable, so landlords just let things go. The commune is home to a mélange of old-stock Europeans combined with residents of Turkish and Moroccan descent. Not far from Schaerbeek is Molenbeek, the minority-majority commune that was home to many of the men who led the horrific attacks on Paris in 2015. And when, in March 2016, terrorists bombed Brussels's airport and metro, killing thirty-two, police arrested one of the plotters in Schaerbeek, only a block from where Judith and Nathaniel and their friends are having dinner.

When asked, most of the young men and women at the table don't know much about their great-aunts and -uncles, though they generally agree there were a lot of them. Danielle recalls that one grandparent had fifteen brothers and sisters. As for the parents, three or four siblings appears to be the norm. They themselves generally have one or two brothers or sisters—"They made small families," Adrien, who's from France, observes of his parents' generation.

Of the six couples at the table, one husband and wife have two children, one couple has one child, and the rest are childless. If these
couples are going to have children, they should be having them now.
But children right now are not a priority. Why not? "Because our
parents told us 'don't have kids. They're very expensive.'" "Because
we're both working." "Emancipation." "Because there is less room;
housing is expensive." "If you want to have children, you have to be
rich." "We work harder. We don't have time for children." Note the
dichotomy between positive and negative reasons for not reproducing: couples are not having children because children are expensive
and the man and the woman are working, but also because they feel
free to have or not have children as they see fit.

Clearly, the people at this table are reproducing far below the
replacement rate of 2.1 children per woman. To reproduce themselves, these six couples should produce thirteen children. But with
only three children thus far, they have managed to achieve a fertility
rate of less than 0.5. Even if there are more babies to come, it seems
highly unlikely that the people at this dinner table will have enough
children to fill another dinner table three decades from now.

These couples are typical. With a fertility rate of 1.8, Belgium is
reproducing well below its replacement rate. And Belgium is hardly
an outlier. In fact, its fertility rate is higher than the European Union
average of 1.6. While the United Kingdom also has a fertility rate
of 1.8, many countries are below that average, such as Greece (1.3),
Italy (1.4), Romania (1.3), and Slovakia (1.4).[100] Those countries are
already losing population. Greece's population started to decline in
2011.[101] Fewer babies were born in Italy in 2015 than in any year since
the state was formed in 1861.[102] That same year, two hundred schools
closed across Poland for lack of children.[103] Portugal could lose up to
half its population by 2060.[104] The United Nations estimates that the
nations of Eastern Europe collectively have lost 6 percent of their

population since the 1990s, or eighteen million people. That's the equivalent of the Netherlands simply disappearing from the earth.[105]

For the people around that Brussels dinner table, a declining population sounds like good news. "More space." "More jobs." "Cheaper houses." "Cheaper everything." But they haven't thought things through. Fewer young people means fewer taxpayers to support their health care and pension costs when they get old. Fewer couples having babies means fewer home buyers, so housing prices decline, wiping out people's savings. Fewer people in the peak acquisition years, from graduation until middle age, means fewer people to purchase cars and refrigerators and sofas and jeans, so less economic growth. When they think about that, the people at the table grow silent.

There is a reason that so many countries in Europe are losing population. That reason is rooted in geography, which made it impossible for the continent to unify, and which helps explain the triumph of the caravel over the junk.

China has been unified, more or less, for four thousand years. Its plains and rivers invite conquest and communication. Periods of disunity were accompanied by chaos, promoting a powerful cultural impetus toward unified, stable government. And unity was often a blessing. As everyone knows, many of the great Western "discoveries"—gunpowder, paper, the compass—were actually discovered first by the Chinese.

So advanced was China that, in 1405—almost a century before Columbus sailed out of Palos de la Frontera—the Yongle emperor launched a great treasure fleet, which, over seven voyages, reached as far as the shores of modern-day Kenya. The fleet was dominated by nine-masted junks that could have been up to 150 meters in length, more than five times larger than the *Santa Maria*, and surrounded by dozens of support vessels.[106] In the early fifteenth century, Chinese naval technology was streets ahead of Europe's.

But a large, united empire requires a powerful central government, which in turn requires a powerful bureaucracy. And that, in turn, invites corruption and decay. After seven voyages, the Yongle emperor's successor ordered the treasure fleet to remain in port. The isolationist Confucian faction at court, which argued the ships were too expensive to maintain at a time when Mongols threatened the borders, defeated the more cosmopolitan eunuch faction. It became a capital offense even to construct a two-masted vessel. The fleet rotted and the technology was lost.

In all of human history, no one has managed to conquer Europe. The plains of central Europe are open enough, if you can get across the rivers, but then you have the Alps isolating the Italian peninsula and the Pyrenees blocking easy access to Iberia. Both Scandinavia and the British Isles are protected by moats of water. The Romans came close to conquering the continent—in Britain, they made it as far as the English-Scottish border, marked by Hadrian's Wall—but they met their match in the Teutonic forests and retreated to the Rhine. Charlemagne briefly unified much of Western Europe circa 800, but the victory proved ephemeral. Napoleon's nineteenth-century conquests were even more ephemeral, and Hitler's more ephemeral still. The greatest European imperial power was Britain, whose empire at its height held sway over a quarter of the world's population. But the British won their empire by sea, not land.

Disunity has been Europe's greatest blessing. It promoted diversity, which is the true mother of invention. No emperor could order the burning of an idea beyond his limited borders. Expel the Jews if you want, but they will find another home. The schism between Catholics and Protestants meant that there was always somewhere for heretics to flee to. This king or that pope could ban this book explaining that theorem, but someone invariably smuggled the plates to a place where the edict held no sway, and the presses rolled. The incessant threat of a Mongol or a Turk or a Hapsburg placed a premium on developing a better sail, a stronger bow, a working musket. Competition between states encouraged economic competition, for any enlightened despot knew that paying to keep an army in the field was half the battle, and sometimes made the battle moot. And with all these principalities elbowing each other for space on a confined continent, and competing with each other to generate wealth, it paid to explore.

In the years when China's treasure fleets probed the Indian Ocean, the Iberian peninsula was a cauldron of conflict and innovation. Conquered by Muslims in the eighth century and gradually reconquered by Christians in the medieval era, it was a place where Christian and Muslim technology jostled and intermingled, fusing to create the caravel, a sturdy ship equipped with a triangular lateen sail that made it possible for a vessel to sail against the wind. Caravels, it turned out, were so well designed that they could leave the shelter of the Mediterranean and sail into the Atlantic's stormy seas. A Portuguese prince, Henry the Navigator, sponsored exploratory voyages along the western coast of Africa, while also establishing an academy dedicated to improving navigation and mapmaking. By the time of Henry's death in 1460, Portuguese explorers had made it as far as present-day Sierra Leone, with the bit in their teeth. In 1480, Bartolomeu Dias rounded the Cape of Good Hope, proving that the Atlantic and Indian Oceans were connected. (He named it Cape of Storms, but people knew a thing or two about marketing even then, and King John of Portugal gave it the more encouraging current title.) Vasco da Gama reached India in 1498, forever smashing Muslim control over trade between Asia and Europe. By now the Spanish had joined the game, sending Columbus west in 1492.

Before long, the English and French were claiming vast territories of their own in the New World, even as Portuguese influence waned. But that was the point: the technology of the caravel was transferrable, and another king was bound to exploit it. Unlike the Chinese, the Europeans after the Dark Ages tended not to lose or squander acquired knowledge.

Technological advances in Renaissance Europe led to scientific advances during the Enlightenment, which led to the Industrial Revolution in the nineteenth century, which forced millions off their farms and into factory towns and cities. We have seen that urbanization is the single greatest factor in reducing the fertility rate, converting children from an asset (more backs to bend in toil) to a liability (more mouths to feed). We have seen as well that urbanization empowers women, who become better educated and more autonomous and who then choose to have fewer children. The influence of kin and the authority of religion also decline. Since the Industrial Revolution was born in Europe, since European society is among the most secular on earth, since European women are culturally more equal than almost anywhere else—even if those men in Brussels do let the women clean the dishes while they smoke—it's hardly surprising that Europe is at the vanguard of population decline.

In England and Wales, the fertility rate sat at 6 around 1800, and then began a steady, unrelenting decline, to about the replacement rate of 2.1 in 1940, more or less in lockstep with the United States and other Western nations. In France, oddly, fertility declines were already underway by the late 1700s. No one is sure why; the ferment of the French Revolution, and the secularization of society that resulted, may have had something to do with it.[107] Whatever the reason, the early-adopter model of reduced fertility had catastrophic consequences for that country's future. The more fertile Germans next door became more populous than the French, defeating them in the Franco-Prussian war of 1870. To prevent a repeat, the French sought allies to compensate for their diminishing population status. The Germans sought allies in turn, leading to half a century of slaughter in the two world wars. Reduced fertility can be a mortal threat to national security.

By the time of the 1930s Depression, many European countries were barely having enough babies to sustain the population. We also know what came next: the suppressed demand for babies created by the Great Depression and the Second World War launched the developed world's baby boom. Intriguingly, an overture to that boom actually preceded that war and might even have continued during it. Fertility rates in Scandinavian countries, after more than a century of steady decline, bottomed out in the mid-thirties and started to recover. England and Wales were at 1.7 and Belgium reached its nadir of 1.9 in 1935; then the trend began to reverse. In what became West Germany after the war, fertility in 1933 was way down at 1.6, well below replacement rate. But then the Germans started making babies again, and the fertility rate started to recover in France as well. Fertility rates appear to have increased in France and Belgium *during* the Second World War, even though both countries were under German occupation or control and supplies such as food and coal were increasingly scarce. For neutrals such as Sweden and Switzerland, the baby boom was already in full swing in the 1940s.[108]

So people in some European countries started having more babies in the second half of the 1930s, perhaps as the Depression began to ease and children became more economically possible. The war disrupted things, but as soon as the war ended, the pent-up demand for children released, launching the baby boom proper. The phenomenon was universal throughout the West, but let's pick

Denmark as an example. In 1930, 29 percent of women in Denmark between the ages of twenty and twenty-four were married. In 1960, the figure was 54 percent. The percentage of young married couples had almost doubled. Marrying young had become a fad: the postwar recovery meant that the young were now affluent enough to marry and have children at a time when living in sin was still considered just that. "Rising nuptiality was a key and very general trend during this period . . . across time periods, generations, and countries."[109] Marrying young meant more time to make babies, so babies also became a fad. By 1960, the fertility rate in Denmark had risen to 2.5. And with growing affluence, the fad was easily affordable.

But fads end. By the 1970s, birth rates in Europe had dropped back to replacement rate, and then continued dropping. Below the 2.1 replacement rate. Birth rates in most developed countries plunged to somewhere between 1.3 and 1.8 children per mother. Finland's is at 1.8. Slovenia is now at 1.6. Ireland, which was one of the last Western European countries to fully modernize, and where the Catholic Church continues to exert considerable influence, is holding steady at 2.0. Italy has hovered between 1.2 and 1.4 since the 1980s. France, with one of the highest birth rates in Europe, is at 2.0. Denmark is at 1.7.

Why this new trend? The answer is simple: there is nothing new about it at all. As we know, birth rates had been dropping for a century and a half. Urbanization, improved public health, increasing affluence, and, above all, increasing autonomy for women had resulted in fewer babies per woman in each generation. The arrival of the pill, easy access to birth control, proper sex education, all played a role as well. The baby boom was a blip. And once that blip disappeared, the trend to a lower birth rate resumed, until it reached what is today its natural state—a birth rate below the replacement rate.

The correlation between the decline of fertility and the decline of organized religion is especially acute in Europe. Prior to the Second World War, both sides of the Christian divide, Catholic and Protestant, influenced public policy in their respective countries. Both condemned sex outside of marriage and discouraged contraception, which led to large families headed by husband and wife in their traditional roles of breadwinner and homemaker. But after the war, because of the rush of communications technology, the elevation of education standards, the decline of deference, a rash of Catholic sex-abuse scandals—choose your reason—the power of the Church declined, including its power to deter contraception. In Belgium, attendance at mass on Sunday was nearly universal as late as the 1960s; today about 1.5 percent of the population in Brussels show up.[110] The Catholic administration in Belgium, one correspondent noted, "could become little more than a heritage agency for ancient churches."[111] The marriage rate today in Europe today is half what it was in 1965.[112] Common law relationships—in Belgium it's called *samenwoning* in Dutch, *cohabitation* in French—are increasingly the norm.

You may be wondering: Why don't societies go into population decline as soon as their fertility rate drops below 2.1? There are two reasons. After the baby boom ended in Europe, there were still all those children, who eventually reached child-bearing age, and even if they had fewer children than they needed to sustain the population over the long term, over the short term there were more than enough kids to keep the population growing. Second, even as the birth rate fell, longevity increased. New treatments, new surgical procedures, new curbs on tobacco use, new health warnings, raspberries in January from Morocco. In 1960, the life expectancy for a male born in the United Kingdom was sixty-eight years, which was typical for a developed country, and which is why the new, elaborate, postwar pension systems that were being developed in the 1960s set a retirement date of sixty-five. You'd work till then, play golf for a few years, and then take your leave.

But by 2010, the life expectancy of a British newborn male was seventy-nine, and that average is expected to continue increasing unless something comes along to flatten the curve, which is why the U.K., like most developed countries, is having trouble financing its pension system. Ninety is the new eighty. All those seniors who are enjoying a retirement that now takes up a fifth of their lifespan or more also help to prop up the population numbers.

But eventually, demographic reality catches up, as fertility rates stagnate below the replacement rate for a second generation. Population starts to go down, as it has started to go down in places like Spain or Bulgaria. With an annual population growth rate of 0.2 percent, the entire continent's population will soon tip into decline.

Not in Belgium, though. Belgium's population is expected to remain stable, even grow a little bit, between today (11.2 million) and 2060 (11.4 million).[113] There's a reason for that. It goes back to a deal made way back in 1964 between Théo Lefèvre and Hassan II.

Being prime minister of Belgium is one of the most precarious jobs in the democratic world, thanks to the bitter differences between the French Walloons and the Flemish. For much of Belgium's history, Wallonia, with coal mines and major industries, was more prosperous, leaving the Flemish feeling marginal and eclipsed. But in recent years, the tables have flipped—just one more irritant in a country full of itches. Cobbling together a coalition following an election can take months, and that coalition may be unstable. So when Théo Lefèvre came to power in 1961, he knew he might not have long to get things done. And one thing badly needed to get done. The country was suffering through a serious labor shortage, with too few workers available for the smelly, dirty, sometimes dangerous jobs that powered Belgian industry. What to do?

Hassan II of Morocco had problems of his own. Only three years into his reign, he faced rebellious tribes in the country's northern region, even as Moroccan claims in Mauritania and Algeria angered his neighbors. He needed foreign aid, and support from Western governments. But security and wealth depended on exports, and Morocco had little to export, apart from its own population. Which was exactly what Belgium needed. In 1964, Belgium and Morocco signed an agreement that sent tens of thousands of Moroccans— mostly troublesome Rif mountain tribesmen—to Belgium as guest workers. Other European nations were doing the same with Turks, Algerians, and others from the Middle East and northern Africa. Their stay was supposed to be temporary, but such things rarely work out that way. The imported workers had children, and those children were born Belgian citizens.

From Pennsylvania to Wallonia, traditional industries went into decline in the 1970s, faced with increasingly successful competition from what used to be called Third World countries, which threw millions of the most marginal workers out of work in the old countries. In Belgium, many of those workers were Moroccan. They looked for new avenues of employment, only to run up against the legendary Belgian bureaucracy; they hoped for a better life for their children, only to find their schools failing, as neighborhoods like Molenbeek sank into poverty and teachers fled. Many Belgians worried that an isolated, impoverished Moroccan underclass was walling itself off from Belgian society, stubbornly refusing to integrate. The Canadian journalist and urban theorist Doug Saunders came to a different conclusion when he studied the problem. "These immigrants weren't retreating into an atavistic Moroccan life; they were trying to survive without the help of the city around them, even if that meant grey-market economies and crime," he wrote.[114] Eventually, the Belgian government took steps to improve things, with better training and educational opportunities. And there are encouraging signs of integration, with Arab Belgians increasingly present in government offices and classrooms. Brussels has become one of the most diverse cities in the world. But for many, the solitudes remain. Belgium, with all these millions of people crowded into this tiny country, with its charming villages and picture-perfect farm fields and gently rolling hills and, it seems, not one tree growing at random, is a collection of solitudes.

The young Flemish artists and professionals at our dinner don't have any Muslim friends. (They don't really have any Walloon friends, either.) They realize that Belgians must do a better job of integrating this new, very different population into Belgian society. "We would like to get to know them better. We must all learn to understand each other more," Judith insists. But it's hard.

Immigration is the means by which advanced societies with below-replacement birth rates can sustain their populations, or at least mitigate population decline. But immigration brings problems as well as promise: isolation, rejection, competing ethnicities, rising tension. And though importing immigrants can make up in part for a declining birth rate, immigrants—including Muslim immigrants— swiftly adopt the native country's fertility rate. New arrivals only take one generation to adapt to the fundamental reality of urban, twenty-first-century life: children are something to be treasured in small quantities.

Europe is destined to become browner and grayer as society ages and immigrants fill the gap in demand for workers gone missing through reduced fertility. The strains are already obvious: as more than a million Middle Eastern refugees flooded into the continent in the wake of the Syrian civil war and the rise of the Islamic State in 2015 and 2016, once-welcoming governments closed their borders and threw up razor fences. Ever wonder why refugees risk their lives by crossing the Aegean or Mediterranean to reach Europe rather than simply walking across the border between Turkey and Bulgaria? One reason is the combination of fences, patrols, and allegedly brutal treatment by Bulgarian border guards.[115] Eastern European countries could well use an injection of immigrants. But they are much more reluctant to admit refugees than their Western European counterparts. "Bulgaria doesn't need uneducated refugees," Deputy Prime Minister Valeri Simeonov told the BBC. Even skilled immigrants are unwelcome. "They have a different culture, different religion, even different daily habits.... Thank God Bulgaria so far is one of the most-well defended countries from Europe's immigrant influx."[116]

The Bulgarian population has already shrunk from almost nine million in 1989 to just over seven million today. It could lose another 30 percent by 2050, thanks to a low birth rate (1.5), an almost total absence of immigration, and migration of Bulgarians to other parts of Europe. The Bulgarians need newcomers. But they don't care. They would rather disappear than live among strangers.

Why are so many European countries, despite clear evidence that their populations are declining, or about to decline, reluctant to accept immigrants? Why are some immigrant groups having such difficulty integrating? Dark arguments swirl around these questions: hysterics and borderline racists such as Bruce Bawer (*While Europe Slept: How Radical Islam Is Destroying the West from Within*) and Mark Steyn (*Lights Out: Islam, Free Speech and the Twilight of the West*) warn of an Islamic cultural and political takeover of Europe that replaces Western constitutional democracy with Sharia law and a new caliphate. In truth, Muslim Europeans will constitute no more than a tenth of Europe's population by 2050[117]—hardly enough to create Eurabia or Londonistan. Most likely the number will be far lower, because fertility rates in the source countries are declining and "with the passage of time Muslim fertility moves closer to the fertility of the majority of the population in the respective [European] countries."[118] A Pew Research Center study predicts that by 2030, the fertility rate among Muslims in Europe will have dropped to 2.0, below replacement rate and less than half a baby ahead of the non-Muslim rate of 1.6. Yet anti-immigrant sentiment—toward both immigrants from Africa and the Middle East and from other European countries—drove 52 percent of Britons to vote to leave the European Union on June 23, 2016. Fear of immigrants stoked the rise of right-wing parties from France to Poland. And who could blame populations subjected to high-profile terrorist attacks for demanding that their borders and neighborhoods become more secure? Europeans of all ideologies and complexions struggle to find a way through the paradox of necessity and resentment that mark the immigration debate.

Of course, one answer to the conundrum of non-European immigration would be to produce more Europeans, to increase the natural birth rate so that the population would grow, and grow younger. Increased child supports, expanded daycare, legislated parental leave—surely there is some suite of incentives that could convince European couples to have the second or third baby. And indeed, some governments have tried. The results are mixed at best.

The Swedish economist, sociologist, and politician Gunnar Myrdal was still a student at Stockholm University in the early 1920s, but already conspicuously brilliant and brash. A professor, so the story goes, once warned him to be more respectful to his elders "because it is we who will determine your promotion." "Yes," Myrdal replied, "but it is we who will write your obituaries."[119] One night, the railway worker's son stopped at a farmhouse while on a cycling trip. There,

he met the farmer's daughter, Alva, and what sounds like the beginning of a joke in poor taste became one of the great marriages
of the twentieth century. Each would win the Nobel Prize separately: he shared the economics prize with Friedrich Hayek in 1974
and she shared the peace prize with Alfonso García Robles in 1982.
The U.S. Supreme Court cited Gunnar's landmark work on racial
inequality in the United States, *An American Dilemma*—the *New
York Times* called it "arguably the most important book about
America... since de Tocqueville"[120]—in *Brown v. Board of Education*,
which struck down segregation in American schools. Alva led a
global crusade for nuclear disarmament. They were also a wonderful, caring, curmudgeonly couple whose marriage spanned six
decades. "People don't realize the great happiness there is in living
to be very old and together all the time," Gunnar once said.[121]

But in the 1930s, their shared obsession was Sweden's dismal
fertility rate. At 4.0 in 1900, it had plunged to 1.7 in 1935. Like every
Western country, Sweden was struggling to overcome the Great
Depression. The Myrdals feared that, on top of its other evils, the
Depression was suppressing the birth rate and endangering the stability of the Swedish population. Until then, "pronatalist" policies
that argued for large families were owned by the political and religious right, where the Catholic Church preached against contraception and abortion. The Myrdals captured the issue for the left,
arguing that population levels could be sustained (Gunnar's obsession) only if women were fully equal partners in the home and in
society (Alva's obsession).[122]

In 1934, they published *The Crisis in the Population Question*,
which rocked the Swedish policy establishment. Deeply entrenched
Scandinavian traditions of social solidarity had brought the Social
Democrats to power in 1932, and the government was spending
massively, deficits be damned, to counter the impact of the

downturn. Following the recommendations in the Myrdals' book, Stockholm implemented reforms that offered free health care for pregnant mothers and generous family allowance payments. It became illegal to fire a woman because she was pregnant or a mother. Swedish women became increasingly comfortable with the notion of combining career and family. As a result, the birth rate increased and the economy improved. Did Sweden's social policies bring about economic growth, and did economic growth lead to an increased birth rate? Untangling that skein has obsessed economists for decades, and still there is no consensus. All we can say is that all three things happened together. The Swedish birth rate gradually rose to about 2.5.

But in the 1960s, the pill became available, and a decade later abortion on demand was legalized. Swedish men were happy to let their wives work, but also happy to let them take care of the housework, leaving women stressed and discontented. In the 1970s, the birth rate began to fall, as it fell everywhere else. But unlike other governments in Europe and North America, Sweden had a decades-old obsession with preserving higher fertility rates. The government expanded daycare and launched campaigns that encouraged men to do their share of the housework and child raising. By 1989, maternity leave had been extended to one full year at 90 percent of income, and the fertility rate had ticked back up to 2.1.

But the programs were enormously expensive, and in the 1990s the Swedish economy went into a tailspin when a real estate and banking bubble burst, bringing on a major recession. Maternal support programs were cut back, along with everything else, as the government struggled to deal with the downturn. Whether because of the cutbacks or fears over economic uncertainty—most likely a combination of the two—Swedish families once again began having fewer kids. By the end of the 1990s, the fertility rate was down to 1.5.[123]

But the recession ended, and the government brought in new programs to bring the birth rate back up. Parental leave now stretches to 480 days, most of it at 80 percent of earnings. Each spouse is required—required!—to take two months off, or forfeit part of the benefit. Along with a generous basic family allowance benefit, each additional child earns you an additional sum, with the per-child amount increasing with each child. In Stockholm, parents pushing prams get to ride public transit for free. Most employers offer paid days off for parents who need to stay home with a sick child. Today, the fertility rate in Sweden is 1.9—better than in many developed countries, but not enough to keep the population stable in the long term. Sweden is increasingly looking to immigrants to bolster its numbers, though there is growing resistance among the native-born to the newcomers.

The Swedish example appears to offer two fundamental lessons for countries that want to improve their fertility rate. Extensive support programs aimed at encouraging parents to have children do have an impact. They can move the needle. But they don't move it a lot, and such programs are very expensive and hard to maintain in an economic downturn. And any such downturn causes parents to hold off having kids. Fear of a gloomier future might also be helping to suppress the birth rate in Japan. Economic uncertainty is a powerful form of birth control.

A similar situation occurred in Russia. When the Berlin Wall fell, the fertility rate was a healthy 2.2 children per woman. But as the Russian economy careened toward collapse in the 1990s, the birth rate plummeted, bottoming out at 1.2 in the late nineties. Coupled with a reduced life expectancy brought on by rampant alcoholism, the Russian population began to decline, from 148 million in 1993 to just under 142 million in 2009. But Vladimir Putin, whatever his other qualities, has succeeded in reversing the trend. Anti-alcoholism programs are paying off, and the country's oil-and-gas-fueled economic rebound has brought the population back up to 144 million, thanks to immigration, and the fertility rate up to 1.7.

You may have noticed a certain irony in all of this. Industrialization, urbanization, and economic growth create the conditions that make women choose to have fewer babies. But after a time, an economic downturn can lead to reduced fertility, and an upturn to an uptick in baby-making. Good times lead to fewer babies, then bad times lead to fewer babies.

Until that dinner party, this topic wasn't on the minds of Judith and Nathaniel and their friends. They were just like everyone else: searching for a decent apartment, worried about finding a job, and then a better job, pushing the boundaries of the relationship to test its strength. Yes, it's that strong; let's move in together. Should we marry? Maybe, maybe not. Should we have a baby? Yes, it's time. Should we have another? No, it's too late.

And Europe wanes.

FOUR

ASIA: THE PRICE OF MIRACLES

Question: Is there anything about South Korea's future that gives Youngtae Cho reason to hope? He pauses, tents his fingers, leans back, then shakes his head.

"I'm afraid not," the demographer at Seoul National University replies. "The future for Korea is not encouraging at all."[124] Cho is not alone. The next day, on the other side of Seoul—and that's quite the distance—at a gathering of North American and Korean intellectuals, one of Korea's most senior statesmen, speaking off the record, concludes his survey of the Korean political and social landscape with the observation: "No one seems to be very happy."[125]

On its face, this makes little sense. Seoul, while hardly the loveliest city in the world, is one of the most vibrant and, depending on how you define its boundaries, one of the largest.[126] And the Korean story, as told in Seoul's architecture, is nothing short of miraculous.

There is a reason why very little of old Seoul survives. During the five hundred years of the Joseon Dynasty (1392–1897), the Hermit

Kingdom, as Korea was known, adopted a policy of strict isolation, having dealings only with China. All this ended in 1910 with invasion and occupation by Japan. The invaders razed the ancient palaces, but also brought some semblance of modernization. The Americans and Russians replaced the Japanese after the Second World War, leaving the isthmus divided. Seoul was virtually obliterated during the Korean War—invaded and reoccupied four times by North Korean and UN troops. That devastating war cost the lives of 1.2 million Koreans in the South (and another million in the North), and left the republic one of the poorest places on earth, with an annual income of less than one hundred dollars a year, even as millions fled Korea's hilly countryside for Seoul, turning the city into an enormous shantytown.

But South Korea's good fortune was the American occupation. In the wake of the Second World War, it was a blessing in many countries to have the Yanks around. American occupation helped lay the foundation for the German *Wirtschaftswunder* (economic miracle). American occupation provided Japan with the foundations for both a democratic constitution and rapid economic recovery. American protection of Taiwan, after China's Kuomintang regime fled there following its defeat at the hands of Mao Zedong's Communists, helped that island develop both a flourishing economy and democratic institutions. And American troops and aid helped South Korea to modernize in the wake of the civil war.

This is not to undersell the collective miracle of the Pacific Asian renaissance. The Japanese, South Koreans, Taiwanese, and Singaporeans seized the opportunity to advance their economies. They worked extraordinarily hard to modernize, lifting millions of people out of poverty in a single generation. Each is an economic miracle. For our purposes, let's focus on the miracle of the Republic of Korea.

A military coup in 1961 launched the period of modernization. Military juntas can be unpleasant to live under, but if they aren't too corrupt, they can instill the economic discipline and social welfare needed to transform a society. Korea's military rulers imposed a series of five-year plans for economic growth, and constructed row upon row (upon row, upon row ...) of concrete apartment towers to replace the rickety slums that proliferated in Seoul after the civil war. Office towers followed, and mile-wide streets that failed to prevent the never-ending traffic jams, virtually but not quite eliminating the narrow and crowded lanes and alleys that you can still find, nestled out of sight behind the glass skyscrapers, where Seoul workers in the know head for lunch. The Korean economic model focused on developing the *chaebol*—state-supported industrial conglomerates—that made Hyundai, Samsung, Kia, and LG household names around the world. From utter poverty in the 1950s, Korea progressed so rapidly that it triumphantly hosted the 1988 Olympics, introducing itself to the modern world. Today, Korea ranks fifteenth on the UN's Human Development Index.

Improved health care after the Korean War, coupled with a birth rate of about 6.0—typical of a rural, impoverished society at the time—brought on Korea's own baby boom, with the population doubling from twenty million to forty million between 1950 and 1985. This enormous cohort of the young proved to be Asia's "demographic dividend," as it was known: a huge number of eager young workers for the factories that produced the cheap transistor radios and their ilk that powered the first wave of growth. Some critics insisted that a large, young population was the only reason Asia soared in the last decades of the twentieth century, but that's bunk— see the Philippines and most of Latin America for examples of a demographic dividend squandered.[127]

But Asian governments feared rather than welcomed their millions of young workers. Seduced by the siren warnings of the

neo-Malthusians, they promoted sex education and birth control—
good things in and of themselves but not necessarily good for
economic growth. Fearing a population bomb, Korea's military
government launched an aggressive and successful campaign to
bring the birth rate down. By the 1980s, the Korean fertility rate was
at replacement rate. But in Korea, as elsewhere, the rate then kept
dropping to today's ridiculously low level of 1.2. The high standard
of living has pushed the life expectancy to just over eighty-two
years, one of the highest in the world. The aging index plots the
number of people over sixty against a baseline of one hundred
people under fifteen. Korea already has a very high aging index
of eighty-nine. By 2040 it will be 289—almost three old people for
every young person. This is why Professor Cho is so gloomy.

Korea is about to pay the price of its economic miracle. But
Korea is not alone.

Masaru Ibuka was a frustrated executive. The co-chairman of Sony
loved listening to opera when he was on the road, which was often,
but the company's flagship portable cassette recorder, the TC-D5, was
too bulky. He asked his engineers to design something more genu-
inely portable for his personal use. Ibuka was so impressed with the
result that he took the machine to Chairman Akio Morita, saying,
"Don't you think a stereo cassette player that you can listen to while
walking around is a good idea?"[128] Enter the Walkman.

The Sony engineers had taken away the cassette recorder's speaker
and recording function, crafted a lightweight set of earphones, and
fashioned a sturdy drive so efficient that it could run on a pair of
double-A batteries. Taking a bit of a flyer—for there was no perceived
demand for a portable music player—Sony introduced the Walkman
in July 1979, hoping to sell five thousand units a month. But sales
jumped instantly to fifty thousand, and the cassette player became an

icon of the 1980s, launching a drive for ever-cheaper, better-sounding portable music systems that led—via the Discman, the iPod, and the smartphone—to the music library you carry in your pocket today. The Walkman represented the peak of Japanese creativity and marketing savvy. And it's been mostly downhill ever since.

If you want to understand what population decline does to a society, just look at Japan. In 1950, as the country struggled to rebuild an economy devastated by the Second World War, the average Japanese woman could be expected to have three babies. But in the 1950s, as Made in Japan became a synonym for cheap and shoddy (think of an old transistor radio), mothers started having fewer babies. In 1975, with Made in Japan increasingly a synonym for quality at a good price (think of the Toyota Corolla), and the country now fully developed, the birth rate of what was now the world's second-largest economy dropped below replacement rate, reaching a low of 1.3 in 2005 before ticking back up to 1.4, where it sits today.[129]

That's not unusual for a major developed country. But Japan is different from the typical European or North American nation. The Japanese are very, well, Japanese. Japan is a *jus sanguinis* state: citizenship is conferred by blood—or, more accurately, by having a parent who is already a citizen. If a Danish couple has a child in Canada, the child will have both Canadian and Danish citizenship. If that same couple has a child in Japan, it will be just Danish. It is theoretically possible to obtain Japanese citizenship, but the paperwork is daunting and must be completed in *katakana*, one of the Japanese writing systems. Inspectors will visit both your home and workplace, and if you are approved, you must renounce your previous citizenship. In 2015, Japan conferred citizenship on only 9,469 applicants.[130] That was down from five years before; in 2010 the number was 13,072.[131] 2010 also happened to be the year that Japan's population peaked, at 128,057,352. Five years later, it stood at

127,110,000. In only five years, Japan lost almost a million people even as it issued fewer new citizenships. That's what happens when a country combines a low birth rate with anti-immigration policies. When describing the demography of Japan today, the word that often gets used is *catastrophic.*[132]

Consider: More than a quarter of all Japanese alive today are seniors, making Japan the oldest society on earth. There are more forty-year-old women than there are thirty-year-old women, who outnumber twenty-year-old women. That's what makes population decline so implacable; once it sets in, it's virtually impossible to stop, because every year there are fewer women of child-bearing age than there were the year before. Even more implacable is the change in mindset that accompanies low fertility. Demographers refer to that mindset as the "low-fertility trap." If a society experiences a generation or more of fertility below the rate of 1.5, goes this theory, then that rate becomes the new normal, a normal that's almost impossible to change. As Sarah Harper of Oxford University describes it, "Employment patterns change, childcare and schools are reduced, and there is a shift from a family/child oriented society to an individualistic society, with children part of individual fulfillment and well-being."[133] Having a child, for a Japanese couple—or a South Korean couple, or a German couple, or a Canadian couple—is no longer an obligation to family and clan, to society, to God. It is a way for that couple to express themselves and to experience life: infinitely more important than the mid-century modern look they choose for the living room, or those two weeks they spent in the Costa Rican jungle, or that amazing—if rather insecure and underpaid—new job in graphic design he just landed, but part of that continuum nonetheless. Does this sound like anyone you know?

By the middle of this century, Japan will be down to just over one hundred million people. By the end of this century, it will be

eighty-three million—less than two thirds of its 2010 peak.[134] It is official government policy to find a way to keep the Japanese population
above one hundred million. But no one has figured out how to do
that. As the young abandon rural areas in search of work and hope in
the cities, "some villages are so depopulated that locals have deco-
rated them with mannequins to provide a semblance of activity."[135]

2010 was a milestone for Japan in yet another respect. That was
the year China replaced Japan as the world's second-largest economy. Chinese growth contributed to the switch, but an even bigger
factor was Japan itself. The year China's economy passed Japan's was
also the twentieth anniversary of the Japanese stock market collapse, leading to the "lost decade," as it was called, of the 1990s, followed by the second lost decade of the 2000s, followed by a third
lost decade that's currently winding up—the Lost Generation. The
proximate cause of the downturn was an asset bubble that burst
when the Bank of Japan hiked interest rates in December 1989, leading to the crash. Banks failed and the survivors refused to lend, anxious to protect their balance sheets. The government responded by
pouring billions into infrastructure to jump-start the economy. That
Keynesian approach might have made things worse by starving the
market of private capital.

But another factor was at work. Along with hard times and growing debt—at 250 percent of GDP, Japan is the most indebted nation
on earth—the rising tide of seniors is a drag on the economy.
Because the retirement age in Japan is only sixty and pay is largely
based on seniority, companies can't keep those older workers who
want to stay on the job. As a result, the population of working-age
Japanese is steadily shrinking, leading to another Japanese record:
the developed world's highest age dependency ratio. That's the ratio
of the working-age, productive population to the combined (and
unproductive) populations of retirees and children. In Japan, the

ratio is sixty-four; in the United States, it's fifty-two; in China, it's thirty-nine.[136] This means there are fewer workers in Japan, compared to other major economies, to fund the social programs consumed by the old (health care) and the young (education). But there's an even darker consequence.

Think back to the Walkman: it might have been designed to meet the needs of a middle-aged opera lover, but the two hundred million cassette Walkmans sold before the machine was finally retired from production in 2010 were mostly purchased by the same people who stream music on their smartphones today: the young. The young consume. Over the decades, they have purchased billions of 45s and LPs and cassettes and 8-tracks and CDs and iPods and smartphones and subscriptions to Spotify or iTunes. As young adults, they buy their first washing machines and sofas and refrigerators and SUVs. They buy a stroller for baby and a simple black dress for the office party. They buy a home, and then a larger home. Workers in their twenties and thirties and forties not only produce most of the wealth that powers an economy; they consume it.

Japan's economy has been mostly stagnant for going on three decades in part because its aging population consumes less and less, leading to less and less demand, and fewer and fewer start-up loans from banks rightly worried that demand is only going to continue to fall. As economists Naoyuki Yoshino and Farhad Taghizadeh-Hesary observed, "The aging population and the diminishing working population is one of the biggest causes of the long-term recession of Japan."[137]

The final cost is also the most intangible. One area in which Japan has never become competitive, even in its powerhouse days of the 1970s and '80s, is the computer. All sorts of explanations—including quasi-racist assertions of a cultural inability to innovate—have been put forward. But one fact does stand out. The digital revolution—the transistor, the silicone chip, the personal computer, the Internet, online shopping, the Cloud—has largely been driven by inventors and entrepreneurs based in Silicon Valley, Seattle, or at elite universities such as Harvard. And if you read their biographies—from Jack Kilby, Robert Noyce, and others who developed the integrated circuit and the silicon chip to Microsoft's Bill Gates or Apple's Steve Jobs, from Facebook's Mark Zuckerberg to Amazon's Jeff Bezos, and on—they have one thing in common. When they came up with whatever breakthrough they were responsible for, they were young. Japan doesn't have many young people anymore. It's hard to innovate when your society is old.

The examples of Japan and Korea repeat themselves through the Asian Pacific in Hong Kong, Taiwan, and Singapore. All five countries have crammed a century's worth of economic modernization into a single generation. All five now have among the lowest birth rates in the world. In Hong Kong, according to one estimate, the fertility rate has actually dropped below one.[138] Other Asian countries that are developing but not yet fully developed are following close behind. Thailand: 1.4; Vietnam: 1.8; Malaysia: 2.0. The move toward or below replacement fertility rate in the large nations of Pacific Asia is one of the great drivers of global population decline.

The Asian tigers lifted a large portion of the planet's population out of extreme poverty in the space of a few decades. It truly has been nothing less than a miracle. But such explosive growth comes at a cost, because societies don't evolve as fast as their economies. Old values clash with new realities. And unintended consequences trip up governments' best-laid plans. As is so often the case with any phenomenon, either natural or human-made, the young feel it the most.

Soo Yeon Yoo is twenty-three and studying economics, Jihoe Park is twenty-four and focusing on international relations, and Soojin Shim, at twenty-three, specializes in international commerce. All three are graduate students at Seoul National University, the top-ranking university in Korea, and over a Japanese box lunch we talk jobs, boys, and the future. As with their counterparts in Brussels, they have many aunts and uncles—their parents, collectively, had twenty-one siblings—but each of them has only one brother or sister.

Articulate, ambitious, and whip-smart, they are focused on marks, graduation, and the jobs that come after graduation. Marriage? Not so much. "My dad encourages me to not get married, because living the single life is much freer, it is freer to live on your own," Jihoe explains. "And also it's really difficult to find the right guy. And my dad says, if you don't find him, just don't get married." As for children, "If I get married, I only want one child," Soo Yeon declares. The others agree. Maybe none, maybe one, but no more than one. "Korean working women face so many other disadvantages," explains Soojin. "It's the glass ceiling in Korea. It's very hard to pursue our career while also raising children."

Millennials in Korea face daunting challenges. Their parents were part of the miraculous, one-generation phenomenon of explosive economic growth. But there was no time for the Korean state to develop a proper pension plan for retired workers. As a result, Korea has the highest poverty rates among the elderly of any advanced nation: 45 percent.[139] To ease their plight, the Korean government raised the mandatory retirement age, so that older workers could stay on the job. But since South Korea also places a high value on seniority, those older workers are clogging the system, keeping younger workers from advancing. This has led to what Korean writer Kelsey Chong describes as an escalating series of sacrifices for the "Give-Up Generation."

First they had to give up dating, marriage, and childbirth: the "3 Give-Up."[140] "When a woman is married and gets pregnant, most employers just let her go," explains Jinhoe. "We know our employer will fire us, and so that is why so many of us avoid getting pregnant." To make matters worse, Korean employers are avoiding the cost of having lifelong workers on the books by limiting young, new hires to contract positions, which makes it harder to afford an apartment in Seoul's pricy real estate market. Lack of permanent employment and a home has converted 3 Give-Up to 5 Give-Up—dating, marriage, childbirth, a reliable job, and home ownership—which becomes 7 Give-Up when you add in students who sacrifice earnings by staying in university to get another degree, and recreation by taking other courses at night, in order to give themselves a competitive edge.

If this is all daunting today, it will become even worse when the great mass of Korean baby boomers hits retirement age, forcing the government to increase health care spending, paid for with the taxes of millennials who are having so much trouble getting ahead that Chong describes their plight as the "'N Give-Up Generation'—N being a variable of exponential growth, with no upper limit."[141]

Professor Cho, remarkably, has not sent his daughters to cram schools—the private tutors that so many Korean parents employ to give their children a better chance of making it into a good university. Those private tutors are expensive—another disincentive to having children in Korea and other Asian countries. But Professor Cho doesn't think his daughters will have trouble getting into one of the 230 public and private universities and colleges in Korea. When he started school four decades ago, there were about a million Korean children in his cohort. When his youngest daughter started school, there were only 430,000. "Many colleges will have to close their doors, or restructure," he predicts. And instead of turning applicants away, universities will be begging students to sign up.

But surely that's an advantage. If the Cho sisters are able to choose their school, won't they also be able to choose their job upon graduation, as millions of Korean boomers retire? Yes and no. "When she goes to college, her life will be much easier than now, and after she finishes college it's going to be very easy for her to find a job," he agrees. "It almost looks as though with less population things will be better. But not really. It's not going to be a permanent job. It's going to be more temporary. And her standard of living will be very low."

Despite being at the front of the pack, Soo Yeon Yoo, Jihoe Park, and Soojin Shim have uncertain job and housing prospects. Employers will be reluctant to offer them lifetime job security, and their standard of living will suffer as taxes needed to support the elderly eat up more and more of their paycheck. No wonder they aren't in a rush to marry and have children.

And there is yet another reason for Korean women to put off marriage and motherhood: Korean men. Although millennial guys insist they are more enlightened than their parents, and more willing to share domestic chores and child-raising responsibilities, statistics suggest otherwise. Granted, Japanese men did three times as much housework in 2011 (ninety-six minutes a day) as in 1996 (twenty-seven minutes).[142] But that's still far less than the three hours the average Japanese woman spends on housework, and also far less than men in most other developed countries spend. A study by the Organisation for Economic Co-operation and Development, a club of major developed economies, showed that Japanese men spend less time as caregivers than anywhere else in the OECD, and less time on housework than any other OECD nation with the exception of Korea, whose men do even less around the house. Household duties, coupled with a seniority-based pay system that penalizes women who leave work to have a child, make it harder for Japanese and Korean women to both work and have children. The system is made even more punitive by national child care policies—or rather the lack of them, compared to other developed nations.[143]

The reasons are cultural. Korean marriages are seen not simply as the union of a man and a woman but as a union of two clans—a concept once universally held around the world that only began to disappear in Europe and North American in recent decades. "The guys our age know they are supposed to help the woman," says Jinhoe. "But I don't know if it's in reality. And also, the family on the guy's side would not want the man to do the woman's work. In Korea, marriage is not just about person-to-person, it's about family-to-family. So we care about what the parents on the other side think, and especially about the mother-in-law. There is a special relationship between a wife and a mother-in-law."

With few benefits, wage policies that punish women who take maternal leave, and social norms that let men get away with doing less work, you might think Japanese and Korean women would stay home and make babies. But they don't. Labor force participation by Japanese and Korean women is lower, but not that much lower, than for non-Asian developed countries: 49 percent for Japan and 50 percent for Korea, compared to 56 percent for the United States and 55 percent for Germany.[144] With little support from the state, the employer, or the husband, and yet determined to work (and probably needing the money), many Asian women put off having babies until they're almost out of time. The mean age for a Japanese woman to have her first child is thirty. In the United States it's twenty-six.[145]

And how does all this translate on the ground? In 2015, according to the Korean statistical agency, the marriage rate reached the lowest level—5.9 marriages per 1,000 population—since records were first kept in 1970. The average age of a woman getting married reached thirty for the first time. Another first: the population of Koreans in their twenties and early thirties declined for the first time ever.[146] As for the prospect of children outside of marriage— of unmarried couples having a child or a woman having a child on her own—forget it. The stigma of bastardy in Korean society remains profound.

We have said that the global tendency toward urbanization leads to the empowerment of women, which leads to a decline in fertility rate, and this is true. But each culture is unique. In our travels, we found many local factors that affect fertility. Among the Asian tigers, one characteristic is the retention of the notion of male superiority. Women are welcome to get an education; they are welcome to enter the workforce. But they are also expected to look after the home, and once they have children, they are expected to sacrifice their career to raise them. This causes women in these countries to have fewer children, and who can blame them?

There is another way to offset a declining population: immigration. But that's not an option in Korea, or in other Asian nations. To understand why, take a look at the refugee situation that plagues the world today.

The 2015 refugee crisis revealed a sharp contrast between welcoming and excluding countries. We've already talked about how the Europeans struggled to accommodate the desperate new arrivals. But how did the Asian countries respond? The simple answer is that they didn't respond at all. They never do. Asian countries do not voluntarily accept refugees. China, the country with the world's largest population, accepts almost no refugees: 0.22 per 1,000. Japan, next door, is even less compassionate, with a refugee rate of 0.02. South Korea sits at 0.03. Remarkably, this is unremarkable. No one expects wealthy Asian nations to accept refugees. Nor do refugees want to go there. And it's not a question of distance. Canada is also an ocean away from the hot spots, and it accepts 4 refugees per 1,000.[147]

We would land ourselves in a world of hurt by trying to speculate on why developed Asian nations prize racial homogeneity so highly.

But for whatever reason, they do. Japan is not alone in rarely granting citizenship to outsiders. China, Korea, and Taiwan also accept
virtually no immigrants or refugees. The people of these countries
see themselves as racially homogeneous, and see that homogeneity
as something to prize and protect. In Japan, "a central tenet of
Nihonjinron—a popular genre of writing on national identity—is
that the Japanese are a homogeneous people (*tan'itsu minzoku*) who
constitute a racially unified nation. While *Nihonjinron* has been
thoroughly discredited in academic writing, it remains deeply
rooted in popular discourse."[148] The Han Chinese, who make up
92 percent of China's population, regard other ethnicities within
their borders as quaint and colorful at best, and dangerously sub-
versive at worst. Foreigners of any kind are unwelcome. "China
today is extraordinarily homogenous," observed *The Economist* in
2016. "It sustains that by remaining almost entirely closed to new
entrants, except by birth."[149] The South Koreans, at least, are embar-
rassed about their xenophobia. In 2011, the military changed its oath
of allegiance, replacing the word *race* with *citizen*.[150] Nonetheless, the
Republic of Korea remains mostly closed to foreigners.

There are four kinds of foreigner in Korea: about two million
Korean Chinese are entitled to return to the old country; Korean
men, usually in rural areas, who are unable to find a wife sometimes acquire one from Vietnam or elsewhere; foreign laborers
are brought in to work the "three D" jobs—dirty, dangerous, and
demeaning—that Koreans are reluctant to perform themselves;
and foreign students study in Korean universities. (We should also
mention the twenty-four thousand foreigners who come to Korea
annually to teach English for a year or two.)[151] But there are fewer
Chinese Koreans emigrating from Korea, thanks in part to economic
opportunities in China. Urbanization has reduced the number
of rural men in search of foreign wives. Temporary foreign workers

have virtually no access to permanent work, much less citizenship. And foreign students rarely stay in Korea after they graduate, because of the difficulty of learning Korean. The problem of language is often cited as a reason for Asian countries' discouragement of immigration—as one Japanese diplomat once explained, Japanese is very hard to learn, and once you've learned it, it's of no use whatsoever outside Japan[152]—but that's a smokescreen. Koreans believe that only Koreans are Koreans. Simple as that.

Asian governments know how much trouble they're in. Unless they can reverse their baby drain, their populations will crater in the coming decades. Since government policies in the 1970s and '80s brought the birth rate down, maybe government policies today can help bring the birth rate back up. Singapore has been particularly creative—with one of the world's lowest fertility rates, 1.2, it has to be. Along with creating the Social Development Unit (SDU), a government-sponsored dating agency—Speed dating! Salsa workshops![153]—in 2012 the government declared the evening of August 12, National Day, to be "National Night," when couples were encouraged to procreate. As the song in the promotional video declared, "I know you want it, so does the SDU . . . the birth rate ain't gonna spike itself."[154]

Korea employs more conventional policies. There are government grants for couples seeking fertility treatments, paternity leave for fathers, and preferred admission to public child care facilities for parents with three or more children. The government in 2010 started turning off the lights in its buildings at 7:30 on the third Wednesday of every month in an effort to get workers to go home early—at least by Korea's workaholic standards—to "help staff get dedicated to childbirth and upbringing."[155] But so far to no avail; there were 5 percent fewer births in 2015 than in the year before.

But South Koreans believe they have a unique demographic advantage: North Korea. Eventually, people fervently hope, the peninsula will be reunited, instantly boosting the population by twenty-five million. And the North Korean birthrate is 2.0, if that country's statistical agency is to be believed—roughly replacement rate and much higher than South Korea's. But whatever demographic dividend unification might bring would be overwhelmed by the challenges of integrating an impoverished and brainwashed (by their own government) population struggling to acquaint itself with the modern world.

The demographic dividend that allowed parts of Pacific Asia to leap ahead, bringing previously unimagined wealth and security to their people, is about to become the demographic drag, as societies age, health care and pension demands increase, dependency ratios move in entirely the wrong direction, and the younger generation struggles to make ends—their own and their parents'—meet. In thirty years, Korea is expected to be the oldest country on earth. At current trends, the last Korean will die round about 2750.

Of course, that won't happen. Already, says Professor Cho, the racial bonds that keep the Koreans from letting others in are weakening. "My daughters are fine with the foreigners in their classes," he says. Still, he remains pessimistic. Koreans, he believes, have yet to come to terms with an approaching era of reduced expectations. "Everything is about growth. Nobody expects that things will diminish."

But they will. National Night in Singapore was a bust.

FIVE

THE ECONOMICS OF BABIES

As we track the decline of fertility across the planet, it's perfectly reasonable to ask: So what? Who cares where the world is decades from now? What does it mean for the life I'm leading today? The answer is: it means everything. Right now, today, economic, social, and demographic forces are pulling at you in ways you scarcely notice, no matter what your age. Those forces are why teens don't have as much sex today as their parents did. They're why the mean age for having a first child is now thirty in many countries, and why most parents in those countries have only one or two children. Not long from now, those forces will compel people to put off retirement; they'll force them to spend more time and energy on looking after their parents than they'd ever planned. Those forces will, in some cases, leave people alone at the end of their life, heartbroken, grieving for the middle-aged child who died before they did.

You don't have to wait decades to see what a world growing smaller and older will look like. All you need do is look at yourself. Because this story is all about you.

Let's start with the most important decision of all: whether and when to have a child. On this front, there's big news. We already know that the mean age of a South Korean woman when she has her first child is thirty. South Korea is no different from Australia, Hong Kong, Ireland, Italy, Japan, Luxembourg, Portugal, Spain, and Switzerland. Most other developed states are in the ballpark. (Canada is at twenty-eight.)[156] The planet-wide trend of women delaying childbirth is one of the most important phenomena of our time.

Children are wonderful. They bring joy to their parents and life to their neighborhoods. They renew and inspire and reward. There is nothing, absolutely nothing, more powerful than the love of a parent for a child. That love is literally written into our DNA. But boy, are they expensive. Child care costs more than university tuition. For an average American family with a child under five, it consumes 10 percent of family income.[157] Then there's food and clothing, to start, and by clothing we mean these sneakers and not those sneakers, this look and not that look, something completely different this fall from last fall. You need a bigger house, with more bedrooms and a yard for the kids to play in, and maybe a swimming pool. The state pays for school tuition, but the state often doesn't pay for the books or the field trips or the new uniforms. There's hockey practice and hockey equipment, or a piano and music lessons. The bike is only two years old and already too small. "But why can't I? Why will you never let me? It's not fair!" And braces. Don't get a parent started on braces: $4,500 at least, and it's never at least. And then there's what he did to the car.

It costs, by one estimate, $250,000 to raise a middle-class child from birth till their nineteenth birthday.[158] Then comes college or university. No wonder that, for most parents, one or two is enough. There are plenty of people who don't have any children at all. They prefer to stay single, or they and their partner decide they would rather travel than raise a child. They get a dog.

Even if you set aside the question of how expensive a child is, there are still plenty of good reasons not to have one. For a teenager, parenthood can be devastating. Having a child that young can endanger the health of the mother and the child—birth weights of children born of teenage mothers tend to be below average. Neither the mother nor the father is emotionally equipped to handle the responsibility of parenting; all too often he simply disappears from the scene. Having a child makes it incredibly hard to stay in school. If the mother chooses to enter the workforce, any available jobs will probably be unskilled, poorly paid, and often exhausting. What income she earns may not be enough for child care, forcing her onto welfare. A child that grows up in a home with a single mother on welfare is vastly disadvantaged compared to a child growing up in a home with a mother and father holding down jobs. The worst impact may be the diminished expectations for the child: mother, other family members, teachers, friends, and ultimately the child herself don't expect her to amount to much, and so she lives down to those expectations. And the cycle repeats. In Germany, which has an extensive social safety net, more than a third of single-parent children live in poverty. For households with two parents and two children, the figure is 8 percent.[159]

The good news—no, the simply wonderful news that is generally ignored when in fact it should be shouted from the rooftops—is that teenagers get this, which is why, contrary to popular perception, the teenage pregnancy rate is plummeting. In the United States, sixty-two out of one thousand teenagers gave birth in 1990; today the number is twenty-two, a decline of almost two thirds. Elsewhere, the drop has been even more dramatic. Teenage pregnancies in Canada have declined by 80 percent since the 1960s, as they have (more or less) in Sweden and the Czech Republic and Hong Kong and Australia and Oman and Mongolia and Maldives and Barbados and most of the developed, and parts of the developing, world. Elsewhere, such as Jamaica or Romania or South Sudan or South Africa, the declines are more like a half or two thirds.[160] Researchers credit improved sex-education programs, along with easier access to contraception and abortion. The relatively recent phenomena of over-the-counter emergency contraception—a.k.a the morning-after pill—and the abortion pill are also helping. Though some socially or religiously conservative groups try to deny it, the evidence is clear. If you want to reduce teenage pregnancies, the key is to teach children about sex and to make contraception cheap and easy to obtain.

The social consequences of fewer teen pregnancies are entirely positive: Fewer young women become trapped in poverty from having a child too early. Governments don't have to spend as much on social programs such as welfare, freeing up money to spend else-where. Crime rates go down—thanks to there being fewer young males from damaged homes at risk of joining gangs or getting into other kinds of trouble—thus reducing police and penitentiary costs. But as women get older and still choose not to have children, the consequences become more mixed.

Although women are still far from achieving full equality, they are closing the gap and banging on that glass ceiling. In 1973, the year the U.S. Supreme Court upheld a woman's right to an abortion in *Roe v. Wade*, a typical woman made 57 percent of what a man earned. By 2016, the figure had reached 80 percent.[161] That's still far too wide a gap, but all trend lines are encouraging. Women outnumber men at universities: 72 percent of woman high school graduates proceed immediately to college, compared to 61 percent of men.[162] Fifty-five percent of the students in medical schools in the United Kingdom are women.[163] In the United States, about 40 percent of chemists and material scientists and 30 percent of environmental scientists and geoscientists are women.[164] This is still not full equality, but again, the gap is closing.

When a woman has an interesting, well-paying job, she is less likely to get pregnant. Childbirth can be a major impediment to career advancement. Even with the most enlightened parental-leave policies, even with the best child care available, taking time off work to have a child can set back a woman's career. Leaving work early because the school calls to say your child is throwing up can raise eyebrows. Sending an email saying you'll be working from home today because the child care arrangements fell through gets noticed. Yes, fathers could and should do more, but they often don't. Studies show that childless women earn about the same as men. It's having children that generates the pay gap.[165]

Good jobs require many years of education, often including a second degree or diploma. That education is expensive: in the United States, seven out of ten graduates carry debt, with the average size of that debt around twenty-nine thousand dollars.[166] Who can afford to have a baby before that debt is brought under control? One of the unintended side effects of increasing college tuition is that it lowers fertility rates.

Once the debt is paid off, there's the question of finding Mr. or Ms. Right. People take that all-important challenge more seriously than they used to. The boomers were encouraged to marry young, which meant many of them married badly. In previous generations, people endured a loveless home, but in 1969, California became the first state to offer no-fault divorce, making it much easier to end a marriage. In 1960 in the United States, when divorce was still something of a *scandale*, there were nine divorces per one thousand marriages each year; by 1980, the divorce rate had peaked at twenty-three per one thousand marriages. But then it began to decline, and today it sits at around sixteen per one thousand marriages.[167] Divorce is traumatic for children; many of those who went through it or witnessed it seem determined not to inflict the experience on the next generation. One option is not to marry at all: marriage rates have declined by 50 percent since 1970. Another is to wait until both partners are older, more mature, more financially secure. In 1960, the typical American woman got married at twenty. Today she is twenty-six.

All of this means that women give birth to their first child later than they did in the past. As we mentioned, thirty is now the typical age for a first child in many countries. More women over forty now give birth for the first time than women under twenty. Amazingly, there is a tiny but rapidly increasing cohort of women giving birth in their fifties: in the United States in 2015, 754 of them, up from 643 the year before and 144 in 1997.[168] Since women start to become less fertile after thirty, the longer they wait to have their first child, the fewer children they are likely to have. But women know this. The decision to wait until they are older to have a first child is part of a larger decision, taken with their husbands or partners, to have only one or two children.

Infertile couples sometimes turn to adoption as a solution. But increasingly, adoption is no solution at all, for reasons that are both local and geopolitical. Domestically, finding available babies for adoption is becoming ever more difficult, thanks to the drastic reduction in teenage pregnancies. And values have changed: unwed mothers, for example, are no longer pressured to give up their babies for adoption.[169]

That leaves the overseas market. Americans adopt more children from other countries than the rest of the world combined. And up until relatively recently, adopt-a-baby was a growth industry. The end of the Cold War allowed parents seeking children access to many thousands of abandoned babies. In the peak year of 2004, 22,989 children arrived in the U.S. as adoptees from other countries. The top five baby-exporting countries were China (which exported 70,026 babies that year), Russia (46,113), Guatemala (29,803), South Korea (20,058), and Ethiopia (15,135).[170] And then the numbers started to go down. And down. And way down. In 2015, the United States brought in only 5,647 babies for adoption, less than a quarter of the number that had come in a decade before. The reasons are many.

As relations with the West deteriorated, Russia banned all foreign adoptions of Russian children in 2012. War in eastern Ukraine made it impossible to take children out of that region. Other countries closed their borders to child exports when it became clear that criminals were buying (or kidnapping) babies and selling them to gullible Westerners. But the single biggest factor was China. As that country's economy grew, and the consequences of the one-child policy started to hit home, the supply of available babies dwindled. Today, virtually all Chinese babies available for adoption are special needs.

Adoption statistics can be hard to come by, because adoptions are primarily handled at a state or provincial level. But the province of Alberta is probably typical. There, even though the number of people seeking to adopt is increasing, actual adoptions declined by 25 percent between 2008 and 2015, and the waiting time to obtain a baby increased from eighteen months to three years.[171]

Tie it all together and this is what you see: Better understanding of contraception and of the social and economic costs of having a child early in life and without a reliable father, along with easier access to emergency contraception and abortion, have led to fewer teenage women having babies. The length and cost of a good education has convinced an increasing number of women not to have a child in their early twenties. The demands of career, the cost of paying off student loans, and the desire to be sure that the man in their life is there to stay encourage an increasing number of women to hold off having a child in their late twenties. When everything does come together to make a child desirable and affordable, many women today are in their thirties, or even forties. Not surprisingly, these women tend to have small families.

We suspect that, no matter what age you are, whether you are a woman or a man, whether you are principally someone's daughter or son, or principally someone's father or mother, all of this resonates with you. These are choices that you are grappling with, or that you have already made. Struggling to pay off loans, struggling to find a decent job, searching for the right person to spend your life with, weighing whether this is the time to finally have a baby, wondering whether the two of you can afford a second one, living with the consequences of that decision—chances are, this is your story. And your choices influence not only your life but the lives of everyone. Because as it turns out, your choices, multiplied by the choices of millions of others, have consequences for everybody.

Small families are, in all sorts of ways, wonderful things. Parents can devote more time and resources to raising—indeed, cossetting—the child. Children are likely to be raised with the positive role models of a working father and working mother. Such families reflect a society in which women stand equally, or at least near equally, with men in the home and the workplace. Women workers also help to mitigate the labor shortages produced by smaller workforces that result from too few babies. It isn't going too far to say that small families are synonymous with enlightened, advanced societies.

But small families are hard on an economy. As we've seen, they reduce the number of consumers available to purchase goods. They reduce the number of taxpayers available to fund social programs. They reduce the number of young, innovative minds. It can be no coincidence that, just as Japan's aging society is a factor in three decades of economic stagnation, so too is the aging of Europe contributing to the stagnation that dogs the economies of so many countries on that continent. The influence of children, or the lack of them, on a nation's economy is profound.

Government programs, such as generous parental leave and child allowances, can encourage parents to have more children. But the impact is minimal, and the programs are so expensive that governments find them difficult to sustain. In any case, small families are also about self-empowerment, the sloughing-off of the social duty to procreate in favor of crafting a personal narrative—life, as told to Facebook. The low-fertility trap, once in place, is irreversible.

There are other consequences—social, political, environmental—of population decline, which we'll look at in the following chapters. But this much at least we can certainly say: economically, a scarcity of babies is a very big deal. And it lies behind one of the more interesting, but least reported, phenomena of our times: the Boomaissance.

Mick Jagger, his face skeletal at seventy-three, his mop of hair suspiciously untouched by gray, greeted the seventy-five thousand fans who filled the Empire Polo Field with sly humor: "Welcome to the Palm Springs retirement home for genteel British musicians." And then he and rest of the Stones proceeded to rock the house.

No, this was not Coachella, the world-renowned music festival that also takes place at the Empire Polo Field. This was Desert Trip, better known by its nickname: Oldchella. The Stones, The Who, Bob Dylan, Neil Young, Paul McCartney, and Roger Waters of Pink

Floyd played the venue over two weekends in October 2016. And
here's the thing: Coachella—which usually generates more revenue
than any other American music festival[172]—raked in $94 million
that year; Oldchella took in $160 million, almost twice as much.

The reason was simple: Oldchella charged an eye-watering $1,600
for a top-price ticket, compared to $900 for Coachella. For that money
you got four-course meals with the finest wines and an art exhibit in
an air-conditioned tent. Every one of the thousand portable toilets
flushed.[173] There were millennials as well as boomers in the crowd,
though people joked the most popular drug at the concert was Viagra,
and when Rihanna joined Paul McCartney in a surprise appearance,
half the audience had to explain to the other half who she was.

Oldchella is a classic example of the Boomaissance: the marketing
offensive to cater to the needs of the baby boomers rather than those
of the smaller and poorer cohort of Gen Xers and millennials. "While
the media remain smitten with millennials, it's the boomers who control 70 percent of the disposable income in this country," one analyst
wrote.[174] And if that weren't enough, boomers are in the midst
of receiving fifteen trillion dollars in inheritance from their departing
parents. Advertisers and marketers are studying how to unlock that
wealth, employing everything from easy-to-understand tutorials on
how to navigate social media to larger fonts on paint cans.[175]

Young people today are investing in expensive educations as the
only way to get a line on a good job. Once they graduate, they have
all that student debt to pay off. And their jobs are insecure, forcing
them to delay the big purchases. Why would you open a restaurant
for hipsters when the only diners who can afford your prices think
the music is too loud, the tables too close—how are you supposed
to fit a walker in there?—and the menu simply ridiculous. (Kimchi?
What the hell is kimchi?) You'd be better off lowering the volume,
making the seating more generous, and offering a nice steak. And if

you live in a decent-sized city in North America, chances are you have at least one cinema with premium-priced tickets that guarantee a reserved, comfortable seat with helpful servers bringing your food and drinks—white wine, not pop—to you. Boomaissance.

But the impacts of an aging society go far beyond marketing ploys. Children and seniors are both dependent populations: they use a disproportionate amount of what the state provides, especially in the developed world. But they are dependent in different ways. Kids need daycare and schools, while seniors need pensions and palliative care. As the median age of the world continues to increase—today it's thirty-one, in 2050 it will be thirty-six, by 2100 it will be forty-two—the agenda will increasingly tilt to meeting the needs of the population that's growing the most: fewer schools and more assisted-living support programs.

A statistic that nicely summarizes the interplay of these forces is the "seniors' dependency ratio." This is the number of working-age people available to support each retired person. Today, there are 6.3 working-age people in the world for every person who is over retirement age. This is a positive ratio, and the world will be in good shape if it holds up. But we already know that it won't. The UN tells us that by 2050 the world's ratio will slip to 3.4 to 1, and, by 2100 it will slide further to 2.4 to 1. That's right, by the end of this century, just over two working-age people will be available in the world to pay for the public services used by each person of retirement age. And that assumes the UN's fertility projections are accurate, and as you know, we don't think they are. So the two-working-people-for-every-old-person ratio could arrive much sooner than many think. Already, several countries in Europe are close to 2 to 1.

This could lead to economic challenges as the state struggles to provide geriatric services despite a diminishing tax base and fewer consumers drive a weaker economy. It could also be deeply, personally painful for some as well. As the Chinese sociologist Feng Wang writes, "Ever more Chinese parents in the future will not be able to count on their children in their old age. And many parents will face a most unfortunate reality: outliving their children and therefore dying alone."[176] Mortality schedules state that the likelihood of an eighty-year-old woman outliving her fifty-five-year-old-son, because he gets ill or has an accident, is 17 percent.[177] And where there is no grief, there may instead be guilt. How many parents around the world will feel shame at being forced to ask for help from children who also struggle to manage their marriage, parenthood, and a job?

The relationship and family choices we are making, or are about to make, or have already made, define our present and future. They shape our society today and will shape it even more profoundly in our future. They will orient social programs, private enterprise, and research technology away from the young and toward the old, not completely—for there is still tremendous value in hooking a young person on your product, perhaps for life—but in part at least. Every year these changes will become more powerful. Your city council will debate converting empty schools into seniors' centers. There will be grief counseling for bereaved parents who have lost an adult child. We may see the return of the extended family: three generations living under one roof.

Welcome to the future of population decline. Or rather, the present.

SIX

THE AFRICA QUESTION

Nairobi's Jomo Kenyatta International Airport is a far cry from what it used to be, and that's a good thing. Five years ago, a traveler who landed at NBO, one of Africa's busiest airports, would find herself in a very long line at immigration control, which ended at a desk staffed by a single bored young man oblivious to the throng begging for his attention. Every now and then, he would look up from his mobile phone, reluctantly acknowledging the traveler who stood patiently before him. After taking the immigration form, along with US$50, he would make an entry in a Dickensian ledger and stamp the traveler's passport. Welcome to Kenya. Next.

Today, if you want to travel to Kenya, you purchase an "eVisa" online weeks before. Upon arrival, you discover that the bored young man has been replaced by immigration kiosks lining a new, modern, brightly lit reception center that would look at home in any Western airport. Once you are in front of an immigration official, you have your picture taken with one of those ball-on-a-stick cameras and your fingerprints scanned, just as you do when entering the United States. There is no ledger, no cash payment. Welcome to Kenya. Next.

We are at ground zero of the debate over the future of our planet's population. The United Nations projects that the number of people on earth will swell from seven to eleven billion over the course of the century because the United Nations doesn't hold out much hope for Africa. It believes the fertility rate will remain high for decades to come, especially in sub-Saharan Africa, powering the last great baby boom before numbers begin to subside in the next century. Grim decades lie ahead as humanity struggles to feed itself and limit the damage it inflicts on a fragile earth.

But must Africa remain dark for so many years to come—its society rural, its people uneducated, its women unfree? Or is Africa, too, following the path of urbanization, education, emancipation? This may be the most important question facing us. Wealth or poverty, war or peace, a warming or cooling atmosphere hinge on the answer. We can't be certain of the answer. But we can at least look for clues. Some of those clues can be found in Nairobi.

Africa, in the second decade of the twenty-first century, is a happening place. In 2016, fourteen of the thirty fastest growing economies— so almost half—were in Africa. Kenya ranked twentieth, with a projected GDP growth above 6 percent each year for the foreseeable future—three times what most Western nations are experiencing.[178] Few doubt that the continent will remain a center of economic growth in the decades ahead.

Some of that growth is self-generating as the continent becomes increasingly important as a consumer market. By 2050, the population of Africa is projected to more than double to 2.6 billion. The biggest national population in Africa today is Nigeria's, at 182 million. By mid-century, Nigeria will be the fourth-largest country, by

population, in the world. Kenya's population will double over that
same period. Meanwhile, Europe's overall population is projected
to shrink by 4 percent.[179] If you were an investor forced to choose,
would you choose Europe or Africa?

Although Africa is our cradle, the place we all come from, it is
also young, with a median age of only nineteen, compared to forty-
two for Europe and thirty-five for North America.[180] In the coming
decades, Africa is expected to be the only region in the world that
will significantly increase its working-age population. On this, everyone agrees: between now and mid-century, Africa will grow both its
population and its economy.

Kenya, which wants to become a regional business hub for international companies chasing opportunities in Africa, is in a race for
modernity with its continental competitors. That upgraded airport
was all about winning that race. Kenya's advantage, like the joke
about the two guys being chased by the bear, is that it doesn't have to
beat the world, it just has to beat the local competition. The country
is centrally and strategically located in East Africa, with the Indian
Ocean, Uganda, and Tanzania on its borders. It also shares borders
with Ethiopia, South Sudan, and Somalia. Yes, it's a rough neighborhood, but Kenya represents a zone of relative calm within the region,
which makes it attractive for international businesses.

That said, the flash of a modern airport represents a bit of a
Potemkin village. About 75 percent of Kenya's workers are still
occupied either full- or part-time in agriculture, which represents
about a third of the economy.[181] Only about a quarter of the citizenry
earns a salary from either a private- or public-sector employer, which
is the very definition of a modern workforce.[182] The unemployment
rate in Kenya could be as high as 40 percent.[183]

Half the population doesn't believe it gets enough to eat and
about a third reports sometimes going to bed hungry.[184] Seven out

of ten Kenyans say they earn less than US$700 per month.[185] Four
in ten live below the poverty line.[186] This is a country in which about
half the population lives the old life of premodern subsistence. But
on the other hand, 75 percent of the population have mobile device
subscriptions.[187] And the rural is slowly giving way to the urban.
Kenya's urban population is growing at a rate of more than 4 percent
annually, centered on Nairobi (pop. four million) and Mombasa
(pop. 1.1 million).[188] In the past three decades, the country's urban
population has more than doubled, from 15 percent of the total in
1979 to 32 percent in 2014.[189] And by now you know what happens
to a country as it urbanizes: the fertility rate starts to go down.

Many Kenyans live two lives at the same time: The first is imme-
morial, agricultural, subsistent, and of course, patriarchal. But in her
back pocket, there's a cellphone. And though she hasn't told her parents yet, she's planning on moving to the city.

Dawn breaks over a Nairobi that bears few traces of its colonial past.
Glass towers, government buildings, electronic billboards, modern
storefronts, greenspace dominate the downtown. The sidewalks
are filled with well-dressed people on their way to work. Roads are
modern and in good repair (except for the occasional apocalyptic
pothole), as are the cars and trucks using them. Traffic's a headache,
but nothing to compare with the hopeless tangles in New York or
Paris. All seems reasonably calm and orderly: a city open and ready
for modern business.

But a few kilometers from downtown Nairobi—a short, white-
knuckle ride by *matatu*, the local minibuses Kenyans use to get
around—is Kibera. The most populous slum in Africa, and maybe the
world, is home to about a quarter million souls.[190] Kibera represents
the flip side of the dual realities of Nairobi: Downtown. Kibera.

The place is an assault on the senses, beginning with an overload

of the color red. Red rust stains the tin roofs laid out as far as the
eye can see. The muddy soil that tracks between the riot of shacks
and makes up the potholed, random dirt roads and paths is red. The
smell, for a pampered Westerner, is hard to describe or forget. There
are no formal sanitary facilities in Kibera, and open sewers run wherever there is open ground. There are also random piles of garbage,
with adults, children, and animals picking through them.

To Western eyes, Kibera is dystopic, hopeless squalor. Not so for
Kenyans. To them, Kibera is a community with a distinct culture
and purpose. It is as much Nairobi as the modern downtown. Kibera
is also the seat of the traditional economy. It is overrun with informal
businesses—food stalls, small grocers, butchers, secondhand clothing stores, repair shops. Some are established stalls or stores, others
are just blankets spread out on the ground with whatever is on offer.
The Kenyan women visiting this day make mental notes about
which clothing shops would be worth a return visit on the weekend.
The men would return for a piece of recycled hardware, or for a part
for an older car. Whatever they need is on offer in Kibera, and at a
better price than in any modern store.

Kibera is also the home for new arrivals—either migrants from
the countryside or those moving from other communities. Manhattan
a century ago had its Lower East Side; Nairobi today has Kibera.
While poverty, terrible sanitation, social pathologies (such as alcohol abuse and teen pregnancies), corruption, and crime are all rampant, these don't make the community a no-go zone for Kenyans
from other parts of Nairobi. Kibera is a distinct center for cultural
and commercial interactions, like any historical ethnic enclave in
a major Western city. Think the Latin Quarter, Little Italy, or
Chinatown. Not today's versions, but the way these places looked
a few generations ago. There's a lot going on in Kibera.

Whether he lives in Kibera, a leafy, affluent neighborhood, or something in between, a Kenyan's personal identity is rooted in tribe, clan, and family. These loyalties supersede any attachment to the Kenyan state. When a visitor asked one of his Kenyan colleagues whether he identified with being Kenyan, he answered, "If you slap me, I'm Kenyan; if a Kenyan slaps me, I'm Luo."[191] For Kenyans, tribe comes first. The same is true across most of Africa.

There are three main ethnic groups in Kenya: Bantus (the largest, at around 70 percent of the population), followed by the Nilotes and Cushites. Each ethnic group has a unique history, culture, lifestyle, language, religion, and food. These ethnic groups are then divided into roughly forty-two tribes, with the tribes subdivided into clans. A clan is equivalent to a family tree. Clan members can trace their lineage back to a common ancestor. Clans can, however, cut across ethnic groups and tribes. Clan is something that someone from the Scottish Highlands would recognize.

Most places on earth are organized around kin or tribe or community. Local and national governments in many countries are some combination of remote, incompetent, corrupt, and menacing. The police are on the make, getting a permit requires a bribe, who you know decides what you get. In such societies, kin is everything. Kin you can trust. Kin won't let you down. Your place in the family or the tribe defines who you are and how you behave.

In developed nations, the modern welfare state has largely replaced tribes, clans, and families as the final source of authority and support in the lives of those countries' citizens. Not so in Kenya. For the average Kenyan, government is simply a plutocracy that generates personal wealth for connected politicians and bureaucrats, not the place you go to for help when times are tough.

Although no one in any part of the world denies the importance of family, things work much, much better when countries are run by reasonably honest governments and the bonds of clan and tribe are weak or nonexistent. You may think your government is inefficient, but if you live in a democratic capitalist society you probably have no idea of what truly inefficient government looks like. Your parents and brothers and sisters and children may mean everything to you, but you probably have little idea of how little your family name, the church you attend, the elementary school you went to, your accent, or the way you dress matters compared to some other societies. You may have given little thought to how much you rely on government for things that really matter in your life. But the dichotomy between government-dominated and kin-dominated societies is roughly the dichotomy between advanced, developed countries and evolving, developing (or in some cases devolving, collapsing) countries.

The dichotomy isn't exact: some nations, such as Greece or Ukraine, act like modern developed states on good days and corrupt pseudo-states on bad days. But Greece at its worst is vastly more functional than Kenya at its best. Postcolonial government in Kenya is chaotic, unruly, sometimes violent, and universally distrusted. The country ranks 139 out of 168 countries measured in the Transparency International Corruption Perceptions Index.[192] It ranks 135 out of 178 nations ("mostly unfree") in economic freedom[193] and scores 51 out of 100 ("partly free") in political freedom, according to Freedom House.[194] Things could be worse, but Kenya still has a long way to go, which is why tribal allegiance in terms of both personal identity and social organization is so strong. Even well-educated and world-traveling Kenyans readily acknowledge that, if you politely scratch, tribal identity is there, just below the surface. As one Kenyan put it, "Government is about yams and knives [money and force], tribe is about trust."[195] And as we've already noted, when kin ties are stronger, fertility rates are higher thanks to family pressure to marry and have children; when kin are replaced with peers and co-workers, the pressure eases and fertility declines.

When young Kenyans go off to school or start a job in a new location, they aren't left to their own devices. Their family connects them to a blood relation, or tribal or clan connection. They may physically stay with this contact; they know they can always reach out in a pinch. Everyone counts on these connections, and everyone is expected to do their part in supporting them. And nobody dies alone in Kenya. People's tribe, clan, and village will take care of them. Most communities or traditional social groups have a "burial society." These are self-help groups that make sure that each member of the community—regardless of their economic status—has a proper burial when the time comes. All contribute to the society, and all expect to access what the society provides.

This communal approach to social organization even finds its way into the epicenter of modern capitalism: the Nairobi headquarters of global companies. As one Belgian expat who arrived in Kenya to take over his company's regional operations quickly learned, there's always a collection going on for someone in the office—a wedding, a soon-to-arrive baby, a retirement.[196] The Kenyans call it *harambee*, which in Swahili means "everyone pulls together." The top executive is expected to set the standard, and will be judged by their willingness to personally contribute to the cause. And this is no token contribution for a birthday card or cake. It's a substantial gift by which others benchmark their own expected personal contribution, depending on where they are in the office hierarchy. The new arrival quickly learned his role when some women in the office took him aside to kindly but firmly explain what was expected of him as the most senior executive.

This unique interaction of modern business requirements and traditional cultural expectations gives demographic modelers conniption fits as they try to predict how populations will develop in the future. While acknowledging that Kenya has halved its birth rate in little more than a generation (from around eight in 1975 to around four today), the UN Population Division predicts a gradual slowing of the rate of decline, so that Kenya won't reach the replacement rate of 2.1 children per mother until around 2075. Other African nations, the UN predicts, will also reduce their fertility rate more slowly in this century than they reduced them in the last half of the previous one. But if the decline continued at something like its current pace, then Kenya would reach replacement rate before 2050, a single generation from now.[197]

Will Kenya, as the UN projects, transition slowly from a kin-based, agriculture-oriented, low-education, high-corruption society whose population grows rapidly due to improved life expectancy and high fertility? Or will it rapidly urbanize and modernize, strengthening the bonds of the state, weakening tribal influence, and empowering women to choose how many children they will have, leading in turn to a continued rapid decline in fertility? We believe the latter will prove to be true, that in Kenya and in many other African countries, the commingling of capitalist and traditional values will very likely slow the massive population growth that most modelers are projecting. Why? Because much of the rest of the world is precedent. Africa is following the global shift toward urbanization, education for women, and a lower fertility rate. This is especially true in Kenya.

The Kenyan government instituted free primary public education in 2003. Free secondary school education arrived in 2008. About two million students are educated in unlicensed "informal schools" that are often faith-based and often quite good. About 17 percent of Kenyan children are still not receiving a decent education, but this is a much lower figure than in previous generations.[198] In recent years, the government has begun to invest massively in postsecondary education. In 2005, there were five universities; a decade later there were twenty-two, with plans for another twenty. Between 2012 and 2014, university enrollment *doubled,* to 445,000 students.[199] Cultural biases that still favor men pose serious obstacles to girls seeking an education in Kenya, especially in the countryside. But the walls of the patriarchy are crumbling. Boys and girls today are equally well represented in primary and secondary classrooms,[200] and thanks to affirmative action programs, women now make up at least 40 percent of the enrollment in Kenyan universities.[201]

Is education leading to empowerment for women and the decision to have fewer babies? According to the Kenyan Bureau of Statistics, fertility in the country has decreased from 4.9 births per woman in 2003, to 4.6 in 2008–09, to 3.9 in 2014. The country has experienced "a one-child decline over the past 10 years and the lowest TFR [total fertility rate] ever recorded in Kenya."[202] And consider this: the Kenyan Bureau of Statistics has also noted a "marked increase in the contraceptive prevalence rate (CPR) from 46 percent in 2008–09 to 58 percent in 2014."[203] That is a big leap in contraceptive use in only five years. It's a small leap from there to faster-declining fertility.

This doesn't mean that Kenya's strong population growth won't continue over the medium term. Young populations—those with low median ages like Kenya's—continue to grow significantly for decades, simply because there are so many young women. And child mortality is also decreasing. While Kenyan women are having fewer children than their mothers did, more of those children survive to adulthood. But as numerous studies have demonstrated, reducing childhood mortality in developing countries also reduces the fertility rate—parents have fewer children when they are confident those children will survive.[204] There are more children who are not being born in Kenya than there are children who are not dying.

The rapid pace of urbanization in Kenya, the rapid increase in education among Kenyan women, the combustible impact of online technology, the transformative impact of international commerce moving to Africa, improved programs in maternal health and education (including sex education) by NGOs—all of these factors are ignored, or insufficiently considered by population models that see Africa's fertility rate as static or in slow decline.[205] The situation is far too dynamic and fluid for such assumptions.

We can fold together all of these myriad economic and social factors—urbanization, education, modernization, and social transformation—by looking at one ancient custom in transition: the dowry. In Kenya it's still around. And as it turns out, there's an app for that.

In Western culture, when two people decide to marry, for the most part they are deemed to be starting a new family that is separate from, though connected to, the families of their parents. Sure, everyone tries to get together during the holidays. But in North America or in Europe, kin relationships usually aren't central to whether the marriage takes place or is a success. Not so in Kenya. There, a marriage is more like a corporate merger. The two families come together to strengthen their mutual social safety nets. While not quite arranged marriages, the involvement of both families in finding and vetting suitable mates for their children is critical, because both families need to believe that the merger will improve the economic and health prospects for both sides. Online dating is largely seen as both bizarre and irresponsible by most Africans. As one Kenyan woman put it, "How would you know if he comes from a good family?"[206]

Since courtship and marriage are about strengthening family networks in Kenya, Kenyans have developed complicated procedures to select appropriate, safety-net-enhancing mates for their children and families. In conversations with an outsider, there is a lot of talk about the role that the "aunties" (who could be female blood relations, close female neighbors, or senior clan members) play in the process. As one woman said, "My aunties will always know someone who knows someone who knows the boy's family. They will check him out for us."[207]

The payment of dowries is also a critical feature in courtship and marriage. This is the same in many other African countries. Dowries are complicated. It's all about negotiating the right number of cows, goats, or a combination of the two to earn the right to marry a woman from a particular family. In some communities, it's a standard number of cows or goats. In others, other commodities (such as other livestock or honey) could also be involved. Sometimes, even though the groom is deemed to be otherwise suitable by the bride's family, he can't afford the initial dowry price. If so, a schedule has to be worked out so that the groom can pay the dowry in installments.

The dowry is based on the perceived value of the prospective bride. There are various pricing factors at play. As one woman noted, this is why Kenyan families have formal parlors in their homes, with graduation pictures of their kids on display. The room provides visual affirmation to the interested suitor's family of their child's accomplishments and his or her potential earning ability after marriage.[208]

One might assume that younger Kenyans, especially women, who have been exposed to the idealized love matches extolled by Hollywood and to the commoditization of sex via the Internet, would be very much against this type of material bargaining for their affection. Yet in conversations with Kenyan women and men, support for the dowry tradition was consistent and strong, regardless of gender or age or marital status, even among senior female executives who were well educated and thoroughly modern in every aspect of their professional lives.

While dowries are a practice from the past, modern thinking and technology have now found their way into today's system. Few families in a place like Nairobi would have suitable facilities to maintain a herd of cows or goats. So they monetize the payment. There are even websites and apps that will calculate what your expected dowry should be, based on your personal profile.[209] This doesn't mean that the exchange of real livestock doesn't happen today. One young Kenyan woman described herself as a "traditional girl" who came from a small village a few hours' drive from Nairobi. She and her family insisted that her future husband pay the dowry in actual livestock. So the first part of her wedding involved a truck containing the appropriate number of cows arriving at the family farm where the wedding was to take place. Everyone went to the barn to inspect the product. Once the bride's family was satisfied with the payment, the wedding party and guests returned to the farmhouse for the joyous celebration.[210]

Wedding traditions in Kenya have evolved over the centuries to strengthen community alliances. They continue to do so today. But thanks to global commerce and urbanization, they have now morphed in ways that can only work against Kenya's high fertility rate. Here's why: If a Kenyan woman wants a good salaried job in the city, she needs a superior education. Obtaining that education and job makes her eligible for better potential mates. Having a college degree and a corner office makes you worth more cows and goats. It also means delaying both marriage and having children. The prospective husband must work longer to accumulate the capital to pay the dowry. And the prospective wife is happy to wait. "We're getting married later," one woman explained. "We want an education, job security, and a nice place to live before we have kids. We now get married when we're thirty because we spend so much time in school. Then the pressure starts from our mothers and aunties to start having kids. But that's hard to do because we are working a lot to be successful in our careers. This also means that we can't have as many kids, even if we want them."[211]

So the traditional institution of the dowry combines with the modern impetus of education and career to delay marriage and delay having children, which has already affected the Kenyan fertility rate, and which will lower that rate further in the years to come. This is another reason why the United Nations population projections for Kenya are off, and the lower population projections produced jointly by the Wittgenstein Centre, the Vienna Institute for Demography, and the International Institute for Applied Systems Analysis—which have Kenya reaching replacement rate by 2060— are likely to be closer to the mark.

Kenya is not Africa. In some parts of the continent, life is still largely rural, and women have few or no rights and little or no formal education. In such places, birth rates remain alarmingly high. Geoffrey York, a Canadian journalist, chronicled the efforts of aid agencies to educate women about sexual and reproductive health using a "contraception boat" that traveled from village to village in the impoverished West African nation of Benin. The women he spoke to well knew the toll that having child after child takes on their health. "I've had too many babies," said Christian Djengue, who has had ten children, eight of whom survived. "I feel sicker and weaker. I suffer illnesses, like hypertension. I get headaches and vertigo and fatigue." But she has little choice. "If you tell your husband that you don't want a large family, he will just go and marry another woman," she explains. "It's a lot of pressure. Our husbands love children and large families." Local religious leaders support the men by preaching against the evils of contraception. "She'll just say exactly what I say," Bourasma Kokossou, a tailor, explained about his wife. "My wife obeys me. Without my approval, she can't do anything. She can't even move."[212]

If Africa rises, as Kenya is starting to rise, then Africa will not produce the millions born in misery that the UN demographers predict. But yes, there is another future for the continent, one of poverty and patrimony and large families. Will more countries move forward, albeit uncertainly, like Kenya, or will most Africans remain mired in deep poverty, at constant risk of disease and violence? One way to answer that question is to look at the rights of women across the continent. For there is no better measure of the progress of a society than the progress of women within that society.

A 2017 report by the African Union observes that some African countries have more women in their legislatures than most Western countries. In fact, Rwanda tops the globe, with 64 percent of its parliamentarians women. Other data, however, is more grim. One in three African women experiences physical or sexual violence. Because many African countries prohibit abortion on any grounds, even if the mother's life is at risk, almost one third of all the unsafe abortions that occur in the world each year occur in Africa. Most of the 130 million women alive today who have undergone female genital mutilation live in Africa, and 125 million of the current population of African women were married before the age of eighteen.[213] "Wherever there are enabling environments in which women are able to exercise and enjoy their rights including access to education, to skills, to jobs, there is a surge of prosperity, positive health outcomes, and greater freedom and wellbeing of not only women but the society as whole," the report concludes.

Nonetheless, many societies resist granting women these rights, thanks to local instability, religious concerns, and "the continued contestation of the universality of human rights vis-à-vis African values," as the African Union report diplomatically expressed it.[214] The best measure of the progress of women within a society is the progress of their education, for everything else flows from that. As the health care philanthropists Baroness Valerie Amos and Toyin Saraki opined, "Girls' education could be the single biggest determinant of development in lower-income countries."[215] UNICEF once called educating girls "a solution to almost every problem."[216] Not only does education equip women for work and increase their personal autonomy, it reduces the likelihood of malnutrition, illness, and childhood marriage. If Africa is to escape the poverty trap, female education is the surest route.

And here, the numbers are positively exciting. In 2000, in almost all African countries, at least 30 percent of girls who should have been in school weren't, according to OXFAM. The exceptions included Algeria (11 percent), South Africa (5 percent), Gabon (9 percent), and a few others. But by 2016, the unhappy club of countries that didn't educate their girls had shrunk to a band of countries near the equator running from Mali in the west to Sudan in the east. Almost every country south of that line had at least 80 percent of its school-age girls in school. Benin reported a female elementary school participation rate of 88 percent.[217]

And in Benin, the fertility rate is starting to come down. It was 7.0 in 1985. It's 5.2 now. The UN predicts only gradual progress for Benin, which is not projected to reach a 2.1 fertility rate until the end of the century. But more girls are now in school. And as the contraception boat makes its rounds, the women listen.

The Muthaiga Country Club opened to great fanfare on New Year's Eve in 1913; a century later, it remains a throwback to a time when the English colonial rulers craved the creature comforts of an

English gentlemen's club in the wilds of Africa. Today's club maintains the impressive original buildings, with their pink and white colonnades, along with many of the trappings and traditions of the past: taxidermied hunting trophies, overstuffed leather chairs, an impressive library, and exceptional wood-panelled bars. Modern touches include a gym, a swimming pool, and more casual dining options. But gentlemen still must wear jackets and ties in the evening. After all, this is the Muthaiga Club. We are dining here thanks to an invitation from the head of a local firm that has recently been acquired by one of those multinationals looking for a foothold in Africa. Fifteen members from the company's Nairobi office are also attending. All except the host and a traveler are African and women.

The lovely, temperate evening begins with drinks in the club's beautiful ornamental gardens, the scent of flowers perfuming the air, before we interrupt our lively, laugh-filled conversation to go inside to the club's impressive Yellow Room, named after the color of its walls. Uniformed Kenyan waiters with white gloves carve and serve a prime rib roast, replete with Yorkshire pudding, from a trolley using heavy silver utensils. Dinner ends with port and cognac from the drinks cart. The British governed their empire this way, and the upper reaches of Kenyan society are happy to continue the tradition.

We discuss tribal identity with a level of frankness unnerving to someone from a more politically correct, Western environment. For the Kenyans, there is a distinct and obvious hierarchy among tribes determined by factors such as cultural history and predispositions, color of skin, height, hair texture, and where people grew up. It is similar to hearing someone from Britain describe the English class system—what you learn from someone's accent, which schools should be embraced or shunned, who is One of Us and who is not— without the least trace of shame. As with all class systems, nuance is everything, and an outsider is oblivious to subtle distinctions that mean everything to the native-born.

The talk turns to family size. The mothers of these women produced a lot of kids. The largest brood consisted of eleven girls and boys; the average was six. The fertility rate in Kenya in 1980 was eight, so given the age of the people at the dinner, that's not too far off the mark. Six multiplied by fifteen gives a total of ninety children. But as parents, the guests at the table are a stingy lot. Some want as many as three children; some want none at all; the average is 1.5. So a total of around twenty-three children, with most of the parents at the table saying they have already had all the children they plan on having. That's a reduction of more than two thirds of the number of children produced in a single generation.

It's true that this table at the Muthaiga Country Club is an elite audience. Most Kenyans wouldn't recognize the lives that these people live. All the African diners had at least one university degree and a well-paying job in the city with an international company. But they are setting the aspirational trend for their society. Provided Kenya remains internally at peace—a challenge for most postcolonial African states, which struggle to navigate tribal tensions and arbitrarily drawn borders—then people will continue to leave the countryside for the city, more women will become better educated, and fewer babies will be born.

Of course, while Kenya's population growth will be limited by lower fertility, it will also be bolstered by increasing longevity. The average Kenyan today lives to the age of sixty-one. This is up from fifty-one at the turn of the century.[218] This is a major increase in the amount of time we can expect each Kenyan to remain on this earth. One factor that's a big unknown for longevity in Kenya is the prevalence of HIV/AIDS. It's estimated that 5.3 percent of Kenyans have HIV or AIDS (the thirteenth highest rate of infection of any country in the world), and that thirty-three thousand die from it every year (ninth in the world). If the prevalence or mortality of HIV/AIDS goes up, then we can expect longevity to go down.[219] The same would apply to any other significant outbreak of diseases such as Ebola. However, the widespread adoption of affordable antiretroviral medicines—spurred in part by initiatives undertaken by the Bush administration in the early 2000s—holds out long-term hope that the HIV/AIDS scourge in Africa can be contained. In any case, more old people being kept alive won't have any impact on the number of kids being born. Though they keep Kenya's population numbers high, the effect is temporary, as each generation is succeeded by one that is smaller, with fewer children.

If Kenya is typical of the path that Africa is on, then expecting African parents to produce the babies that people in other parts of the world aren't having is unrealistic. Kenyans are already having fewer babies, and are likely to have even fewer in the years ahead. The complex interaction of culture, capitalism, urbanization, technology, and the education of women is forming local vortexes of change that will shape the future of humanity, a humanity that is smaller and older, with fewer clusters where the population continues to grow than most of us can grasp. Yes, some countries defy this trend. But we hope and believe the future of Africa is brighter than the UN demographers predict, that there will be more Kenyas than Benins, and that Benin's future may be brighter than skeptics imagine. Almost everywhere on the continent, more girls are getting educated each year than were educated the year before, and we know what that leads to. The day may come sooner rather than later when the cradle of humanity no longer grows the population of the earth.

SEVEN

SHUTTING DOWN THE FACTORY IN BRAZIL

We are in São Paulo in search of answers to a mystery. That mystery is a number: 1.8, the fertility rate of Brazil. Poor, chaotic, plagued by corrupt government and self-defeating policies, the world's fifth-most-populous country should be a cauldron of population growth. But it isn't. From a typically developing world level of six children per woman in the 1960s, Brazil's fertility rate has cratered, reaching replacement rate at the turn of the millennium and then continuing to fall to the below-replacement rate of today. United Nations projections have Brazil's fertility rate stabilizing and even increasing slightly over the course of the century, but that seems odd. If fertility has fallen so far, so fast, it doesn't make sense to assume, as UN demographers assume, that it will level off and even go back up. So, the mystery: Why did Brazilian women stop having so many babies, so quickly, and what are the prospects for future population growth or decline?

This isn't simply a Brazilian question. Fertility rates are falling rapidly in the developing nations of the Western Hemisphere. Back in 1960, the average fertility rate for Latin America and the Caribbean was 5.9. Today it's 2.1, replacement rate. Seventeen of the thirty-eight countries in the region are at or below replacement rate. The two largest, Brazil and Mexico, have populations of 205 million and 125 million respectively. Today, Mexico is chasing Brazil, with a fertility rate of 2.3 and falling. If Latin America had a stable fertility rate of 2.1, that would be one thing: the region's population would grow slowly and predictably in a prolonged Goldilocks phase. But it's not. Fertility rates continue to go down—by the equivalent of half a baby since 2000 in the fourteen biggest countries in the region. This isn't a gradual, smooth decline. This is collapse. What happened?

"Brazil is the country of the future . . . and always will be" quipped Charles de Gaulle, and the same could be said of Latin America as a whole. A region rich in natural resources always seems to be on the brink of shaking off the shackles that have oppressed its people for centuries, but the shackles stay on just the same. The reasons for failure are many: The Spanish and Portuguese were brutal masters, who took the gold and sugar and left little in return but Catholicism. Any society infected with slavery does not easily heal; Brazilians still use the phrase *para Inglês ver*, "for the English to see," referring to the nineteenth-century Potemkin ports shown to the Brits, who had prohibited slavery, even as a brisk trade went on elsewhere. Anything today intended to impress outsiders while hiding the grim reality is "for the English to see." Caste systems based on race and class threw up oligarchies who viewed the business of government as protecting their businesses. Occasionally the people would rebel, but each populist strongman seemed worse than the last military junta. Corruption flourished along with a (quite justified) lack of trust in the institutions of the state, including the police and courts.

Chile, the most democratic and developed state in South America, has found a way forward, Argentina might finally be righting itself after decades of bad government, and for a while it looked as though Brazil might also escape the poverty-and-corruption trap. In 2001, Goldman Sachs's then chief economist, Jim O'Neill, coined the term BRIC to encapsulate the rising and developing economic powers of Brazil, Russia, India, and China, which he predicted would surpass the old developed economies by 2041. From 2003 to 2011, Brazil was governed by the wildly popular President Luiz Inácio Lula da Silva, who landed the 2014 World Cup and 2016 Olympics for Brazil, while also passing progressive reforms that improved living standards. But then commodity prices fell, the economy went south, and the inevitable corruption scandal emerged, a political crisis that led to the impeachment and removal of Lula's successor, Dilma Rousseff. The final indignity: Lula himself was convicted in July 2017 of corruption and money laundering, and in April 2018 began to serve a twelve-year sentence. He continues to protest his innocence, and to be fair, he was only working within the system he inherited as he sought to implement his progressive agenda. "*Rouba mas faz*"—"he steals, but he gets things done"—as Brazilians like to say about some politicians. As more than one observer noted, it was Lula's efforts to clean up the law-enforcement system that produced the dragnet that ensnared him.[220] Some people believe that the emerging generation of millennial Brazilians will finally put an end to the old, corrupt ways.

Still, times are tough. After a severe recession, growth has returned, but the OECD outlook remains cautious, due in part to Brazil's reluctance to open its closed economy.[221] Brazil is a country with an ever-receding future once again.

———

The University of São Paulo's buildings are scattered across a huge, attractive, but rather run-down and unkempt campus. In the School of Philosophy, Languages and Literature, and Human Sciences and Letters building, there is no apparent sign of air conditioning, despite the brutal mid-summer heat. Funding cuts, we are told, have led to neglect and disrepair across the university. We are here to talk to the Brazilian equivalent of the university students in Korea, the dinner party in Belgium, the young professionals in Nairobi: the upwardly mobile, educated, professional, ambitious members of a society. How do their experiences and perceptions differ, or match up, with their counterparts in other parts of the world? The results surprise us.

Professor Lorena Barberia, from the university's political science department, has assembled a dozen students attending a graduate summer program. These are bright, driven, career-oriented young women, ranging in age from mid-twenties to mid-thirties, fluent in English and determined to realize their full intellectual and career potential. One of the students is married, with one child. A few have boyfriends; most are single but hope to marry and hope to have one or two children—one hoped for more, but doubted she could accommodate that and her career goals, especially given the expense of raising a family in São Paolo. As it turns out, the role of children in their lives is something they have been thinking about a great deal. What was to have been a question-and-answer session turns into something resembling group therapy.

Like young, well-educated women everywhere, these students struggle to reconcile the challenge of advancing their academic goals while also having a family. How to obtain both a Ph.D. and the right life mate? They have scorned hook-up apps, preferring to find Mr. Right the old-fashioned way—meeting the friend of a friend, being introduced to someone at a social or sporting event. But this is getting harder to do as they get older. "Everybody seems to be together already." "We women have higher standards now." "It's so hard to meet someone when you are as busy as we are." A few of them are thinking about freezing some of their eggs for future use.

The conversation becomes increasingly personal, and tense. One woman struggles to explain how much pressure she is under from her parents to marry and have children. Others nod. One of the students quietly starts to cry. The others offer support, and hugs. Afterward, Professor Barberia, a warm, empathetic role model who cares deeply about the future of these women, explains that they are pursuing advanced degrees in an effort to inoculate themselves from the machismo still prevalent in Brazilian men. "Brazil remains a very sexist society," she observes. A Ph.D., these women hope, will help level the playing field, both professionally and at home. She shakes her head. "I don't know how many will succeed." State cuts to education have made tenure-track positions difficult to obtain. Finding a husband who respects and understands their ambitions, even as they struggle to translate their degrees into a secure career, is an almost insurmountable challenge. For Professor Barberia, this is personal: "I have struggled with this myself throughout my career." She is married, with three children.

Middle-class professional Brazilian women face the same challenges in the effort to balance career and family as their counterparts in other parts of the world—made more difficult, perhaps, by the antediluvian attitudes of some Brazilian men. But these young women will, inevitably, have fewer children than their parents had. For the middle class, at least, the fertility rate in Brazil will continue its downward curve. But most Brazilians are less affluent and less educated than these students and their professor. Many of them live in poverty. If Brazil's fertility is low, it must be low because of them. Yet conventional wisdom holds that poor and poorly educated women have more children than their middle-class counterparts. So what gives?

We know that urbanization leads to declining fertility as children become an expense rather than an asset and women obtain greater autonomy and control. Brazil is one of the world's most urban countries, with 80 percent of the population living in cities. Latin America's most populous nation reached a level of urbanization in 1950 that Asia and Africa didn't achieve until 2000. The reasons for this urbanization are many and complex, but in essence: The Portuguese overlords did not encourage colonization and agriculture, preferring simply to extract the wealth of their colony and ship it to the homeland. In the twentieth century, Brazilian governments promoted industrialization through import-substitution policies (high tariffs that kept out competitors and encouraged local industries to flourish), which spurred workers in rural areas to move to the city in search of factory jobs.[222]

Urbanization undoubtedly played a role in lowering the fertility rate in Brazil. It may also play a role in another factor that plays into declining fertility: the waning influence of religion in much of Latin America. A Pew Research Center study shows that in societies where Islam is dominant, the fertility rate is 3.1; in Christian societies, it's 2.7; Hindus have 2.4 children per woman and Buddhists 1.6.[223] What matters here is not simply religion but religiosity, the firm adherence by members of a society to whatever religion is dominant within that society.[224] Both Europe and sub-Saharan Africa are predominantly Christian, but Europeans in general are a less intensely religious lot than Africans, and also have much lower fertility rates. Muslim societies are, generally speaking, less secular than their Christian counterparts.

Though Latin America is home to almost 40 percent of the world's Catholics, it has been experiencing a crisis of faith in recent decades. Ninety percent of people in Latin America identified as Catholic in the 1960s; today the figure is 69 percent. This is partly explained by the growth of evangelical Protestantism in the region, from 9 percent of the population to 19 percent in the same period, and partly by an increase in the number of people not affiliated with any denomination—essentially agnostics and atheists—which has doubled from 4 percent to 8 percent.

Evangelical Christians oppose abortion, sex outside marriage, and the full equality of women every bit as fiercely as Catholics, but they do permit (though don't necessarily approve of) contraception. Historically, Protestant fertility rates have been lower than Catholic fertility rates, (though the distinction disappears in more economically advanced societies).[225] But perhaps even more important than the shift away from Catholicism toward Protestantism is the shift in the degree of religiosity in the region, or at least parts of it. One way to measure that shift is to examine attitudes toward same-sex marriage, something both Catholic and evangelical authorities strongly condemn.

According to another Pew study, either a large minority or a majority of the population in Brazil (46 percent), Chile (also 46 percent), Mexico (49 percent), Argentina (52 percent), and Uruguay (62 percent) support the right of same-sex couples to marry. (Same-sex marriage is legal in Argentina, Brazil, and Uruguay.) Guess what? These countries also have some of the lowest fertility rates in the region. (Chile is at 1.8, Uruguay 2.0, and Argentina 2.4.) They also, with the exception of Mexico, have above-average numbers of nonbelievers in their midst. And the societies where same-sex marriage has the least traction, and where nonbelievers are rare, also have some of the highest fertility rates: Paraguay (fertility rate: 2.6), Honduras (2.7), and Guatemala (3.2).[226]

Conclusion: with minor variations, the higher the fertility rate the lower the support for same-sex marriage and the greater the degree of religiosity in a society. Research also demonstrates that "countries that have the greatest gender equality also have . . . the most positive aggregate attitudes toward lesbians and gay men."[227] So declining religiosity leads to increased tolerance toward LGBT citizens, greater equality for women, and a declining birth rate. Fertility rates are declining in Latin America because religiosity is on the decline as well.

But there is a nagging problem with this thesis. Brazil has an extremely high level of income inequality. While the top 10 percent of Brazilians own half of the country's wealth,[228] at least a quarter of the population lives below the poverty line.[229] Surely poor Brazilians are having more children than their middle-class counterparts. And if so, then how can Brazil's fertility rate be so low? This is the mystery that most needs answering. And it is here that we find our own complacent, conventional assumptions upended.

Like the rest of Brazil, São Paulo is a cluster of contradictions. There is the conspicuous opulence in the gleaming office towers and luxury condos that dominate its downtown skyline. But even more than in gated American communities, the middle- and upper-middle-class neighborhoods—attractive, modern homes that would not be out of place in, say, Phoenix—are fortresses, surrounded by elaborate security walls, iron gates, razor wire, and CCTV cameras. Crime is corrosive in Brazil—in 2015, there were more violent deaths there than in civil-war-torn Syria[230]—and fear defines the streetscape, with the middle class literally walling itself off from the rest of society.

While the middle and upper classes struggle to protect their property and personal safety, millions more struggle just to get by in what Eduardo Marques, an expert on Brazil's urban issues, calls "precarious accommodation," the most famous of these being the favelas.[231] Favelas were created by Brazilians migrating from the rural north to the urban south starting in the 1950s, driven by the job opportunities created by Brazil's rapid industrialization.

Favela residents are squatters—they, or those who came before them, simply occupied the land that they now live on. Some of the land originally had private owners, some of it was public land, but Brazil's various levels of government have tolerated the confiscation over the years. Governments have even brought in some municipal services, such as electricity and roads, partly in hopes of building political support. They have also accepted addresses in some favelas as state-recognized residences. In São Paulo, having a residential address is extremely important. It confirms a person's citizenship, gets them an ID, and makes it possible to participate in the formal economy and receive the limited government services that exist in Brazil.[232] The Brazilian government, following the recommendations of the Peruvian economist Hernando de Soto, has in some cases granted property rights to favela dwellers, who make up about 20 percent of the urban population. However, critics contend that this simply leads to gentrification as developers purchase and redevelop the properties, pushing the poor to the extreme edges of the city, making it harder for them to get to work or access services.[233]

One thing Brazilians will tell you about favelas without hesitation is that they are dangerous places. As one local noted, "You need to watch your GPS when you're driving in São Paulo because sometimes it will pick a route that goes through a favela. That could prove to be fatal."[234] The danger in favelas has intensified with the increase in drug dealing and gangs. Even visiting a favela these days for research purposes requires the permission of the local drug gangs.

Vila Prudente is São Paulo's oldest favela, with an estimated population of roughly one hundred thousand souls, though formal numbers don't really exist. It is described by those we spoke to as a safe favela because it isn't considered to be "hot" (the scene of active drug trafficking). Nonetheless, the colleagues who arranged the visit went to great lengths to describe the proper protocol: don't look at people, don't leave the group, be mindful of the time. Things are riskiest when people are on the move, heading to or from work.

On the day of the visit, our driver drops us off a short distance from the favela and we enter on foot. Passing through the wall that divides the two communities is like stepping through a portal into another world. While the surrounding neighborhood is modest, it's worlds away from what greets us.

The accommodation in Vila Prudente is sturdier and more permanent than what is on offer in Nairobi's Kibera slum. But the random piles of human detritus—garbage, broken bricks, and broken asphalt—are similar, as is the sour smell of rotting garbage. After a rainstorm, the paths become mostly brown, gelatinous mud, weaving through a maze of tightly packed shacks, some of them selling groceries, batteries, snacks. Most of the shacks, however, are people's homes. It's easy to spot the difference between the two because what's happening on the inside is mostly visible from the outside.

Eventually, we are met by a team from a charity called Arca do Saber, which runs a drop-in center for preteen youth living in the favela. The center is supported by the French and British embassies, as well as by several private companies and the City of São Paulo, which provides half the budget.[235] Arca do Saber supports about 120 favela children every day. Evelyn, the president of the charity, and her associate, Frédéric, lead us around the drop-in center and the parts of the favela they considered safe enough to walk through. But we aren't allowed to speak to any residents, which could incite the anger of the local gang. Both Evelyn and Frédéric are French nationals. With them are two young women—idealistic and committed university graduates from France who have come here to make a difference.

Arca do Saber aims to help the youth of Vila Prudente make better choices in their lives, such as getting an education, staying away from drugs and violence, and avoiding teen pregnancy. The aid workers spread these messages to the children who attend the drop-in center, as well as to their families. They are most worried about the boys, especially the smarter boys. The girls find it easier to stay in school, but the boys are pressured by their families to find work. The smarter boys are often recruited by the drug gangs.

Teen pregnancy remains a problem in Vila Prudente. Too many girls are getting pregnant at around fifteen or sixteen years of age. The mean age at which mothers have their first child in Brazil is still quite young, at twenty-two, which should push up the birth rate.[236] But what the statistics don't capture is that women all over Brazil, including in the favelas, are choosing to stop having children earlier than their parents did. Although they give birth at a younger age than their more affluent counterparts, they also choose to stop having children at an earlier age than previous generations.

Part of this choice by poorer Brazilian women can be explained by the universal phenomenon of increasing education and literacy that comes with moving to the city.[237] But there are other factors, such as the influence of Brazil's wildly popular television soap operas, called *telenovelas*, whose plots involve smaller families, empowered women, rampant consumerism, and complicated romantic and family relationships. As the footprint of the Globo TV network, the main producer of the *telenovelas*, expanded, researchers noticed that in communities where *telenovelas* became accessible, there were spikes in children being named after popular *telenovela* characters, as well as declines in fertility.[238] The government aided this process by expanding Brazil's power grid and providing access to consumer goods, such as TVs. Women in favelas now have a new set of role models that show them a different life to both admire and aspire to. As Brazilian demographer George Martine puts it, "The family image presented is typically that of the small, egalitarian, and consumer-oriented unit. Moreover, new themes—such as extramarital sex, family instability, female empowerment, and nontraditional family arrangements—are frequently portrayed on the screen and, as a result, have become part of the daily discourse."[239] For these women, as for women in other parts of the world, having a child is less of a fulfillment of the obligations to family, church, and state, and more a personal fulfillment. Not having more than one or two children is even more fulfilling.

Another contributor to decreased fertility is both unintended and astonishing. It's called *a fábrica está fechada*, "the factory is closed," or "shutting down the factory."[240] Brazil has a very high rate of caesarean sections for delivering babies. It also has an uncommonly high rate of female sterilization. The two are linked. The cost of a caesarean is covered by the public health system, and the procedure is more profitable for the attending physician to perform than natural childbirth. Sterilization, while not covered directly by the health system, is commonly available through a "special" payment to the attending physician. As George Martine tells it, "a common ploy is for a doctor to have his patient classified as being at high risk for pregnancy complications. He then arranges for her to have a caesarean section, based on her high-risk status, and to have her privately defray the costs of the tubal ligation that will be carried out simultaneously. The financial advantages of this for the often underpaid medical attendants in the official health system can be seen as an important part of the explanation for Brazil's exceptionally high rates of caesarean sections and sterilization."[241] Another incentive to proceed with tubal ligation is that abortion remains illegal in Brazil.

"Shutting down the factory" (which can also mean any form of birth control) by *laqueadura tubária*, "tying the tubes," is a middle-class phenomenon as well. Urban anthropologist Teresa Caldeira observes, "In the last twenty years, I have talked to countless women in Jardim das Camélias [a lower-middle-class neighborhood in São Paulo] who do not want to have large families anymore. This is not strictly for economic reasons but because, like any middle-class woman, they want time for themselves to do other things, including getting better jobs than being maids. They do not want to be prisoners of necessity, and many have chosen to be sterilized after the birth of a second or third child. They consider it a true liberation. They have learned—and television with its portrayal of upper-class women's behavior and family patterns has taught them a great deal in this matter—that to control their sexuality and fertility can offer immense liberation not only from the burdens of nature but also from male dominance."[242] In developed countries, women choose to marry later, and so have fewer children. In some developing countries like Brazil, women have no choice but to marry early, but they limit their family size through sterilization.

As we have seen, local circumstances—from the pressures of career in Korea to the cost of the bride price in Africa to the popularity of soap operas in Brazil—influence how and why women decide to have children. But almost everywhere, provided they have a choice, women choose to have fewer. And the desire for a small family is becoming a universal phenomenon. An Ipsos survey of 18,519 people in twenty-six countries asked: "What is the ideal number of children for a family to have?" The answer in almost all the countries was close to two. The average was 2.2, which was also the Brazilian average. The answer didn't vary by any of the key demographic groups—gender, age, income, or education level. This shows that the norm hasn't just been adopted by the affluent, better-educated, and younger population. It has become a new standard for nearly everyone, almost everywhere.

While an overall average of 2.2 should be enough to maintain the overall size of the world's population, it's not enough to get us to the UN's estimate of 11.2 billion people by the end of the century. Especially since the small-family norm has taken such a strong hold in the world's two most populous countries, China and India, a subject we will explore further on. In any case, for reasons both universal and local, Brazil is no longer capable of replacing its population. The speed of this transition is amazing. It took Europe and other developed nations almost two centuries to take their birth rate from a Stage One rate of six or more children per family to Stage Five, below replacement rate. Brazil and many other nations in Latin America have accomplished the same shift in two generations, with other countries in the region following close behind. Latin America is setting the standard for curbing the growth of humanity.

EIGHT

PUSH AND PULL MIGRATION

Even now, years later, just thinking about it brings a stab of pain. A young boy, lying face-down on the beach at the water's edge, curled up as though he were sleeping. Alan Kurdi drowned when the boat carrying his family and a dozen other Syrian refugees capsized. More than three thousand refugees lost their lives in the Aegean or Mediterranean in 2015, many of them children. But that photograph by Nilüfer Demir struck the conscience of the world. Donations poured in; European politicians encouraged each other to accept more refugees and berated those who refused. In Canada, where a federal election was underway, news that the Kurdi family had been denied admission as refugees because their papers weren't in order may have helped to defeat the governing Conservatives. Syrian refugees became the most important story on the planet. The world was in the grip of a migration crisis.

Yet that tragedy and its aftermath obscured and distorted some important truths. In the broader context, refugee movements are insignificant. The real tectonic force reshaping societies and economies is the decade-after-decade flow of economic migrants from poorer countries to richer countries. That shift in labor isn't accelerating; it's slowing down. It will slow down even more in the future. We are faced with a looming shortage of migrants. Unfortunately, popular suspicion of immigrants and refugees, especially those from Muslim lands, fuels opposition within national populations to new arrivals, a sentiment stoked by populist, nativist politicians. These policies are self-defeating, for in countries with a below-replacement fertility rate—which is pretty much every country in the developed world—economic migrants are essential to counteract the impact of population decline. And immigrants are going to become increasingly hard to come by as incomes rise in developing countries, even as fertility falls. If politicians were statesmen, they would confront these realities and explain them to voters. Instead, many of them pander to prejudice, even as their populations age and begin to diminish, despite the millions of would-be immigrants who could reverse the trend, if only they were let in.

We were born to move. Our ancestors came down from the trees of East Africa sometime between six and seven million years ago and began to experiment with standing upright and walking. It was this unique adaptation to walking on two legs that separated the first hominids from the other apes.[243] It helped our brains grow. Once we took to moving, we never stopped. Our mobility helped us to find and follow distant and migrating sources of food, as well as to react to changes in our local climate and habitat. When the food was gone, we simply moved on. The discovery of agriculture about twelve thousand years ago settled us down a bit.[244] But there were always more children than available land. And there was always the horizon. So we kept moving, in search not of game, now, but of worlds to conquer, soil to till, people to oppress or convert, glory.

Humans began their migration from Africa to the rest of the world about fifty thousand years ago.[245] As we moved, we invented breakthrough technologies such as the wheel and the sail to help us traverse the vast oceans and continents. We got so good at moving that by the early twentieth century, most of the world that could be settled by humans had been. And still we move, for reasons both as ancient as the race and as new as the latest headline. Things push us and pull us. Push: war, famine, upheaval, ethnic or religious persecution, catastrophe. Things that make it too dangerous to continue living where we are. We flee for our lives. Pull: There are richer fields or better jobs over those hills, or on the other side of that sea. There's a chance for a new and better life for us, or at least for our children.

Pull movements tend to be gradual but inexorable: *Homo sapiens* leaves Africa in search of land and game; millions leave Europe for the New World in search of a better life; Filipinos travel to the Gulf states in search of work. Push movements often arrive unannounced and unforeseen, creating chaos. Push movements are things of horror: millions fleeing from rape and death as armies approach, from starvation after yet another harvest fails, from flood or eruption or tremor. Pull movements are far more powerful, but harder to detect because they happen slowly, over decades, or generations. Push movements get all the headlines.

Events within living memory that pushed us include the boat people fleeing the brutal unification of Vietnam, the victims of Somalia and Sudan, the 2010 earthquake in Haiti, the Syrian civil war, and the rise of ISIS. The pull movements are older but more transformative: the promise of gold and silver and other treasures in the Andes, word that the Great Plains could sustain cattle and wheat, a letter from your brother saying there were jobs in Chicago or Toronto and, given your grim Sicilian existence, why not? Of course, people are still pulled today. The war is over, things are calmer, let's go back home and start again; we must leave our Guatemalan village to work in California fields during the harvest, so that we'll have food; this knowledge I have is wasted in this economy, but in Europe or North America, I could make my way. A common thread in pull-based migration is a surplus—and thus impoverished—population in one place and opportunity available in another.

And yet, although we were born to move, most of the time we prefer to stay where we are. Family is here, and the familiar. Before the Industrial Revolution, travel took place only at walking speed. Most people never ventured farther than the next village, unless the men were recruited for war. Even today, most Americans have never traveled outside the United States.[246] Unless we are pushed or pulled, home is where our hearts are.

And the truth is, we are not moving as much as once we did. The great migrations of the distant past, from the Old World to the New, are over. The great migrations of the present, from the developing world to the developed, are stable, perhaps even slowing down. In 1990, about three quarters of 1 percent of the planet's population migrated; by 2010, the number was down to six tenths.[247] The Middle East refugee crisis increased those numbers, but like many push-based migrations, the tide will subside, and even reverse, when the crisis subsides. The nations in Europe that agreed to accept Middle Eastern refugees did so expecting that once Syria and Iraq and other strife-torn nations in the region returned to some semblance of normalcy, people would move back.

It's odd that we're becoming more sedentary. After all, getting around has never been easier. The democratization of global air travel has made migration relatively painless. (Those who lament the lost days when a plane flight was a pleasure and not an ordeal have forgotten what the ticket used to cost.) It wasn't always like that. Even in the not-so-distant past, traveling put your life at risk. For example: There are people alive today who knew people who knew people who risked their lives to travel from Europe to North America during the Irish famine. Over six years, starting in 1845, blight destroyed the potato harvest in Ireland. A million died; a million more came to the United States and Canada in search of a new start.[248] One of them was Thomas Fitzgerald, who fled the starving village of Buff in County Limerick in 1852 as a young man in his twenties. He came to America on one of the "coffin ships," filthy and crammed (typically with twice their legal capacity of passengers) and slow (it could take from five weeks to three months to make it across, depending on the weather and the skill of the crew), riddled with lice and typhus, and supplied with little food or water. People would lie in the filth and disease waiting to see if they would live or die. Typically, the trip killed a fifth of the passengers, though mortality rates of 30 to 40 percent were common.[249] But Fitzgerald survived, and so did Patrick Kennedy, a cooper from Dunganstown, County Wexford.[250] Both men settled in Boston, where they scrapped and scraped to survive in the face of deep hostility from the Anglo-Protestant toffs up on Beacon Hill. Illiterate, they worked as laborers and grocers, married, had children, died. Today, it takes less than eight hours to fly from Dublin Airport to New York's JFK, named after these two men's great-grandson, John Fitzgerald Kennedy.

One reason we don't migrate as much as we did is that famine and other pestilence are now rare and often controllable at the source by local government or foreign aid. Another reason is that the world is a far, far wealthier place, reducing the surplus-population phenomenon. Between 1900 and 1915 alone, three million Italians, mostly from that country's southern regions and the island of Sicily, immigrated to the United States, driven by rural poverty, to work in the sweatshops of New York and other industrial cities.[251] Sicilians don't leave home to work in the sweatshops of New York today. There are no sweatshops, and although Sicily is still poor, at a per capita GDP of around US$18,000 (almost half the national average), people get by. As for migrations from poorer countries to wealthier ones, they continue. But as we've already noted, even the poorest parts of the world are much wealthier today than they were a generation ago. The number of people living in extreme poverty (less than US$2 a day) has declined from more than 1.8 billion in 1990 to fewer than 800 million in 2015.[252] The end of extreme poverty within this century is not only possible but probable. People who are not poor are less likely to move.

And though the terrible migrations from the Middle East in recent years are every bit as dangerous and difficult as those our ancestors endured, they mask a larger truth: the refugee situation is more stable than it looks.

The United Nations' warning was stark: The world's refugee population at the end of 2015 had reached 19.9 million, higher than it was even at the end of the Second World War.[253] With the world in turmoil, tens of millions had been displaced from their homes, many of them reduced to a life placed on hold in refugee camps. The need is great. Who will help?

Except the UN was torquing the numbers. There may have been more refugees in 2015 than in 1945, but the planet's population is triple what it was then. And if the plight of Muslim refugees is dangerous, desperate, and terrifying, the millions of Germans who fled from East Prussia as the Soviet armies advanced, or who were expelled by Poles or Czechs or Hungarians who wanted their land, fared far worse. Millions of Poles were displaced, in turn, from eastern lands that the

Russians took for themselves. The scenes were equally chaotic in the Balkans. At its peak, fourteen thousand people a day were crossing, or being pushed across, the border between the Soviet-occupied and Western-occupied zones. Many thousands drowned in overcrowded freighters that capsized in the Baltic Sea. Those who couldn't or wouldn't leave, and who ended up trapped behind Russian lines, sometimes resorted to cannibalism. Many eventually ended up in Soviet labor camps. At the same time, Western authorities sent about two million Soviet citizens, many of them prisoners of war, back to their homelands, where in many cases they were never heard from again. And hundreds of thousands of Jews who had survived the Holocaust struggled to make it to the Jewish homeland in Palestine. It took fifteen years before the last of the refugee camps in Europe were closed.[254] In all, as many as fourteen million Germans were displaced at the end of the war, and about five hundred thousand died as a result.[255] And on the other side of the world, one study counted thirteen million Chinese displaced or homeless in 1947.[256] This figure was only an estimate, and didn't account for the one hundred million who were displaced by the civil war between the Nationalists and Communists that went on before and after the Second World War.[257] The death toll also isn't known, but it must have been horrific. The planet, in short, was in far greater turmoil in the wake of the Second World War than it was in 2015.

In fact, were it not for the chaos in Syria and Iraq, added to the chronic instability of Afghanistan and Somalia and the state of nature that Libya descended into, the current refugee situation would be relatively stable. According to the United Nations Development Program, in 2015 there were 244 million international migrants—people not living in the country in which they were born—spread around the world.[258] While a quarter billion people may seem like a lot—it is, after all, equivalent to the population of

the world's fourth-most-populous country, Indonesia[259]—it's just
3.3 percent of the world's total population, up from 2.9 percent in
1990, but not up by a lot, in the grand scheme.

How much is the crisis in the Middle East obscuring the overall
stability of refugee trends? Consider: In 2015, more than half (54 percent) of the world's refugees came from just three countries: Syria
(4.9 million), Afghanistan (2.7 million), and Somalia (1.1 million).[260]
And although some Europeans claimed that their continent was being
inundated with refugees, most of those refugees—86 percent of the
global total—were camped in developing rather than developed
regions. Forty percent of displaced people were being temporarily
housed in refugee camps in the Middle East and North Africa, and
30 percent in sub-Saharan Africa. The top three host countries were
Turkey, which had taken in 2.5 million refugees, Pakistan (1.6 million),
and Lebanon (1.1 million).[261] And as Western-backed Iraqi and Kurdish
forces handed ISIS one defeat after another, and the violence of the
Syrian civil war began to wane, refugees began trickling back—half a
million in the first half of 2017.[262] Chancellor Angela Merkel said she
expected all the refugees in Germany to go home once the Middle
East returned to something approaching peace.

The rest of the world's movers—three quarters of the total—are
being pulled, not pushed, from middle-income countries to higher-
income countries.[263] About 40 percent of them come from Asia.[264]
The biggest diasporas—people living in countries different from
where they were born—today are from India (sixteen million
people), followed by Mexico (twelve million), Russia (eleven million), and China (ten million).[265] Migration today is less about
humanitarian crisis and much more about strivers looking to cash
in on the economic opportunities another country has to offer them
and their families. About a fifth of them end up in the United States,
the perpetual land of opportunity. Germany, Russia (taking in

migrants from poorer countries on its periphery), and Saudi Arabia (a magnet for guest workers) are also key destinations.

Put it all together and, as the chart below shows, people on the move are both pushed from countries to whoever takes them in, and pulled from middle-income to high-income countries in search of a better life.[266]

TOP DESTINATIONS (2010–2015) (in thousands)

United States **1,002**

Turkey **400**

Lebanon **250**

Germany **250**

Oman **242**

Canada **235**

Russia **224**

Australia **205**

United Kingdom **180**

South Sudan **173**

TOP SOURCES (2010–2015)

Syria **806**

India **520**

Bangladesh **445**

China **360**

Pakistan **216**

Sudan **160**

Indonesia **140**

Philippines **140**

Spain **119**

Mexico **105**

All in all, local conflagrations aside, the migratory situation has been pretty stable now for a couple of decades. But those conflagrations pose a risk, not just to migrants but to people in advanced economies who are being hornswoggled into believing there is some kind of migratory crisis. There isn't. Thinking there is hurts both the migrants and people in the countries they want to migrate to.

Despite all the political ructions in Europe over immigration from the Middle East and Africa, of the twenty-seven million international migrants in Europe who have relocated over the last twenty-five years, nearly half (45 percent) were born in Europe. These are Europeans moving between European countries. For the United States, about half of the immigrants who arrived between 1990 and 2015 were born in Latin America and the Caribbean.[267]

In most parts of the world, migration appears to follow local corridors. North Africa and the Middle East supply Europe; Latin America supplies the United States. Despite the ease of global travel today, most migrants still prefer to move to someplace close to home. This was reflected in the Middle East refugee crisis. Most European-accepted refugees were expected to return to their home countries once the situation quieted down; only those taken in by Canada and the U.S. were considered permanent adoptions. (To leave Syria for a refugee camp, and then a refugee camp for Vancouver, is to leave for good.) Asia is also the principal destination for Asian migrants. More than fifty-nine million Asian immigrants today live in another Asian country, making that continent the world's biggest migrant hub.[268]

This is important to remember: Most people in the world don't want to move from where they are; those who do want to, or who are forced to, move to someplace close, where the language and the culture may still be familiar. Maybe they'll go back. At the least, it will be easier to visit family. The great global migrations between continents, surplus populations filling empty lands, are over. The lands are no longer empty, and as developing economies become more prosperous, the populations are no longer surplus. In the United States, since the economic crisis of 2008, more people have gone back to Mexico and Latin America than have come north to the U.S. Researchers studying the phenomenon cite a weakening American economy, greater availability of jobs in Mexico, and the declining Latino fertility rate.[269]

Remigration will be an increasing phenomenon in the years ahead, as immigrants are tempted to return whence they came, back to their family and their people and proper food. Developed countries in need of migrants to sustain their populations should be doing everything in their power to keep them. Instead, they have become increasingly hostile to newcomers, which is a highly self-defeating attitude.

Keith Ellison had a warning. It was July 2015, and the congressman from Minnesota was appearing on ABC's popular Sunday morning talk show *This Week with George Stephanopoulos*. "Anybody from the Democratic side of the fence who's terrified of the possibility of President Trump better vote, better get active, better get involved," he warned, "because this man has got some momentum." The other panelists instantly burst into laughter. "I know you don't believe that," Stephanopoulos grinned.[270] After all, Trump had launched his campaign for the Republican presidential nomination the month before by declaring that Mexican immigrants were "people that have lots of problems, and they're bringing those problems with us [*sic*]. They're bringing drugs. They're bringing crime. They're rapists. And some," he added generously, "I assume, are good people."[271] He would build a wall to keep them out. Six months later, in the wake of shootings in San Bernardino, California, he vowed to ban all Muslims from entering the United States, until authorities were able to "figure out what the hell is going on."[272]

The question is not how President Trump has implemented those promises; the question is how they helped him get elected. This isn't a book dedicated to analyzing the disconnect between liberal elites and angry, nativist voters. What matters is that the anger is real, not only in the United States but in Europe, where far-right-wing anti-immigrant parties are on the rise, and where Great Britain voted to leave the European Union in part due to popular anger over what many saw as uncontrolled immigration.

In July 2016, Ipsos Public Affairs polled people in twenty-two countries on what they thought about immigrants. Half of those polled agreed with the statement "There are too many immigrants in my country." The numbers were even higher in countries whose populations are declining or on the brink of decline, such as Italy (where 65 percent of citizens agreed with the statement) or Russia (64 percent). In Hungary, which stands to lose 20 percent of its population by 2060, support for immigrants stood at 6 percent. Some of the resentment, no doubt, is driven by fear of changes to their country's cultural, religious, or racial makeup brought on by immigration. But another reason is economic. In the poll, only about a quarter of those surveyed thought immigration was good for their economy. Half believed immigrants placed strains on social services. Three quarters believed that immigrants compete with them for available jobs.

These popular perceptions are flat-out wrong. To cite just one, particularly comprehensive, survey, a 2016 study by the National Academies of Science, Engineering, and Medicine concluded that legal immigrants to the United States—more than half of whom had postsecondary education—filled gaps in demand for highly skilled labor, created jobs through their entrepreneurial drive, and rarely generated competition for jobs between immigrants and the native-born. "Immigration enlarges the economy while leaving the native population slightly better off on average," the report concluded, "but the greatest beneficiaries of immigration are the immigrants themselves as they avail themselves of opportunities not available to them in their home countries."[273] And as we've already demonstrated, immigrants provide the bodies needed to drive consumption and to pay taxes for services consumed by those no longer working. Immigration is a win-win for both immigrants and the native-born. It is the very opposite of a zero-sum game.

The cold hard fact is that, without migration, population growth in most of the developed world would already be screeching to a halt. This is especially the case for Europe. In that continent, the population would have fallen between 2000 and 2015 had it not been for migrants.[274] In the rest of the developed world, principally the United States and Canada, immigration will become the sole driver of population growth starting sometime in the 2020s.[275]

Politicians should be educating voters on the vital importance of immigration to their economic security. They should be pursuing policies that favor applicants with the language and job skills needed to find a job in their adopted country. And they should be ensuring that new arrivals have the necessary supports in place to help them integrate quickly and easily. Instead, too many surf the fears revealed by the Ipsos survey, warning of jobs lost and lives threatened. Yes, it doesn't help that the Middle Eastern refugee crisis has generated local acts of terrorism from extremists posing as refugees. But long before the Syrian civil war or the rise of ISIS, national populations chafed at what they saw as the infiltration of their societies by foreigners. ISIS didn't create Donald Trump in the United States, or Marine Le Pen in France or Viktor Orbán in Hungary. The seeds had already been sown.

But the blame for this sorry state lies not only with the populist, nativist nationalists on the right. Defenders of immigration on the left contribute too, by characterizing immigration as a test of personal compassion and tolerance. To oppose immigration, for them, is to be selfish at best and racist at worst. People do not respond well to such insults. They tend to lash out at their accusers, damning them as out-of-touch elites, and then voting for the politician they think will have their back. What sensible politicians of both the left and the right need to explain is that accepting immigrants isn't a question of compassion and tolerance. It's good for business. It grows the economy. It increases the tax base. People are much more easily moved to act in their own selfish interests than to sacrifice for the sake of others. The Latino and Asian immigrants arriving in the United States today are simply the latest wave that began with religious dissenters arriving in New England and continued with the Irish and the Germans and the Slavs and all the other waves that made America great long before Donald Trump came along.

Immigration is not a permanent solution to the problem of an aging and declining population. For one thing, migrants aren't all that young; their median age is thirty-nine, according to the UN.[276] At thirty-nine, most people are pretty much done producing children. So the fertility potential for much of the migrant population is actually quite weak. For another, immigrants quickly adopt the fertility pattern of their new home. "The big reason immigrants' birth rates are falling is that they tend to adopt the ways of their host communities," *The Economist* observed. "This happens fast: some studies suggest that a girl who migrates before her teens behaves much like a native."[277]

Besides, immigrants may soon be hard to come by. Fertility is declining everywhere, even in the poorest countries. And incomes

are rising in nations that once were very poor, decreasing the incentive to leave. China was once Canada's largest source of immigrants.
Today it's a distant third. Remember, as the data show, most of us
prefer to stay in the country where we were born until we are either
pushed or pulled to move. And we're not talking about a gentle
nudge here; a hard shove is usually what it takes to prompt people
to uproot their lives and risk a new start in a foreign land. Still, for
now, the best way for any country on the brink of population decline
to stave off that decline is to up the immigrant intake. In the end, it
doesn't matter whether they were pushed or pulled to ask for admission. You need them as much as they need you.

When we said that migration patterns were relatively stable, disas-
ters aside, we weren't telling the whole truth. There is one hugely
important movement that has been underway for the past six
decades. It is the movement from rural to urban, and it is reshaping the world.

In 1950, only 30 percent of the world's population was urban,
though in the developed world it was much higher. But as the developing world began to catch up with the developed, people increasingly moved from the country to the city, where the jobs—first in
industry, then increasingly in services—were to be found. By 2007,
the world's urban population surpassed its rural population for the
first time in history.[278] Today, the number of urban dwellers is at
55 percent. By 2050, two thirds of us will live in cities, reversing the
rural/urban split of a century before. The global rural population
has already reached its peak and will soon begin an absolute decline.
This is a massive change in the human condition, and it's taking
place within a single century.

Although most of us live in cities of one million or fewer, the
stars of the show are the megacities, with populations of ten million

or more. This table lists the ten largest megacities and their population in millions:

> Tokyo, Japan **38.1**
> Delhi, India **26.5**
> Shanghai, China **24.5**
> Mumbai, India **21.4**
> São Paulo, Brazil **21.3**
> Beijing, China **21.2**
> Mexico City, Mexico **21.2**
> Osaka, Japan **20.3**
> Cairo, Egypt **19.1**
> New York–Newark, United States **18.6**[279]

Only three of these megacities are in the developed world, and
two of those are in Japan. And Japan's population is shrinking. This
is no coincidence. As we know, urbanization leads to population
decline. At an astonishing 93 percent, Japan is one of the most
urbanized societies on earth. It is also experiencing one of the highest rates of population loss.

Let's roll things forward and look at the top ten in 2030. Here
they are:

> Tokyo, Japan **37.2**
> Delhi, India **36.1**
> Shanghai, China **30.8**
> Mumbai, India **27.8**
> Beijing, China **27.7**
> Dhaka, Bangladesh **27.4**
> Karachi, Pakistan **24.8**
> Cairo, Egypt **24.5**
> Lagos, Nigeria **24.2**
> Mexico City, Mexico **23.9**[280]

Osaka is gone from the top ten and Tokyo has lost a million people as depopulation gathers steam. But we have some new arrivals, including Lagos. And this is big news.

Nigeria's hopelessly corrupt federal government simply can't handle the tribal and religious rivalries that are tearing the country apart. But Lagos is a different story. A succession of efficient regional governments, major Chinese investments, and corporate interest in the city's low-wage workforce and its emerging middle class are transforming the city and the region. There is a new deepwater port under construction, new office and residential developments, new public transit—including the first sub-Saharan metro outside South Africa—and a new ten-lane superhighway, for both cars and rapid transit, that will link Lagos to Accra in Ghana and Abidjan in Côte d'Ivoire. Economists and demographers are predicting that, by 2050, fifty-five million people will live along the Trans–West African Coastal Highway, making it a much larger version of the I-95, the spine of BosNYWash, the acronym for the conurbation encompassing Boston, New York, and Washington. As the author and journalist Howard French observed, "The continent's biggest cities are spawning enormous urban corridors that are spilling over borders and creating vigorous new economic zones that are outstripping the ability of weak and plodding central governments to manage or even retain their hold on them."[281] And here's the thing. Nigeria, Ghana, and Côte d'Ivoire have fertility rates of between 4 and 5. But we know that the fertility rate in the LagAcAbid corridor, or whatever they end up calling it, won't be anything like that. It will be close to replacement rate, because that's what happens when people move to cities. So why does the UN continue to predict such high fertility rates for Africa?

Every region in the world is getting more urban every day. About 80 percent of the Americas and the Caribbean are now urbanized;

it's better than 70 percent for Europe; 50 percent for Asia; and
Africa is at 40 percent and growing fast. The urban world we are
becoming will be dominated by a geographically concentrated,
older, less fertile population. And because this is happening most
acutely in places that traditionally produce the surplus population
that migrates, and because poverty in those regions is also on the
wane, immigrants in the not-too-distant future may be hard to come
by. That's why developed nations with fertility issues should be
throwing open their doors. Instead they're closing them. Folly.

NINE

THE ELEPHANT RISES;
THE DRAGON DECLINES

The children born, or not born, in China and India today will shape the future of humanity. More than a third of us live in one of these two countries. How many are born this year, and the next, and the next, and how long these new arrivals are with us, will become the baseline for the world's future population. Population modelers must get China and India right. The fate of the environment, the global economy, the rise and fall of powers all depend on it.

The United Nations Population Division predicts that China's population will peak at more than 1.4 billion people around 2030 and then decline to just over one billion by 2100—a dramatic loss of population, by any measure. India's population, according to the UN, will reach something like 1.7 billion by 2060 and then begin to gently decline.[282] We believe these predictions are likely to be wrong. China's population will not just decline, it could practically collapse. India's population may never reach 1.7 billion. Here is why.

———

The Chinese National Bureau of Statistics is housed in a drab, gray, low-rise Beijing building that was never in contention for an architectural award. The interior of that building is phobically clean. As we enter, a group of older women dressed in cleaner's uniforms patrols the lobby with the Chinese equivalent of Swiffers, scrubbing invisible grime off a gleaming marble floor. In the lobby, women in identical azure-blue, short-sleeved, crew-necked, knee-length dresses, their hair pulled back into severe buns, stand at attention, like flight attendants at inspection. After our hosts arrive—a delegation of Chinese state statisticians who want to discuss developments in social research and polling with us—some of the women follow us as we walk down the pristine hallways; others are stationed along the hallway, waving us toward the appropriate room, as though the statisticians didn't know their own building.

The room itself is a windowless interior meeting space of the sort that can be found in drab office buildings the world over, well equipped with computers, projectors, and the like. Women assume stations behind each chair. If you take a sip of the green tea provided to each of those seated, one of them instantly pours a refill. If you use the warm hand towel placed thoughtfully beside the notebook, with its perfectly sharpened pencil, the towel is instantly replaced. God only knows what might happen if you used the pencil. Afterward, a Chinese colleague explains. The government has a policy of full employment—or at least as full as they can make it. These women were recruited from the countryside and brought to Beijing to perform these tasks. Any work, even pointless work, is better than being idle.

As the world's most populous nation, China has a huge, cheap workforce at its disposal—so huge and so cheap that many Western companies have decided to move their plants and jobs there, leading to accusations that low-wage Chinese labor has undermined

American manufacturing. That criticism may once have been valid, but it is less so today. Yes, China's per capita GDP is only a third that of the U.S., but living standards have improved drastically and growth rates still outstrip those of any developed economy.[283] The economist Branko Milanović believes the real gap in wages today is not between China and the United States, but between high-wage and low-wage earners in both countries.[284] And the Chinese labor market is about to shrink, because the Chinese have largely given up on having babies. The world's largest nation has a very low birth rate; it has had a low birth rate for decades. Because the Chinese don't accept immigrants, inexorable math dictates a declining and rapidly aging population, a shrinking workforce, and an increasingly dependent society. China is becoming Japan.[285] The only difference is that Japan became rich before it became old. China will not be so lucky.

On a recent trip from Shenzhen (a city of twelve million that links Hong Kong to the Chinese mainland) to Beijing, we were startled by the absence of babies. Parents with their children on a trip are a common sight in most airports. Strollers are a constant hazard at security lines. ("I've never seen a stroller collapse in less than twenty minutes," George Clooney's character says in *Up in the Air*.) But strollers are so rare in both Shenzhen and Beijing that in each airport they can be counted on the fingers of one hand, with fingers left to spare. And we looked everywhere.

Alarmed by the dearth of births, the Chinese government finally eliminated its odious one-child policy in 2016.[286] That policy was a product of ideology and bureaucracy gone mad. After the civil war that created the modern Chinese state, Mao Zedong encouraged the Chinese people to have babies to help fulfill a combination of military and economic aspirations. It proved to be too much of a good thing. By the end of the 1950s, overpopulation contributed to the famine that killed tens of millions of Chinese.[287] In the wake of that famine, the regime took a 180-degree turn and created the Birth Planning Commission. At the launch of the fourth Five-Year Plan in 1971, the government inaugurated a campaign they called "Later, Longer, Fewer," which urged citizens to marry later, have fewer children, and wait longer between having children.[288]

That would probably have been enough to bring the fertility rate down to replacement rate. By 1979, it had already fallen from 6.2 in 1960 to 2.5, thanks to state encouragement and urbanization. (In 1960, only 16 percent of China's population lived in urban areas. Today, the figure is 54 percent. By 2050, it will be 76 percent.)[289] But planners love to plan. In that year, Deng Xiaoping imposed a compulsory one-child policy. There were many exceptions (ethnic minorities were exempt, and in many cases a second child was permitted if the first child was a girl), but state officials estimate four hundred million births were prevented by the time the policy was phased out in 2016.

The one-child policy was authoritarianism at its worst. Instead of incentives—such as education and free birth control—the state resorted to coercion, which led to heartbreak for parents who longed to raise a second or third child, and loneliness for the only sons and daughters. And like most acts of state coercion, the policy was counterproductive, pushing the birth rate below replacement rate even as the mortality rate also went down, thanks to economic development and improved health care. The average Chinese person now lives to seventy-six years of age, an astonishing increase of eighteen months over the life expectancy in 2010.[290] This means that China's elderly, dependent population will continue to climb through the century while the baby-making part of its population will continue to shrink. By 2040, one quarter of all Chinese will be senior citizens, compared to a global average of 14 percent.

We need to stress this point: large populations aren't necessarily fertile populations, especially if the average age skews older. In 1960, the median age of China was just twenty-one; today it is thirty-eight; by 2050, it will be will be fifty.[291] By then, China will be much closer in median age to Japan (53) than to the United States (42), its main competitor as a world power.[292]

Demographer Feng Wang sums China's population dilemma up neatly with one number: 160. "First, the country has 160 million internal migrants who, in the process of seeking better lives, have supplied abundant labor for the nation's booming economy. Second, more than 160 million Chinese are 60 years old or older. Third, more than 160 million Chinese families have only one child, a product of the country's three-decade-old policy limiting couples to one child each." Wang's sobering conclusion is that population decline and an aging society could bring on a crisis of political legitimacy. "Political legitimacy in China over the past three decades has been built around fast economic growth, which in turn relied on a cheap and willing labor force. An aging labor force will compel changes in this economic model and may make political rule more difficult."[293]

China's authoritarian child policies have had another, tragic, consequence: the removal of a huge number of women from the Chinese population through gender-specific abortions. The one-child policy, coupled with the traditional emphasis on producing a male heir, is the reason for the skew. Normally, there should be 105 boys born for every 100 girls born.[294] In China, there are 120 boys born for every 100 girls.[295] This gender imbalance is even more extreme in some rural areas of China. Between 30 million and 60 million Chinese women are "missing," though some of them might simply not have registered in rural areas.[296]

If at least thirty million women are in fact missing, then at least thirty million Chinese men will not be able to find wives.[297] In addition, even though the social norm in China is for women to marry, many Chinese women are now fighting hard for the right to pursue a professional career. This means getting married later, if at all, to accommodate their educational and career aspirations.[298] China could soon have millions of lonely and sexually frustrated young men on its hands—never good for social stability.

Chinese authorities assumed that, once the one-child policy was lifted, the country would have its own baby boom. So far, that boom isn't happening. As we've seen elsewhere, once small families become the norm, they remain the norm generation after genera- tion. The low-fertility trap conditions expectations. This is especially true in China, which has propagandized the virtues of smaller fami- lies for decades. Further, sterilization is a popular method of birth control in China. Fully half of the women of reproductive age in China report that either they or their partners are sterilized.[299] So even if potential mothers and fathers are now allowed to have a second child, many are physically incapable.

The Ipsos survey on ideal family size underscores this. An almost unanimous 93 percent of Chinese respondents say the ideal family should have two children or fewer. Twenty percent even say one or none is ideal. And, showing the depth to which the small-family norm has burnt itself into Chinese culture, even when Chinese women leave China, they continue to carry the norm with them. In Canada, Chinese women have the lowest birth rate of any of the major immigrant groups—even lower than the already low rate for native-born Canadian women.[300]

And yet, despite the overwhelming evidence that the Chinese fertility rate will remain low, the United Nations projects that it will increase from 1.59 in 2020 to 1.75 by 2050 and to 1.81 by 2100. This would keep China's population at about a billion at the end of the century. But given all the evidence that families will stay small, the estimates of Wolfgang Lutz and his colleagues in Vienna are probably closer to the mark. Factoring in the impact of improving education for Chinese women, they predict the birth rate will hold at 1.4 or 1.5 for most of the century. If so, the Chinese population will fall to around 754 million by 2100, a quarter billion people below the UN's medium estimate, and an astonishing 630 million fewer people than are alive in China today. China's population could decline by almost half in this century. And even that is not the lowest-case scenario. If either Lutz's Rapid Development Model or the UN's low-variant projections turns out to be accurate, the population could collapse to between 612 and 643 million. Seven hundred million people could disappear from the face of the earth.

Could these low-variant projections possibly come true? Not only could they come true, they could be conservative. The Chinese statistics bureau pegs the fertility rate at 1.2.[301] That number has been discounted by analysts as too low, due to unreported births.[302] But what if it isn't low at all? Some demographers quote data from a 2016 survey by the Chinese State Statistics Bureau that cites a fertility rate of 1.05.[303] Other studies say the fertility rate has been at or near this level for almost a decade, and that it will remain at or near this level at least through 2035.[304] This is not as implausible as it sounds. After all, Hong Kong and Singapore are also reporting that their fertility rates have dropped to 1.0 or below. Major cities such as Beijing and Shanghai reportedly have fertility rates below 1.0, and millions of people continue to stream into the cities from the countryside, where fertility rates are much higher.[305] If Chinese parents are following suit, the Middle Kingdom will have a population of just 560 million by the end of the century. China will not be much larger, in terms of population, than the United States. In any case, China appears to be on the verge of a deliberate, controlled, massive collapse of its population. Nothing like this has ever occurred. We will look at the economic and geopolitical consequences of this shift later in the book, but none of them bode well for the Middle Kingdom.

One way the world population could get closer to the UN's predicted 11 billion by 2100 is if India maintains the torrid pace of growth it experienced in the last century. In 1950, India's population was just 376 million. Fifty years later, it had more than tripled to a billion. India will replace China as the world's most populous country within the next few years, with the UN predicting an astonishing benchmark of 1.7 billion people crowded onto the subcontinent by 2060. Then it will start to gently decline. How likely is it this future will come to pass? Let's take a look.

Traveling between India and China can be a bit of a shock. Beijing, despite its enormous population of twenty-two million people, is remarkably orderly. Yes, the air pollution can be horrific, but much of the city center was built in this century. Even in the poorest neighborhoods, the government is in control and crime is low, and the city's harsh winters ensure the absence of favela-like slums.

New Delhi, on the other hand, is a study in random contrasts. On one side of a street is a modern office building. On the other, enormous black feral sows and their piglets roll happily in the dust of a vacant, overgrown lot. Protests and religious celebrations materialize out of nowhere. Monkeys clamber across roofs while cows and goats stroll about freely. And the dogs. So many stray dogs. Lying in front of food stands, meandering down the sidewalks, relaxing in the lobbies of office buildings and university concourses. No one controls them. And in this Hindu society, culling them is out of the question.

The streets are choked with ancient and modern cars, trucks, buses, green-and-yellow auto-rickshaws, motorbikes, and carts being pulled by various draft animals. A new Mercedes reluctantly shares the road with a donkey straining to pull an overloaded cart. If you think the sound of honking car horns in New York City is annoying, try the cacophony of a New Delhi roundabout. On the back of one of the ubiquitous auto-rickshaws—three-wheel motorbikes with an attached passenger cab—a sticker in Hindi and English promises: "This responsible rickshaw respects and protects women," which says a lot about the lives of women here. India remains a deeply patriarchal society. That sticker matters because, as several women told us, "Delhi is the rape capital of India." The problem extends to cab and auto-rickshaw operators, which is why Delhi's Transport Department holds gender sensitivity classes for drivers. The one-hour class is mandatory for anyone who wants an annual auto-rickshaw licence.[306]

But the most fraught relationships for many Indian women are not with strangers but with their husbands, fathers, uncles, brothers, adult sons, and even brothers-in-law or male cousins. Men determine almost every aspect of their female family members' lives—education, employment, marriage, and family planning. As one woman told us, male control even extends to whether a female family member can travel.[307] The control of men over women is more rigid in rural areas than in urban, though it exists to some degree everywhere.

Almost everyone in India marries, and the marriages are arranged by the families of the bride and groom.[308] This practice is reinforced by religion (both Hinduism and Islam), as well as by the pervasive clan and caste systems. "Love matches" do happen, but they are rare. If a woman wants to elope and marry someone not approved by her family, she might be taking her life into her hands. Women who bring "shame" to their families by marrying without permission can and do become victims of so-called honor killings. In 2015, 251 murders in India were classified by authorities as honor killings.[309] Many others may have gone unreported. Again, the practice is more common in rural than in urban areas.

While remaining single is a viable option for women in many cultures today, it is a radical act in India. As Indian demographers K. Srinivasan and K.S. James explain, "In spite of various efforts made by governments, non-governmental organizations, and a few political parties, gender equalities on a scale achieved in the West will not be realized in India in the near future. Indian women tend to be valued by society in relation to their role in the family—as a wife, daughter-in-law, and mother. Women who fall outside of these roles, such as widows and single women, face discrimination and, in many cases, loss of property. Since a woman is considered incomplete without marriage, unmarried adult women, widows, and divorcees face strong social stigma."[310]

One of our female colleagues in India, who is in her late thirties, told us about the ordeal she's been through with her family because she decided to remain single.[311] She did this, she says, because she didn't want to surrender control over her life to a strange man through an arranged marriage, which she calls "India's adventure sport." Instead, her dream was to get an education, land a good job, and earn an independent income. The price she pays is to live with her parents, where her father as patriarch still controls, either directly or through societal pressure, many decisions about her life.[312]

Not surprisingly, given social and familial pressure, Indian women tend to get married in their late teens or early twenties. The groom is typically five years older than the bride.[313] One reason for this is that in Indian culture, the family of the bride pays a dowry to the family of the groom (the opposite of the tradition in Kenya). To warrant a strong dowry in the Indian marriage market, a prospective groom needs time to get the type of education and job that would make him a good investment for the bride's family. Especially desirable are university-educated men with government jobs.

Since men and women marry universally and early in India, you would think Indian couples would have lots of babies. Back in 1950, when India's fertility rate was 5.9, this was certainly the case. Today, however, India's official fertility rate has dropped by 60 percent, to just 2.4. While this is still above the replacement rate, and well above China's current fertility rate, the small-family norm has now found its way to India, too. The question is: why? Since the mean age when a woman first becomes a mother in India is still very low, at just twenty years; since women have so little power within the relationship; and since two thirds of the population still lives a rural existence, Indian women should be having far more babies than is good for India or them. As it turns out, other forces are also at work. Those forces include government policy and changing cultural practices. Governments, especially state governments, have been propagandizing for small families—"complete families," people call them—for decades. The complete family has two children, with at least one of them a boy. Or, as the government markets it: "We Two, Our Two." Once you've had your two, you should be done.[314]

"We Two, Our Two," and its many variants, are India's version of China's one-child policy and are motivated by the same official concerns about rampant overpopulation. But India has pursued its version of family-planning policy with a zeal that might make even China's state planners anxious. While some of the birth control measures are voluntary, such as the distribution of free condoms and education about birth control, India also has a disturbing history of forced and semi-forced surgical sterilization—for both sexes, but especially for women. There are still state governments in India today that run sterilization camps where masses of mostly rural Indian women are bribed to be sterilized.[315] Female sterilization remains by far the most prevalent method of birth control in India, regardless of all the efforts to promote less intrusive and more reversible methods. Only 4 percent of Indian women take a birth control pill, while 6 percent manage to convince the man to put on a condom. As K.S. James tells us, it's typical for an Indian woman to be sterilized immediately after her second child, at around twenty-five years of age.[316]

While many Indian governments now promote methods of family planning that are less intrusive than sterilization, many women still prefer to go the surgical route. While anecdotally you hear about bureaucrats trying to make their quota, or husbands having their wives sterilized and then pocketing the cash—1,400 rupees, or about US$20, a not insubstantial sum, given India's median annual income of $616—Indian women we spoke to had the surgery of their own free will. And when they explained why, they sounded a lot like their Brazilian sisters.

Srinivaspuri is a large urban slum located in southern Delhi close to busy highways and office blocks. It's difficult to say how many people live there because large portions of the Delhi population are clustered in unauthorized communities.[317] The residents, who are largely migrants from neighboring, rural states, come and go every day. Let's just say that based on what we saw, it's a lot of people. Communities like Srinivaspuri are the leading edge for fertility change in India. These rural emigrés are discovering for the first time that children are expensive, now that they can no longer contribute to the family's labor pool as they did on the farm. Many of the women are being exposed for the first time in their lives to education, employment, and modern technology. So what impact are these forces, which have reduced birth rates around the world, having on Srinivaspuri?

The slum is a jumble of makeshift buildings constructed with rough bricks and recycled building materials. These one-room hovels are artfully jammed into wherever it's possible to build a wall.

The only features that define their placement are the footpaths of broken concrete that snake through the community. Most of the buildings have curtains across the front that are either open or partially drawn. A few have doors. Inside are single rooms with large carpets covering their earthen or concrete floors. All of life happens in that one room—cooking, sleeping, and the rest of what we do as human beings. Pots and pans and other kitchen items and groceries are either stacked on the floor or hang from the walls.

The narrow walkways are interrupted by random ladders—some homemade, some prefab—that ascend to additional units built on top of the buildings at street level. Laundry hangs colorfully everywhere. Most units appear to have some form of electricity, but the seemingly random wires that snake in all directions wouldn't pass any safety code. Along both sides of the walkway are single, uniform, shallow trenches, each about a foot wide. These are open sewers. As for toilet facilities, we didn't see any. But, the smells in the air suggest that whatever was being used could best be described as primitive.

It's about ten on a pleasantly mild Friday morning in March, and Srinivaspuri is a very busy place. The walkways are teeming with people, young and old. The women are dressed in brightly colored saris, their long, dark hair covered with a scarf or tightly pulled back. The men wear Western clothes—logoed T-shirts and shorts or trousers. As for footwear, both genders wear sandals. Everyone is expected to take off their shoes before entering a home. Given what we are walking through, that seems like a very good idea.

Our destination is a preschool located thirteen minutes from the slum entrance. Our local colleagues have organized two focus groups for us with women living in the slum. A total of fifteen women have agreed to participate. They are both married and single; the oldest is thirty-five years of age, the youngest is seventeen. Four are Muslim, the rest are Hindu. We spoke to the married and unmarried women separately. The discussions were in Hindi, with the colleague who moderated the groups repeating what was said in English.

As in the residences, a single large mat covers the earthen floor of the tiny, one-room school. The walls are adorned with tattered alphabet posters, as well as charts of shapes, colors, and animals. One of the alphabet posters is in English. We remove our shoes and enter the room. Everyone sits on the mat. There is no door or curtain to close, just a raised cement threshold to step over. The room is open to the street.

One of the women who joins us breast-feeds a baby under her shawl. The women are all dressed in brightly colored saris, and adorned with assorted jewelery, including bangles, finger and toe rings, and nose jewelery. Some also have painted nails and henna tattoos. These women spend considerable time attending to their appearance.

But they are shy in conversation, and we are discussing a sensitive subject in a public forum. After some introductory "getting to know you" chatter, our moderator gets down to business. "How many kids do you plan to have?" she asks. For those who haven't started a family yet, or for those with only one child, the answer is universal: "two." Our moderator asks why, and things start to get interesting. The younger women say that they want to live different lives than their mothers, whom they regard as cautionary tales. They want to have fewer kids because they aspire to having the independence that would come from a good education and the earning potential that it brings. Having their own source of income would give them leverage, they believe, in negotiating with men, including their husbands, over the big issues in their lives.

The other reason for having two children is the desire to create a "complete family." It seems the "We Two, Our Two" norm is hitting home. As several women tell us, they wouldn't want to have just one child. That's because family responsibilities (especially the care of elderly parents) in Indian families are considerable, and it would be too much of a burden for one child. But more than two children would be an unaffordable expense (although one woman said she had five children and was making do). To quote one participant, "Doing what needs to be done to raise two children seems all that's possible, given the expense of raising and educating children."

While the women want complete families, they are also quick to remind us that it isn't their decision to make. As one participant tells us, "The husband decides on the number of kids, not the mother." "It's all about having a boy," one mother explains. "I had three daughters but had to keep going until I had a boy." The one woman in the married group who has five children says that this was the result of having daughters to start.

One subject the women are reluctant to discuss is birth control. It is clear, though, that for them, the more certain the solution (i.e., sterilization), especially after two children, the better, since their men won't consider using condoms or getting sterilized themselves. For the Muslim women, sterilization was not an option for religious reasons.

There is little talk of romance in the room, no longing among the single women for ideal mates and fairy-tale weddings—ironic, given the idealized romances featured in popular Bollywood movies. These women do not hold their husbands in high regard. Their men are unreliable providers and hard to live with. Most are day laborers who only work when they feel like it and spend too much of the proceeds on alcohol and gambling. Drinking is repeatedly raised as a big issue in their marriages.

For all, marriage and children are responsibilities, not aspirations. And yet, though they want to be wives and mothers, they also dream of doing as much as possible on their own terms. A thought occurs: as these young women pass their aspirations for independence on to their daughters, that demand for greater autonomy is likely to grow—slowly but inexorably, generation by generation. In the slums of Delhi, family planning involves economic need, clashing traditions, the power of religion and the patriarchy, the aspirations of women to have control over their lives. This can only lead to greater independence and fewer children. The struggle for the rights of women goes only in one direction.

A surreptitious proof of how that struggle will end reveals itself as we talk. From time to time, the women reach under their robes and glance at a backlit screen. Even in the slums of Delhi, women can access a smartphone, a carrier plan, and a network. Even in the slums of Delhi, they hold the sum of human knowledge in their hands.

Will India's population, as the UN predicts, peak at 1.7 billion in 2060? On this, at least, Wolfgang Lutz and his colleagues at the International Institute for Applied Systems Analysis basically agree. But over and over again during our stay in Delhi, demographers and government officials conducting local research told us, *sotto voce*, that they suspected the fertility rate had already dropped below 2.1. If so, then India is a decade ahead of where both the UN and the Vienna school have it. If India is already at or below 2.1, then it is unlikely to reach much past 1.5 billion, according to the low-variant models, and will be back down to 1.2 billion by 2100.

If the UN modelers are right, China and India could help the world reach something close to eleven billion. But China and India are sending strong signals that those predictions are too high, that both countries will peak in population sooner than many expect, and then join most of the rest of the planet in shedding population.

Of course, we could be wrong, but we don't think so. We keep thinking of those women in that school in a Delhi slum, checking their smartphones beneath their robes.

TEN

THE SECOND AMERICAN CENTURY

A t noon, they break for lunch—half an hour, using a portable grill to cook the beef, which goes on crispy, flat tortilla shells, along with salsa. There are about a dozen of them, all Mexican immigrants, the youngest in his twenties, the oldest in his fifties, working on the renovation of this grand, mid-century Palm Springs bungalow, joking and teasing in the way of workers who know each other well. Most of them are family or friends. The contractor who hired these men eats with them. He hires only Mexican laborers, he says, because they work so hard and so well. Some of these workers are legal immigrants; some are undocumented, working on the down-low.

They all come from the same city, San Miguel, which is typical of migrant workers. Years ago, one migrant arrived, scoped out the job scene, found work, then began sending messages back to family and friends. Some of these guys are recent arrivals; most have been here for many years: they married their wives here; their children were born here.

In many ways, their lives are very American. Their children attend local schools. They work and pay taxes. But there is always that worry. One man's brother-in-law, who had lived in the United States for decades and had American-born children, was pulled over by police on a traffic violation. When officials discovered he was in the country illegally, he was deported. It took him five years to reunite with his family.

The undocumented workers miss Mexico deeply, but they can never go back. As one of them put it: "You can't go bury your parents, unless you have fifteen grand for the coyote."

"The U.S. is no longer a world power. It is a declining power. Forget about it," one Pakistani diplomat said at a conference in 2016, perhaps not aware that his words were being recorded.[318] He's hardly alone in this opinion. The financial crisis of 2008, the rising economic power of China, the renaissance of Russian power under Vladimir Putin, quagmires in Iraq, Afghanistan, and Libya, all point to a giant on the wane. At home, racial strife is endemic in major cities, with African Americans and police seemingly at war; infrastructure decays and global test scores embarrass American students. Donald Trump's shocking presidential victory, and the refusal by many progressive Americans to accept the reality of that victory, suggest that political polarization has become so toxic that the stability of the republic itself is at risk. No wonder the National Intelligence Council concluded recently that the "unipolar moment is over and Pax Americana—the era of American ascendancy in international politics that began in 1945—is fast winding down."[319]

Perhaps. But there is a whole lot of "on the other hand." However large the Chinese economy, the average American makes eight times their Chinese counterpart; the American dollar remains the unchallenged global reserve currency; despite massive new investments in

China's military, the U.S. outspends its rival in defense three to one, with a global-power-defining eight hundred military bases in fifty countries around the world; ten of the world's twenty highest-ranked universities are located in the United States;[320] eight of the world's nine largest high-tech companies are U.S.-based; the American-invented Internet is dominated by such U.S. giants as Google and Facebook and Amazon; a once-energy-dependent United States has become a major energy exporter; and last but most important, America is a democracy and China and Russia are not, and the arc of history, to rephrase Martin Luther King, bends toward freedom.[321]

America's cultural hegemony is unshakable. Netflix is available in 190 countries. You can buy a Big Mac in 119 countries, sign up for Apple Music in 113 countries, and watch *Star Trek: Discovery* in 188 countries. The ten highest-grossing movies of 2017 all came out of Hollywood. The highest-grossing movies *always* come out of Hollywood. The best-selling book of all time by a living author is, sadly, *The Da Vinci Code*, by Dan Brown.[322] And music? Gospel, the blues, jazz, Broadway, country, rock and roll, hip-hop, rap. We could go on.

As analysts Ely Ratner and Thomas Wright wrote, "The United States is blessed with a superior combination of sound fundamentals in demography, geography, higher education and innovation. That ensures it has the people, ideas and security to thrive at home and on the world stage. There's a reason elites around the world remain eager to send their fortunes, and often their families, to the United States."[323]

American declinism is as old as American exceptionalism, and both are as old as the republic. Alexander Hamilton warned that, unless the states coalesced around a powerful central government, the United States was doomed to "poverty and disgrace." (The warning worked, which is why Hamilton is on the ten-dollar bill, and

Broadway.) There were plenty of opportunities in the nineteenth century to predict the demise of the republic, not least during the War
of 1812 (which the Americans lost, though to this day they refuse to
admit it) and the Civil War. Isolationism in the 1920s and the Great
Depression of the 1930s appeared to leave the U.S. alone and adrift.
At the very height of the American empire, its critics predicted its
imminent demise: after Russia's launch of the Sputnik satellite in 1957;
after the riots and assassinations of 1968; after Watergate, the loss
of Vietnam, and stagflation in the 1970s; after the rise of Japanese economic power in the 1980s. As the writer Josef Joffe likes to say, "Decline
is as American as apple pie."³²⁴ And yet somehow the republic always
rights itself, and rights the rest of the world along with it.

Declinism has never been more ill-suited to the American story
than it is today. The twentieth century has been named the American
Century. The twenty-first will be American, too. American economic and cultural power, along with its geopolitical and military
heft, will grow rather than weaken. Provided Americans don't close
themselves off from the world, they will influence the world more
than ever before. Those Mexican workers eating lunch in Palm
Springs are part of the reason why.

Despite the endless, acrimonious debate over immigration policy,
Americans continue to welcome newcomers. A 2016 Pew Research
poll showed that 60 percent of Americans agreed with the statement that immigrants "strengthen our country because of their
hard work and talent," while only 35 percent believed immigrants
"are a burden on our country because they take our jobs, housing
and health care." Twenty years ago, those numbers were essentially
reversed. The divide is political and generational. While eight in
ten people who identify as Democrats welcome immigrants, only
about a third of Republicans feel that way. And while three quarters

of millennials support plenty of immigration, only about half of the boomers concur.[325]

Although Australia and Canada bring in more migrants as a share of their population, the United States dwarfs all others in terms of the absolute volume of legal immigrants—typically around one million people per year, more than twice as many as any other country. The disparity would be even higher, were Europe not playing temporary host to people displaced by the civil wars in Syria and Yemen, campaigns by ISIS, chaos in Libya, and the like.

But there is a second stream, the Mexican, and other Latinos crossing the southern border into the United States illegally. An estimated eleven million undocumented immigrants live and work in the United States.[326] Despite the controversy surrounding their presence, they contribute richly to the American economy and society. They help make up the gap created by a native-born population that is reproducing below replacement rate. And the higher birth rate of immigrants pushes the overall fertility rate in the U.S. higher.

The disparity between American, Chinese, and Russian birth rates is another U.S. asset. The United States' fertility rate is 1.9; Russia's is 1.5. Officially, the Chinese rate is 1.6, although as we have seen, it may in fact be much lower. The United States is reproducing more robustly than its largest geopolitical competitors. Thanks to immigration and a higher fertility rate, the U.S. is far better placed than most major developed nations to sustain its population through the course of this century.

Another secret weapon is the American attitude. The United States welcomes new arrivals, and people from all over the world want to move there. China doesn't permit immigration, and Russia has trouble convincing anyone to come. America's willingness to supplement the gap between babies produced domestically and babies needed to sustain the population through immigration is the crucial advantage that will secure the American hegemony.

The American fertility rate is higher than in most other developed countries because African American and Latino women have more babies than white women in the U.S. or than women in Europe or China or other major industrialized societies. But in fact the trend line is headed toward fewer births for all American women, regardless of race, which is why immigration is more important than ever for keeping the American dream alive.

Among millennials, especially, the fertility rate is very low. Between 2007 and 2012, the birth rate among Americans who came of age after 2000 dropped by 15 percent, to the lowest birth rate ever recorded in the United States: 0.95, less than one baby for every mother.[327] The Great Recession was certainly a factor during those years: as we've seen before, in advanced societies with below-replacement fertility rates, bad economic times will depress baby-making even further. But whatever short-term cause convinced millennial women to put off having children, the long-term impact is profound. Millennial American women have, in the main, opted not to have children in their twenties. This means that these women, when they do have children, will have fewer children than they would have had otherwise, which means the generation produced by the millennials will be smaller than the millennial generation itself.

But here's what's really startling about the recent birth dearth in the U.S. Among white American women, fertility declined by 11 percent during the recession. Among African American women, it declined by 14 percent. Among Latino women, it declined by 26 percent.[328] This completely upends an age-old assumption about the American birth rate: that high fertility among blacks and Latinos will offset declines in fertility among whites. Precisely the opposite is happening. The birth rates among ethnic minority groups in the United States are dropping like a stone. To look at it from a different angle, the fertility rate among white, non-Latino women in the United States has remained relatively unchanged since 1991, at about 1.8 children per woman of reproductive age (though the millennial figures might eventually suppress that). During that same period, the Latino fertility rate has dropped from 3.0 to 2.1.

And it isn't just native-born Latinas and legal immigrants who are imitating their European counterparts in having fewer babies. Between 2009 and 2014, the number of children born annually to undocumented women declined from 330,000 to 275,000. This is a serious decline over five years, more than can be accounted for by undocumented immigrants returning home during the recession.[329] Latino Americans have lost, on average, one whole baby per woman in the past generation. Meanwhile, the African American fertility rate has gone from 2.5 to 1.9.[330] There is now little difference in the fertility rates among whites, blacks, and Latinos in the United States, a statistic that rarely gets mentioned but that will have a massive impact on the United States' demographic future.

"This shift in fertility rates is simply not getting enough attention," David Drozd, a demographer with the Center for Public Affairs Research at the University of Nebraska at Omaha, believes, and we couldn't agree more.[331] Declining and converging fertility rates in the U.S. should have a positive impact on race relations going forward. The struggle of African Americans and Latino Americans for full equality is not over—it is not even close to being over. But if fertility rates in these communities are coming down, then it can only mean that African American and Latino women are becoming better educated and more empowered.

The fertility decline is especially acute among African American teenagers. In 1991, there were 118 births for every thousand African American teenagers aged fifteen to nineteen—more than one African American teenage woman in ten got pregnant in any given year. But by 2013 that number had declined by two thirds.[332] Why are fewer African American teenagers becoming pregnant? For one thing, like all teenagers, they're starting to have sex later.[333] For another, they're doing a better job of practicing contraception.[334] But why are they acting so responsibly? Improved sexual education programs are almost certainly a factor, along with the highly public campaigns warning about the spread of HIV/AIDS. Governments and doctors are making contraception easier to obtain, and use of the morning-after pill has increased substantially in recent years.[335]

Growing affluence among African Americans could also be a cause. Many studies report that teens delay sex and practice it more safely if they feel close to their parents. That means they have a stable situation at home, and that suggests financial security. Even as controversy surrounds police shootings of African Americans and the protests of the Black Lives Matter movement, life for black Americans has been getting steadily better.[336] We don't want to overstate the case. The net worth of an average black family is 6 percent of that of the average white family, largely because black families are more likely to rent than to own, and home ownership is how Americans typically accumulate much of their wealth.[337] The black unemployment rate is twice that of whites. The poverty rate in the United States is 15 percent, but among blacks it's 27 percent, almost double. Still, that poverty rate is less than half the 60 percent you found among blacks in 1960.[338] And according to one study, college enrollment among African Americans is now higher than the national average (71 percent versus 68 percent).[339] Another study found that two years after they enter university, eight out of ten white students are still enrolled; for African American students, the figure is seven in ten. So there's a gap, but it's not huge.[340] The decline in teenage pregnancies among African Americans in the United States parallels a general increase in education and income, which is cause for celebration.

The Mexican workers having lunch in Palm Springs tell a familiar story. Back home, indigenous Mexicans from the state of Chiapas are migrating to the cities, putting downward pressure on wages in the factories, and sending workers north across the border. Urbanization is universal, but its effects are local: in Mexico, migration from countryside to city prompts a second migration, from Mexican city to American city.

Another universal phenomenon with local consequences: as Mexico urbanizes, the hold of the Roman Catholic Church on society weakens. As one of the workers explains, his grandmother gave birth to twenty-four children, twelve of whom lived, because the Church taught her that contraception was a grave sin, and the role of the woman was to raise a family of many children and make the home a refuge for her husband returning from work. Today, everyone practices contraception. And as one worker puts it, "Women go to school, they drive cars, they hang out together—" "They drink tequila like a man!" another interjects. All of these workers have, or expect to have, two or three children, reflecting right where the Latino fertility rate currently sits. "You have eight children, that's eight pairs of shoes," one of them points out. In Palm Springs, for Mexican immigrants, both documented and undocumented, economic logic dictates fewer children, and the women are dictating it, too.

Latinos are achieving their own share of the American dream. As we've seen, Latino fertility rates are approaching those of non-Latino white Americans. Teenage pregnancies among Latinos are declining in lockstep with those of their African American counterparts. And here's one simply amazing statistic: between 1996 and 2016, the Latino high school dropout rate fell from 34 percent to 10 percent. The black rate went from 16 percent to 7 percent. For whites, it was 8 percent to 5 percent.[341] Dropout rates have almost completely converged. The kids are going to be all right.

Decades of legal and illegal immigration from Latin America into the United States have wrought profound changes on the ethnic and psychic makeup of the country. Latinos now outnumber African Americans, further blurring the racial divides. In 1995, a year after Canada, Mexico, and the United States signed the North American Free Trade Agreement, there were three million unauthorized Mexican immigrants in the United States. By 2008, that number had peaked at seven million—out of a total undocumented population estimated by Homeland Security at around twelve million—before the recession convinced many of them to return home, leaving an estimated 5.5 million undocumented Mexicans in the country today.[342]

While progressive voices and Democratic politicians search for ways to provide an amnesty and path to citizenship for unauthorized immigrants—or at least for those who were brought into the country illegally as children—many Republican politicians and other conservatives oppose amnesty. President Trump is actively seeking to deport as many as he can. But this cause is lost. Caucasians are on track to become a minority in the United States by around 2044. The Latino population as of 2016 was about fifty-seven million, or 18 percent of the overall population. By 2065, Latinos will make up a quarter of the American population, and whites, at around 46 percent, will have lost majority status. African Americans will be well back, at 13 percent, roughly tied with Asians.[343] America will be browner, more Catholic and less Protestant, and Spanish will supplement English as the common tongue. Even now, more minority than white babies are being born every year in the United States.[344] Although, to be honest, even saying whites will be a minority by 2044 represents outdated thinking. Fifteen percent of marriages in the United States today cross racial lines. As those lines blur and begin to dissolve, the Census Bureau will have the challenging task of trying to define what ethnicity or combination of ethnicities a person might be. The final stirring of the melting pot will be happily underway.[345]

A caveat: "We are becoming a more diverse society, but not a post-racial one," the sociologist Richard Alba noted. The history of slavery, segregation, ghettoization, and other forms of discrimination are still too raw to airily dismiss. "But we need to admit that these categories are at best rough approximations when it comes to understanding who we are becoming," he adds. "Our society, transformed by immigration and new forms of assimilation, hasn't yet developed the vocabulary to capture the nuanced realities of this evolution."[346]

Whatever hopeful signals a declining birth rate might send for future racial reconciliation, the fact remains that aging, low-fertility populations face deep challenges as their workforce and then their entire population begins to shrink. The steep reduction in fertility rates among African Americans speaks to increasing affluence and autonomy, especially for African American women; decreasing fertility among Latinos speaks to the universal tendency of immigrants to align their child-bearing habits with those of their adopted country. In both cases, the implications for racial harmony are heartening, but they speak to a future United States that is older and no longer able to reproduce itself through domestic births. If America is to remain great, it must remain a nation that welcomes immigrants.

For that to happen, Americans must once again overcome the worst angels of their nature.

A dark thread of racist, nativist, populist intolerance flows though the American story. The latest immigrants are not like us. They don't share our British values, our Protestant religion, which are the true, founding American values and religion. They will never assimilate. We should stop bringing them in and keep a close watch on those already among us. They're a threat.

You find that talk surrounding the Alien and Sedition Acts of 1798, which (among other things) sought to keep French immigrants and French influence from corrupting the new republic. You find it in the Know-Nothing movement of the 1850s, which fought to stem the flood of German and Irish Catholics who were the latest contribution to the American melting pot. After the Civil War, white Protestants sounded the cry over the "yellow peril," the tens of thousands of Chinese immigrants who carried out the hard, dirty, dangerous, and ill-paid work of building the transcontinental railroad. They also worked in the mines and in the fields. The Chinese Exclusion Act of 1882 prohibited Chinese immigration. Chinese migrants already resident could not marry white women or obtain citizenship.

In the late 1800s and early 1900s, steam-powered vessels made it possible to bring many more immigrants to American shores. Labor surpluses in the Mediterranean and Eastern Europe drove millions of men and women across the Atlantic in search of work. Persecution and pogroms forced Jews to abandon Europe in search of safety and a better life. These swarms of new arrivals settled in urban ghettos—overcrowded, disease-filled tenements that must have made these newest Americans wonder what they had gotten themselves into.

The story was always the same: People fleeing war, poverty, or oppression came to a new and still largely empty land looking for a new future. They took hazardous or poorly paid jobs shunned by the native-born. Employers urged the government to keep the flood-gates open; they needed the new arrivals for the factories and farms. But the old stock resented the alien arrivals, convinced they were driving down wages, convinced that Catholics owed their first allegiance to the pope, convinced that Asian and Caucasian could never mix, convinced that whatever new group turned up could never truly be Americans. And they were proved wrong, as the latest wave of yearning masses blended in. And then the pattern of immigration shifted, new waves washed up on America's shores, and the old stock sounded a fresh alarm.

One of the most powerful voices was Charles Edward Coughlin, a Catholic priest in Chicago who raged against Jews and Communists. By 1938, he was a flat-out fascist, predicting, "When we get through with the Jews in America, they'll think the treatment they received in Germany was nothing."[347] Other voices, tragically, were far more mainstream, and far more powerful. In the worst single act of government-sponsored race hatred in American history, the federal government interned one hundred thousand Japanese Americans and Japanese residents in camps during the Second World War, fearing they were disloyal. Of course, they were loyal. The American government placed its own citizens in concentration camps (and the Canadian government shamelessly aped their cruelty) out of sheer, racist fear of the Other. Figures as progressive as Franklin Roosevelt and Earl Warren, then the governor of California, allowed themselves to be blinded by animus and prejudice. Today, the Japanese internment stands as a shocking legacy of American inhumanity toward its own people.

But the racist, isolationist, anti-immigrant stream that fouls the American narrative never prevails. Millions listened to Coughlin's tirades, but millions more ignored him. His efforts to defeat Franklin Roosevelt in the 1936 election came to nothing. Forty years after the Japanese internment, a federal commission called the incarceration a "grave injustice" motivated by "racial prejudice, war hysteria and the failure of political leadership."[348] President Ronald Reagan issued a formal apology, and the federal government provided each survivor with twenty thousand dollars in compensation. In his memoirs, Warren—who went on to become one of the United States' greatest chief justices of the Supreme Court—said he "deeply regretted" the removal order. "Whenever I thought of the innocent little children who were torn from home, school friends, and congenial surroundings, I was conscience-stricken."[349]

And after each backlash dissipates, the flood resumes. After the war, the U.S. welcomed more than two hundred thousand Displaced Persons—DPs, they were called—fleeing chaos and Soviet armies in Europe. Then the migration patterns shifted, from horizontal to vertical. Starting in the 1960s, Mexican and other Latino migrants began crossing the border to the United States illegally, once again in search of the low-paid work others wouldn't take. A succession of amnesties that aimed to close the border to new arrivals while granting citizenship to those who were already established failed to stem the flow. By 2007, when Congress next debated—and defeated—an amnesty bill, an estimated twelve million undocumented immigrants bolstered the lowest ranks of the American economy.

One of the workers we talked to at lunch came to the United States from Mexico via Canada, crossing an unguarded border near Bellingham, Washington. A relative drove up from California and they met at a designated rendezvous, then headed back down south. Others used the more conventional route of crossing between Mexico and the United States, using the services of a coyote: people who smuggle people into the U.S. The fee, we're told, is about fifteen thousand dollars, part of it paid in advance, part of it paid over the years from the worker's salary. There are people around whose job it is to collect the payments.

Today, many white Americans, either implicitly—through anonymous posts on the web, for example—or explicitly—through the so-called alt-right movement—complain that the United States is losing its identity as a mostly white, Christian nation, which is why they supported Donald Trump in the 2016 election, and support as well his plan to build a "big, beautiful wall" at the Mexican border to keep out "illegals." Others fear that immigrants of all kinds steal jobs from "real" Americans and depress wages. The notion that immigrants steal jobs is a fallacy. The very opposite is true. More than half of all U.S. start-up companies worth more than a billion dollars today were founded by immigrants.[350] As for whether low-skilled and undocumented immigrants suppress wages for low-income Americans, the evidence is mixed, though it appears they are most likely to suppress the wages of other immigrants.[351]

Yes, the situation is corrosive. Just about anywhere you live in the United States, you know you are benefiting from the labor of undocumented immigrants. They cut your grass or clean your house or make the bed in your hotel room or pour concrete for the new building. The country's dependence on undocumented workers makes a mockery of the rule of law and reveals an American economy that still depends on unregulated, low-wage labor. However, the flow may be starting to ease, or even reverse. The recession of 2008 contributed to this shift, an improving Mexican economy helped as well, and today there are fewer undocumented immigrants than there were a decade ago.[352] Still, everyone complains—from the right, that these workers flout the law and should, somehow, be deported en masse (though this is quite impossible); from the left, that these workers deserve legal protection and a path to citizenship.

Meanwhile, unemployed and underemployed white workers, cast aside by governments and employers alike in the rush to globalization, blame the Latinos for their misery. It isn't fair, but on this sorry issue, nothing is ever fair.

The United States is a nation of immigrants in spite of itself. For nigh on 250 years of American history, anti-immigrant sentiment has plagued the American narrative. But history teaches us that the forces of reaction have seldom prevailed for long. From the Alien and Sedition Acts to Donald Trump, nativist, racist opposition to immigration has, sooner or later, always had its day, and then another day dawns. And a good thing, too, for those immigrants are America's secret weapon.

The United States could and should, for its own good, be taking in far more than the one million people who arrive annually. (If they were following Canada's example, they would be taking in three million.) With a streamlined and more open system for attracting talented economic-class immigrants from around the world, the Yanks could suck up many of the world's best brains. But even with their complex, restrictive, and self-punishing regulations, a million people a year is still a lot of people. Immigrants account for about 15 percent of the population of the United States. In China, the figure is less than 1 percent.

Immigrants, whether documented or undocumented, both mitigate the effects of an aging population and bolster the number of American babies. And history tells us that it doesn't matter whence they come, how much education or what job qualifications they have, what language they speak. Inevitably, they, too, become American. The soup in the melting pot might change its hue over time, but the result is always the same.

Of the three global nuclear superpowers, only America will be growing its population during the present century, provided it continues to take in newcomers. Even at current levels, it is expected to grow from 345 million today to 389 million by 2050 and 450 million in 2100—a solid 100 million more than today, and closing in on a much-diminished China. Whatever else might be added to the geopolitical calculations, demographically the American advantage is decisive.

And in case anyone still needs to be convinced, consider: In 2016, seven Americans won Nobel prizes. Six were immigrants. (The seventh, Robert Zimmerman, is better known as Bob Dylan.)

Immigration may be America's greatest competitive advantage in the twenty-first century. Ultimately, as the developing nations advance and fertility rates continue to fall, the migration of peoples will slow. Remigration will see immigrants returning to the land of their birth, lured by good new jobs and family back home. With populations aging and declining almost everywhere, countries may one day be competing for immigrants. In such a struggle, the United States will always have the upper hand. From jeans and a T-shirt to HBO, Americans' cultural values rule the planet. The U.S. economy remains a vibrant, if chaotic, place in which to invest. American politics are no less vibrant, and no less chaotic. In entrepreneurship and creativity, America continues to lead the pack. People looking for new opportunities and a better life will continue to flock to this wild, gleaming, messy, ill-planned, magnificently-executed-in-spite-of-itself city on a hill. That city will never cease to flourish, provided it never closes its gates.

ELEVEN

CULTURAL EXTINCTION IN AN AGE OF DECLINE

W earing his signature black hat, Mick Dodson tucks into a burger with pepper shrimp at the wonderfully named Hoi Polloi, a restaurant in the Old Parliament House in Canberra, once home to Australia's parliament. Though he may be the most distinguished Aboriginal Australian—the first to graduate law school; counsel for the Royal Commission into Aboriginal Deaths in Custody; co-author of *Bringing Them Home*, the report on Australia's equivalent of Canada's residential school system; and the 2009 Australian of the Year, perhaps that nation's highest honor—in person he is modest, funny, eyes glinting mischievously at times behind the reading glasses perched on his nose. His dining companions include another famous Aboriginal Australian, the former rugby star Katrina Fanning. But it is Dodson who does most of the talking today, about the troubled past and uncertain future of Australia's Aboriginal community.

He was born in 1950 in the Northern Territory, to an Aboriginal mother and a non-Aboriginal Australian father. Orphaned at ten, he was sent to a boarding school in the town of Hamilton, Victoria. Boarding schools, like Canada's now abandoned residential school system, could be mills of abuse and assimilation, part of a systemic effort by the Australian government to extinguish Aboriginal culture through forced assimilation. Dodson is credited with being the driving force behind then prime minister Kevin Rudd's historic formal apology in 2008 for wrongs committed by past governments against generations of Aboriginals.

Even now, though, "It's very difficult for Aboriginal youth to get an education unless they move away from home," Dodson explains.[353] A quarter of all youth currently in boarding schools are Aboriginal. "It's either boarding schools or nothing." Youths who leave their home and family to attend boarding school are likely not to return. They will move instead to cities and often lose their ability to speak their native language or to remain connected to their culture. As more Aboriginal youth migrate to urban centers, "that means the best and brightest are no longer there to lift the community," Dodson observes. Many Aboriginal Australians only return home at the end. "Lots of people go home to die."

Like indigenous populations around the world, Aboriginal Australians struggle with above-average rates of poverty, crime, violence, and substance abuse. But as more and more migrate to the cities, a new and growing middle class has emerged, and with it the desire to preserve Aboriginal culture and, especially, language. "New South Wales has as many languages as Europe," Dodson points out. But preserving these languages in an urbanizing Aboriginal environment is difficult, despite government efforts to make them part of the school curriculum.

"The new Aboriginal experience will be an urban experience," Dodson predicts. And that means an experience in which English is dominant, more Aboriginal students graduate and attend post-secondary schools, the Aboriginal middle class expands, and fertility rates decline. "In twenty-five years, [fertility] will be the same as for the general population," he believes.

By now, we hope we've dismantled some myths about population growth. No, we are not going to keep adding bodies until the world is groaning at the weight of eleven billion of us and more; nine billion is probably closer to the truth, before the population starts to decline. No, fertility rates are not astronomically high in developing countries; many of them are at or below replacement rate. No, Africa is not a chronically impoverished continent doomed to forever grow its population while lacking the resources to sustain it; the continent is dynamic, its economies are in flux, and birth rates are falling rapidly. No, African Americans and Latino Americans are not overwhelming white America with their higher fertility rates. The fertility rates of all three groups have essentially converged.

These myths can be hard to dispel, because even when a country's fertility rate has reached replacement rate, there is still one last large generation of young, presenting an illusion of population growth. Walk down the teeming streets of Bangkok and try to convince yourself that Thailand is in the midst of a population bust. Impossible! But Thailand's fertility rate is 1.5. Even though the United Nations inexplicably expects the fertility rate to modestly increase throughout the century, it predicts Thailand's population will start to decline after 2030, reaching a low of fifty million at the end of the century after a high of seventy million. More likely, Thailand's fertility rate will not increase, and may even decrease, leading to an even larger population loss.

Here's another myth: the birth rates of indigenous people are very high, much higher than in the general population. Because they are so high, indigenous populations are young, and many young women get pregnant when they and their partners lack the resources to care for their children, contributing to and reinforcing cyclical indigenous poverty and contributing also to militancy, especially among the young. Because indigenous fertility rates are so high, the population as a share of the general population is expanding and will continue to expand. A growing and impoverished indigenous underclass is a moral and social crisis that poses a grave threat to economic and social stability for the larger population.

We're not going to minimize the problem of indigenous poverty in Western society: it is real; it is pressing. Governments from Canberra to Ottawa face no greater social policy priority than to break the cycle. But the fertility rates of these populations are actually not all that high. They are at or close to replacement rate, and they are falling. In at least one case, they are even lower than the national average. The current large cohort of young native people will be the last. Indigenous populations will soon start to age, along with the general population, and they will face the same resulting challenges. And because they are so few in number, relative to the general population, they will find it ever harder to preserve their languages, cultures, and autonomy within the larger society. The challenge for indigenous populations in Canada, Australia, the United States, and New Zealand is that there are not too many babies being born, but too few.

On June 11, 2008, the same year that Kevin Rudd apologized on behalf of his country to the Aboriginal people of Australia, Prime Minister Stephen Harper apologized on behalf of all Canadians to Canada's Indigenous peoples for their treatment at residential schools. "We now recognize that far too often these institutions gave rise to abuse or neglect or were inadequately controlled, and we apologize for failing to protect you,"[354] Harper declared, in the pin-drop-silent

House of Commons. From soon after Confederation until the 1970s, many thousands of First Nations children (still called "Indians" under the Canadian government's Indian Act) were taken from their families and reserves and educated in boarding schools operated by Catholic and Protestant churches. Physical and even sexual abuse were rampant; the scars of Ottawa's efforts to "kill the Indian in the child,"[355] as one government official put it, remain with those students and their descendants to this day.

Canada's population of Indigenous peoples (the preferred term that includes First Nations, Métis, and Inuit) has grown in the past decade from 4 percent of Canada's thirty-six million people to 5 percent, largely as a result of people living longer and more people self-identifying as Indigenous.[356] Though some First Nations reserves are flourishing, many of those in remote areas such as northern Ontario, northern Manitoba, and the territory of Nunavut struggle with poverty, substance abuse, and violence. Sixty percent of First Nations children living on reserve live in poverty.[357] One reserve in six lacks clean drinking water.[358] Suicide is the leading cause of death for Indigenous Canadians under the age of forty-four; Indigenous youth are five or six times more likely to kill themselves than non-Indigenous youth.[359]

Indigenous communities already form large minorities in Prairie cities such as Winnipeg and Saskatoon, and the general assumption is that those minority communities will continue to grow far into the future. But those assumptions are wrong. This large generation of Indigenous young will be the last large generation of Indigenous young. The next generation will be considerably smaller, and the generation after that smaller still. The Indigenous population, as a percentage of the Canadian population, will stabilize, and then start to shrink.

Back in the 1960s, the Indigenous fertility rate was 5.5, more than twice that of the general population. But by 2001, it had fallen to 2.6, compared to 1.5 for the general population. By 2011, it was only 2.2, while the general population had a fertility rate of 1.6.[360] The fertility rate of Indigenous Canadians is both plummeting and converging with that of the general population. By now, it has probably dropped below replacement rate.

Indigenous fertility rates are declining for the same reason they decline in every other place among every other group: the women in this population are becoming empowered through urbanization and education. While Indigenous leaders stress the honored place of women within their culture, until recently women's legal rights were restricted (and in some ways still are). According to one estimate, up to 80 percent of women living on reserve experience some form of sexual abuse, four times the national average. "It's nothing less than a goddamn embarrassment in this country," fumed Senator Roméo Dallaire.[361]

Indigenous women and men (who are victims of homicide at twice the rate of women living off reserve) are at elevated risk of poverty, violence, you name it. But look at this: The on-reserve high school graduation rate is 40 percent. Off reserve, the rate is 70 percent. For Canada as a whole, the figure is 90 percent.[362] More than half of First Nations people live off reserve, and 70 percent of Métis.[363]

As Indigenous peoples urbanize, and their fertility rate declines, they are destined to become a smaller, not a larger, component of the Canadian social fabric. Canada brings in three hundred thousand immigrants a year. Most of these immigrants are from the Philippines, India, China, and other Asian and Pacific countries. Out of an overall population of 1.7 million Indigenous Canadians, there are only 328,000 First Nations living on reserve—a little more than one year's worth of immigrants.[364] With 20 percent of Canadians not born in Canada, the Indigenous population as a share of the overall population—and in particular the First Nation population living on reserve—is certain to decline over time, becoming even more marginalized in a racially complex and increasingly less European society.

Declining indigenous birth rates are hardly unique to Canada. In Australia, where 3 percent of the population identifies as Aboriginal, the Aboriginal birth rate in 2015 was 2.3, about the same as in Canada, while the overall birth rate for the country was 1.8.[365] Compare that with an Aboriginal birth rate in the 1960s of 5.8.[366] New Zealand is a special case because the Maori constitute 15 percent of the population, which means their statistics influence the overall statistics. As elsewhere among indigenous peoples, the Maori fertility rate has plummeted, from a high of 6.9 in 1961 to a replacement rate of 2.1 by 1986. There has been an upward blip in recent years, probably as a result of the baby-boom echo, to 2.8.[367]

No indigenous community has been chronicled as extensively as Native Americans, even though most of that chronicle, authored by Hollywood, is utterly false. Here is what we can truthfully say. At the time of European colonization, the Native American population was probably in the range of five to seven million. Disease, war—really, campaigns of extermination—forced relocation, poverty, and famine drove their population down to something like 250,000 by 1890. By then, their situation had become so precarious that many observers predicted that Native Americans would eventually become extinct.[368]

Instead, the population grew, as fertility rates increased beyond that of other racial groups. By 1980, with fertility rates dropping across the board, white fertility rates had declined to 1.7 children per woman, while Native Americans and Alaska Natives (as defined by American statisticians) were having 2.2 kids. But then the strangest thing happened. The Native American birth rate swooned, dropping below the white fertility rate in 1999, and then continuing to fall. By 2014, it had gone all the way down to 1.3, the lowest of any racial group in the United States, and one of the lowest fertility rates found anywhere in the world.[369] White women were reproducing at 1.8. Native Americans had fallen half a baby behind. At these fertility levels, Native Americans will one day find their numbers dwindling, with simple demography the villain this time. And yet, as the authors of a 2017 study note, there has been virtually no research in the research-obsessed United States into why Native American and Alaska Native women are having so few children.[370]

Australians are working hard to preserve Aboriginal culture—for posterity. An estimated 130 people are currently at work digitizing languages and other aspects of Aboriginal culture. Though Mick Dodson approves of the effort, he notes, "It's difficult to keep your culture as a living idea this way." Aboriginal Australians—indigenous cultures everywhere—are not alone. The global decline of fertility is putting a plethora of cultures at risk, leaving them with a future that could be far more homogeneous and far less interesting.

Islands are special. Islanders are special people. They are different from mainlanders, and think of themselves as different. Cultures evolve differently on islands, and the roots of those cultures are often deeper than on cosmopolitan continents. Islanders are invariably proud of their difference, suspicious of those across the straits or the sea. The sea governs; the rhythms of the sea seem to permeate the land and air. People go about their lives on Island Time, at a slower pace, and with less respect for the tyranny of deadlines.

The sea can make islanders outward-looking; it is their highway, after all. The Britons are a seafaring people; they used the ocean surrounding them to forge an empire that spanned the globe. But the Brits are also famously insular: the English Channel is a moat. "The wogs begin at Calais," they used to say, when you could get away with saying such things. They shocked the world and themselves in

2016 when 52 percent of them voted to leave the European Union, in part because of opposition to immigration.

Like indigenous peoples, island peoples fight to protect the special qualities that make their islands unique. Like indigenous peoples, they are losing. The mixed blessings of satellites and fiber optic cables make it possible for islanders to connect with the whole world, but they also bring the world to the islands, causing the young to move to the mainland in search of jobs and nightlife. And as with indigenous people, declining fertility makes islanders more vulnerable to extinction or assimilation. Let us look at two Atlantic islands, as different as different can be. Each is unique. Each is at risk.

St. Helena Island (not the one Napoleon died on) is one of the one hundred or so Sea Islands along the coasts of South Carolina, Georgia, and Florida. Flat, low-lying, marshy, only 165 square kilometers in total, it is so close to the South Carolina mainland—it would be part of it, but for the Beaufort River—that you can cross over on Highway 21. The Spanish colonized first, then the French, then the British. For two centuries, men and women were brought over from West Africa as slaves. After the Civil War, the area's remoteness and ethnic homogeneity—the majority of the population is black—encouraged the development of a unique culture and creole language: Gullah, which has been described as "the most intact West African culture in the United States."[371] (The Georgian equivalents are known as Geechee, with the Gullah–Geechee corridor stretching from the northeastern edge of Florida to the southern border of North Carolina.) About 250,000 people in the region speak Gullah.[372]

There are about 8,400 people on St. Helena Island. Their incomes are below the South Carolina average, and the median age is forty-four, compared to thirty-eight for the rest of the state. But they are also intensely proud of their Gullah heritage. While nearby islands, such as Hilton Head, have been consumed by development, local politicians successfully campaigned to protect St. Helena from commercialization. The local Penn Center seeks to preserve the language and culture.[373]

In St. Helena, the residents typically have small families. The island average is 3.1 people (parents and children) per family, compared to the state average of 3.2 and the United States average of 3.3. St. Helena families are stable; children on the island are more likely to have both a mother and father at home than is the case elsewhere in the state or country, but that relatively low family size means the Gullah language and culture of St. Helena is threatened by more than development; it is threatened by low fertility.

Across the sea, a very different island confronts a very similar problem. The people living on the Isle of Man descend from Vikings and English and Scots—as you might expect for an island in the Irish Sea roughly equidistant from Scotland, England, and Ireland. A millennium ago, it was much fought over, but the English eventually won out. Yet the Manx remain a fiercely independent people; this self-governing crown dependency claims that its Tynwald, having sat without interruption for more than a thousand years, is the oldest continuously sitting legislative body in the world. (This may or may not be true; Icelanders make the same claim, though their Althing has at times been suspended.) The Isle of Man is self-governing, with the United Kingdom responsible only for foreign policy and defense. It isn't even part of the European Union, which means the British are moving toward imitating the Manx. The Manx are loyal subjects of Elizabeth II, Lord of Mann.

Once rural and poor, dependent on fishing and farming, today the Isle of Man is a banking center (or tax haven, if you're more cynical about it). The population is 88,000; the combination of ancient isolation and recent affluence has made the island attractive to investors and newcomers. But lately, the growth of the working population has flattened, and the island government is pushing hard to attract new workers. The goal is to bring in 15,000 workers by 2030, bringing the overall population to about 110,000 or so, depending on the number of dependents. If that target isn't met, the Manx government warns, the island economy will soon have to support a population almost half of whom will be over sixty-five.

Many on the island resist. Fifteen thousand new arrivals, with partners and dependents, "would have a disastrous impact on Manx culture, identity, the very existence of the Manx as a people," warned one critic, calling the policy cultural "genocide."[374] But even as the Manx debate, the island's population has started to decline, by almost 1,200 people between 2011 and 2016. "We are losing young people, especially in their 20s," said the author of a report on the island's population. "The birth rate is falling in relation to that and this has the risk to become cumulative as fewer people grow up here and few people enter the workforce."[375] Less than half (49.8 percent) of the Manx population was born on the island.

Every new arrival erodes efforts to resuscitate the Manx language. For a century, that language had been on the decline, as parents encouraged their children to speak English rather than the island's unique form of Gaelic. "*Cha jean oo cosney ping lesh y Ghailck,*" the saying went: "You will not earn a penny with Manx."[376] By 1900, the population of native speakers had dropped below 10 percent. Ned Maddrell, the last native speaker of Manx, died in 1974. UNESCO declared the language extinct in 2009. But the death certificate was premature. Local enthusiasts have been teaching themselves and each other the tongue, based on recordings, and Manx is now offered as a course in some schools. As many as 1,800 Islanders now speak Manx with varying degrees of proficiency, and UNESCO has upgraded the language's status to "critically endangered."

But the long-term prospects for the Manx tongue are bleak. Immigrants to the island are unlikely to take an interest in learning an obscure language spoken nowhere else on earth, and by only a tiny percentage of people on the island itself. Of course, if the children of the old stock were taught the language in school, they might import it into their homes, eventually producing the first native speakers of Manx since Ned Maddrell passed away almost half a century ago. But it hardly seems worth the effort. The fertility rate on the Isle of Man is 1.7, about the same as Great Britain's. With fewer than ninety thousand souls, many of them new arrivals, and with all population growth to come from immigrants, the Isle of Man is bound to homogenize, to become just another English-speaking outcrop on the edge of Europe. And the Manx are not alone in their plight. We could just as easily have profiled the Shetland Islands (Shetland Scots) or the Orkneys (Orkney Scots) or Denmark's Faroe Islands (Faroese). These most remote outcrops in the North Atlantic have little hope of preserving the old ways in the face of modern culture and declining fertility.

The examples cited above are situated in advanced, developed countries. But literally thousands of other indigenous cultures are in jeopardy of disappearing within developing countries.

The Boni people of Kenya number four thousand today; half a century ago there were twenty-five thousand. Honey is a staple of their diet; gatherers sing to birds who lead them to hives. The Boni also hunt game, which puts them at odds with the Kenyan Wildlife Service. (One person's hunting is another's poaching.) The Boni want access to decent health care and education for their children—why wouldn't they? But this puts them in direct contact with modern Kenya, threatening the unique Boni language and culture. "Our way of life is disappearing," Boni tribesman and municipal councilor Omar Aloyoo told a reporter. "There is a danger that the Boni people will disappear."[377] Fighting between the Muslim insurgent group al-Shabaab and the Kenyan military in Boni territory makes the situation dangerous as well as difficult.

Some Boni tribesmen have mobile phones, which are shared communally. To access a signal, it's sometimes necessary to climb a tree—a unique combination of old and new technologies, as one Boni member observed.[378] But when a young man climbs a tree with a smartphone, he catches more than a signal; he catches a glimpse of the future of better jobs, better food, better living standards, and fewer babies. And with only four thousand Boni left, a declining fertility rate is the very last thing they need. But there is no reason to believe the Boni are unique. Declining fertility is a constant, even in a remote Kenyan forest. As the Boni integrate within the larger Kenyan society, there will be fewer babies, and then fewer Boni, who are already so few.

"The right to culture is central to the enjoyment of a whole host of other rights, from education and health to language and livelihoods," a report from Minority Rights Group International, an NGO, concluded. "Without it, a fair and equitable life is impossible to achieve."[379] But globalization, climate change—which can imperil island and low-lying communities—displacement by war, the vandalizing of monuments by occupying forces, deforestation for agricultural use, religious intolerance, or sheer bloody-mindedness threaten thousands of minority cultures around the word. Whatever the cause, or combination of causes, "the end result is the silencing of marginalized communities and the atrophy of their unique traditions."[380]

To this menacing mix must also be added the impact of declining fertility, as marginal and vulnerable communities join the global trend toward having fewer babies. For Finns or Chileans, fertility decline is an issue; for the Boni or Gullah or thousands of endangered cultures around the world, the threat is existential.

And the whole earth was of one language, and of one speech. . . . And they said, Go to, let us build us a city and a tower, whose top may reach unto heaven; and let us make us a name, lest we be scattered abroad upon the face of the whole earth. And the Lord came down to see the city and the tower, which the children of men builded. And the Lord said, Behold, the people is one, and they have all one language; and this they begin to do: and now nothing will be restrained from them, which they have imagined to do. Go to, let us go down, and there confound their language, that they may not understand one another's speech. . . . Therefore is the name of it called Babel; because the Lord did there confound the language of all the earth: and from thence did the Lord scatter them abroad upon the face of all the earth.[381]

The Lord brought down the Tower of Babel and confounded the common tongue, or so the Book of Genesis tells us, because he understood that having a single language would catapult human progress, that "nothing will be restrained from them, which they have imagined to do." In scattering us from Babel, He made it infinitely more difficult for us to understand each other, culturally as well as linguistically. The Other speak a babble we can make no sense of, another reason to shun and fear them.

But Babel is once again under construction.

There is nothing special about English, apart from the fact that, unlike most European languages, it lacks gendered nouns and elaborate verb conjugations. (Third-person singular present takes -s. Form the past using -ed. Form the future by adding *will*. Class dismissed.) English became the new Latin, for the same reason that Latin became the old Latin: conquest. Latin, which was the lingua franca of educated Europeans for a millennium and more, was the legacy of the Roman Empire. Great Britain conquered and/or colonized one quarter of the world's land surface; its progeny, the United States, has been the dominant economic and geopolitical power for a century. As mass communication evolved, American culture spread around the earth, with both English and the Golden Arches ubiquitous.

Today, global corporations routinely use English in-house, even if, like Siemens of Germany, they are not located in an English-speaking nation.[382] Most major scientific research is published in English-language journals. English is the language of global air traffic control. English is the language of globalization, the conference, the Internet, Hollywood. Although only the third-most-spoken language in terms of native speakers (outranked by Mandarin and Spanish), English is the most common second language in fifty-five countries, making it by far the most common second language globally. Far more people speak English as a second language (1.2 billion) than as a first (360 million).[383] As God feared, having a common tongue accelerates the pursuit of knowledge, and brings those who have been scattered across the earth together again, at least virtually.

But if English makes it easier for everyone to get along as they get around, it also contributes to cultural vulnerability. There are an estimated seven thousand languages spoken around the world today, but the numbers of people speaking each language differs hugely.[384] About 1.2 billion people speak Mandarin or Cantonese Chinese. But for about two thousand languages, there are fewer than a thousand speakers each.[385] Those languages are under threat. Forty-six languages are down to a single remaining speaker.[386] Twenty-five languages are lost every year.[387] That rate is likely to accelerate, thanks to urbanization and globalization. A century from now, the world could be down to six hundred core languages,[388] dominated by Mandarin, Spanish, and English, the new global tongue. Something precious is lost when a language is lost, for every language is unique, and the syntax and grammar of a language influence the worldview of the speaker. If humanity is enriched by diversity, then the disappearance of languages and cultures impoverishes the human inheritance.

Declining fertility is simply another challenge to fragile cultures and communities already under threat. Different societies attempt different, and often contradictory, strategies to protect and advance their culture. Do we bring in more immigrants to bolster our aging, dwindling population? But then how shall we preserve the old ways and the old tongue? Can we use social media and new communications technologies to chronicle our past and preserve what remains unique about us? But doesn't that put us at greater risk of homogenization and assimilation? Should we simply cut ourselves off from the larger community: preservation through isolation? But then what will become of us?

Through it all runs this implacable narrative: however large the population of the young is today, for much of the world the next generation will be fewer in number, and the next generation fewer still, until finally there will be fewer of us, period, every year. Against that threat to cultural extinction no one has found any cure.

TWELVE

THE CANADIAN SOLUTION

The first thing the visitor heard as he approached the cab rank outside the airport was a lively discussion in Arabic, which brought him up short. Inuvik is a town of about 3,500 souls on the delta of the Mackenzie River, two hundred kilometers north of the Arctic Circle, in Canada's Northwest Territories. On this June day, the sun never sets; for thirty dark winter days each year it never rises. The population is roughly 40 percent Inuit, 40 percent First Nations, and 20 percent everyone else—with the everyone else including about forty Arabs, some of whom drive taxis. There is even a mosque in the middle of town—the most northerly mosque in the world—which was transported from the south by barge in 2010.[389] To the visitor's ears, this was Canada's most multicultural moment.

It is also typical of the world's most cosmopolitan country. People from everywhere on earth stock this northern land. Twenty percent of Canada's population was not born in Canada, and that percentage climbs every year. Half the population of the Greater Toronto Area, now North America's fourth-largest urban area, is foreign-born.[390] A country of 35.2 million souls—5 percent more than there were five years earlier, according to the 2016 census[391]—brings in 300,000 people each year, and there's a push to increase that number to 450,000, with a goal of bringing Canada's population to 100 million by 2100.[392] That would be the equivalent of reproducing the country's tenth-largest city (actually, the tri-city conurbation of Kitchener, Waterloo, and Cambridge, in southwestern Ontario) every year. But even at current levels, Canada's population is expected to grow to around fifty million by 2060, Statistics Canada projects.[393]

This is extraordinary. In a century when most developed nations will see their populations decline, Canada will continue to grow, robustly. In a world where populations are aging, Canada's ages more slowly, because the average age of immigrants is seven years younger than the general population.[394] Yes, Canadians worry about the boomers growing old; yes, health care is perpetually under stress; yes, politicians argue furiously over whether to raise the retirement age, improve public pensions, or both. But they argue less fiercely than elsewhere. And Canadians have accepted levels of immigration, year after year, decade after decade, that would flummox people in most countries, including the United States to the south. (To repeat: to equal Canada's intake, on a per capita basis, the U.S. would need to accept about three million legal immigrants a year, three times the current level.)[395]

Do these migrants sink into poverty, living in dingy gray apartment towers in high-crime neighborhoods where police fear to tread? Emphatically not. Immigrants to Canada are, on average, better educated than native-born Canadians.[396] They contribute to, and flourish in, a peaceful, prosperous society. The half-foreign-born City of Toronto, with a population of 2.6 million (the Greater Toronto Area sits at 6.4 million) usually has fewer than sixty murders a year, making it the eighth-safest city on earth.[397] Like most major Canadian cities, Toronto is a vibrant yet well-ordered mélange of people of every color, language, and background, living and working together in the same offices and the same neighborhoods, making love and fusion cuisine together, complaining to each other about the subway, which is far too overcrowded, and enjoying life in the world's most diverse city.[398]

The message is stark. Any country that wants to stave off the economic effects of population decline—the sluggish or nonexistent growth; the declining tax base and growing debt; the intergenerational resentments between old and young, with the young always fewer than the old—must adopt the Canadian Solution: an immigration level of 1 percent of population annually, or close to it. Every nation in Europe and Asia with a birth rate at or below replacement rate has this simple choice: become like Canada, or decline. Yet that might be an impossible choice.

The interview was not going well. A Swedish reporter doing research on Canadian immigration policy had called a Canadian journalist for background on the subject. But the two seemed to be at cross-purposes; the answers that came from Ottawa didn't make sense to the interviewer in Stockholm. Eventually, they figured out the problem: they had totally different understandings of the meaning of the word *immigrant*.

Sweden has a proud tradition of admitting refugees. Thousands of Danish Jews found refuge from the German extermination camps during the Second World War by fleeing to a welcoming and neutral Sweden. The breakup of Yugoslavia sent more than 100,000, mostly Bosnians, north to their new home. And when the collapse of civil order in Syria and Iraq sent people fleeing in search of safety, Sweden stepped up like no other country, taking in 160,000 asylum seekers in 2015, when the migration crisis was at its peak. For a country of only 9.5 million people, this was extraordinary.

But the strains soon began to show. So many, so soon, from such a desperate part of the world. So many of them young men. How quickly could they learn Swedish? What jobs were there for them? Homelessness increased, and unemployment and crime and resentment. The Swedish government imposed restrictions on new arrivals, and offered those who had arrived money to leave. Anti-immigrant planks appeared in the platforms of conservative (for Sweden) parties.[399] So the Swedish reporter wanted to know how Canada was able to take in so many refugees, hundreds of thousands of them, year after year, and integrate them successfully.

Except, that's not what Canada does at all, the Canadian explained. Typically, about 10 percent of the people who are granted permanent resident status (which puts them on the path to citizenship) each year are refugees; the rest are either immigrants brought in because they will contribute to the Canadian economy or family members of economic-class immigrants. The Swedish journalist was shocked. "Immigrants have always been accepted to Sweden for humanitarian reasons," she observed.[400] This is the fundamental difference between Sweden and Canada. Canada brings in immigrants for reasons that are entirely selfish, which is why immigration works better in Canada than in Sweden.

Good public policy is always based on communal self-interest. Each of us is in it for ourselves. In most cases, "ourselves" includes our immediate family and, in diminishing importance, our neighborhood; our village, town, or city; our region; our country; our planet. Of course we have empathy, of course we act for reasons of altruism. But you will only do something because it's the right thing to do for so long, before you start asking yourself: "Why am I making this sacrifice? What's in this for me or my family?" There are curbs on nakedly self-interested behavior: traditional codes of duty combined with the power of collective self-preservation still dictate that, in an emergency, women and children go first. But in the main, effective public policy reflects collective self-interest: it's good for everyone. This is particularly true of refugees and immigrants.

During the refugee crisis, Sweden took in, on a per capita basis, 1,667 immigrants per 100,000 population, which was incredibly generous. Germany took in 587 per 100,000. "We can do this," Chancellor Angela Merkel told the German people, as a million asylum seekers poured across its borders. Across the European Union, each country took in an average of 260 immigrants per 100,000 population.[401] But very few countries were average. Hungary initially took in more refugees than any other country, almost 1,800 per 100,000 population, but almost all of these were in transit to Germany, and the number quickly fell when that country closed its border with Croatia. Other Eastern European countries were no more generous: Poland took in 32 refugees per 100,000 population; Romania took in six. Social services, officials explained, were insufficient for the native-born population, let alone for asylum seekers. And, it must be said, many Eastern Europeans shared Hungarian prime minister Viktor Orbán's anti-immigrant sentiments. Nativist, populist, frankly racist parties emerged in countries throughout the region.

Parts of Western Europe were not much more generous. Great Britain brought in only 60 per 100,000, even as Britons voted to leave the European Union, in part over fears of uncontrolled immigration; France took in 114, half the EU average. And as we have seen, the backlash in 2016 against the influx of 2015 caused even the most generous countries to close their doors.

In Canada, the refugee crisis peaked in the middle of a federal election. Stephen Harper's Conservative government had been pro-immigration, increasing the annual intake above the levels of its Liberal predecessors. But the Conservatives were less welcoming of refugees, tightening the rules of entry after a boatload of Tamil asylum seekers arrived in a rusting hulk off the British Columbia coast in 2010. Harper had been in power for a decade, and was probably going to lose the election no matter what happened, but once people learned that the family of Alan Kurdi, the three-year-old Syrian boy who drowned in the Mediterranean, had been denied entry to Canada, that was that. The Harper government's apparent heartless-ness drove voters to the Liberals and their young and charismatic leader, Justin Trudeau, who promised to admit twenty-five thousand Syrian refugees before the end of the year if elected.

One of Trudeau's first acts as prime minister, in November 2015, was to keep that promise, or at least try to: rigorous security screen-ing and bureaucratic logjams kept the total from reaching twenty-five thousand until February. But people were forgiving; they understood the government was working flat-out. Officials put in punishing hours; public servants voluntarily canceled their own Christmas vacations and pitched in. The prime minister himself greeted the first arrivals at Toronto's Pearson Airport shortly before Christmas. "You are home," Trudeau told them. "Welcome home."[402] There wasn't a dry eye in the country. By the end of 2016, fifty thou-sand Middle Eastern refugees had arrived in Canada, behind the intake of Germany or Sweden, but well ahead of many other coun-tries, and especially generous since these refugee arrivals were expected to settle in Canada permanently. Next door, the United States, with almost ten times Canada's population, had taken in fewer than thirteen thousand.[403]

Did Canada admit more Syrian refugees than the United States because Canadians are nicer people? Not at all. Canadians had learned that, if handled the right way, it is in the country's interest to bring refugees in. They had learned that lesson almost forty years before.

Historically, Canada had a rather shameful record of accepting people in distress. When the steamship *Komagata Maru* arrived in Vancouver in 1914 filled with Sikhs in search of a new home, the Canadian government turned them away. Far worse, when the *St. Louis*, a steamship filled with almost one thousand Jewish refugees, arrived in Halifax harbor in 1939, the ship was ordered to return to sea. When a Canadian immigration official was asked how many Jews Canada should let in, he replied: "None is too many."[404] Eventually, the *St. Louis* returned to Europe, where many of its passengers ultimately met their deaths at the hands of the Nazis.

The infamy of the *St. Louis* was much on Ron Atkey's mind when the immigration minister met his Progressive Conservative cabinet colleagues in July 1979. The United Nations had issued an urgent appeal: Hundreds of thousands of Vietnamese had fled their country by boat in the wake of South Vietnam's takeover by the Communists from North Vietnam. Those who hadn't drowned or been killed by robbers were huddled in refugee camps in miserable conditions. A poll showed that most Canadians didn't want them. Should the government listen to the poll? As cabinet members arrived, each found a copy of *None Is Too Many*, Irving Abella and Harold Troper's landmark study of the *St. Louis* tragedy, on the desk in front of them. "Do we want to be known as the government that said no?" Atkey demanded of his Conservative colleagues, "or as the government that saved the day?"[405] Cabinet voted to save the day. But it imposed a condition: Canada would accept up to fifty thousand Vietnamese refugees, but it asked citizens and community organizations to privately sponsor them. The country responded, magnificently, as church groups, service clubs, and families or groups of families banded together to bring in each new arrival. In the end, sixty thousand Vietnamese boat people came to Canada, earning the country the Nansen Refugee Award from a grateful United Nations.

Canadians learned several valuable lessons from the experience. First, refugees make great immigrants. The Vietnamese quickly integrated into society; people joked that every corner store seemed to be owned by a Vietnamese husband and wife; two decades later, it seemed as though every top-of-the-class student in the country's universities was the son or daughter of those grocery-store owners. Second, private sponsorship was an excellent way to integrate refugees, who were dispersed across the country and who were well supported by the local community, preventing ghettoization. Private sponsorship became a permanent facet of Canada's refugee program, especially during times of crisis. About half of the fifty thousand Syrian refugees who came to Canada in 2015 and 2016 were privately sponsored. There were far more volunteers ready and willing to sponsor refugees than there were properly vetted candidates.

Canadians embrace refugees and immigrants, not because Canadians are particularly nice, but because they have learned it is in Canada's own interest to welcome them. That discovery is part of Canada's historical DNA—and the unintended consequence of an uncomfortable truth that, as nations go, Canada is pretty much a failure. That failure to gel a nation was the secret sauce in Canada's postnational, multicultural success.[406]

In 1896, Clifford Sifton confronted just about the biggest problem a politician can have. The new Dominion of Canada, barely a quarter century old, was in danger of failing. People didn't want to live there. Many of those who did live there wanted to leave. To the south, the American giant, recovered from its civil war, surged ahead, as millions streamed from Europe to its shores, then to the western frontier. But the Canadian frontier was empty. Too cold, too remote. In the settled portion of the new dominion, stretching along the north shore of Lake Erie and Lake Ontario, then along the St. Lawrence River and in the Maritime provinces, many wondered whether it wouldn't be easier and more profitable for Canadians to throw in their lot with the United States. Union was both inevitable and desirable, "Canadian nationality being a lost cause," the writer and pundit Godwyn Smith maintained. For him, "in blood and character, language, religion, institutions, laws and interests, the two portions of the Anglo-Saxon race on this continent are one people."[407] Canada was cold and weak and poor—the economy sputtered throughout the 1870s and '80s—and the United States to the south wasn't. The new government had already put down, with difficulty, a Métis rebellion in the Prairies, which had so few people that it risked being simply absorbed by American settlers. The odds for Canada's future did not look good.

But Clifford Sifton wasn't willing to give up. The solution, simply, was to try harder. That had been the secret to his own success. A Canadian-born son of Anglo-Irish stock, Sifton moved with his parents from southern Ontario to Manitoba in the 1870s, when he was a teenager, giving him a keen sense of both the English heartland and the western frontier. He had been partially deafened as a result of scarlet fever, which he overcame through iron self-discipline. Top-of-his-class smart at law school; a skilled negotiator from a young age; energetic, meticulous, thorough, inevitably successful at everything he took on, and politically ambitious, Sifton found himself minister of the interior in the cabinet of Wilfrid Laurier, Canada's first and greatest Québécois prime minister, when he was only thirty-five.[408] It was his job to find a way to increase immigration and fill the Prairies before the Americans got there. He solution was, for the time, incredibly radical: aggressively recruit immigrants from Eastern Europe.

The idea was anathema to many Canadians. The country was already divided between French Quebec and the rest of Canada, a division that threatened the unity and very existence of the dominion from the moment of its birth in 1867. Diluting the Protestant, Anglo-Saxon culture in English Canada would further weaken national bonds, critics warned. The new arrivals would be Catholic or Orthodox, speaking not a word of English. They would never integrate. But Sifton didn't care; he needed bodies and he needed them now. Immigrant agents were stripped of their salaries and put on commission; the Canadian government flooded Scandinavia, Germany, the Balkans, Ukraine, and everything in between with leaflets in every language, touting Canada as the "Last, Best West," "the New Eldorado," with "rich virgin lands" that were "protected by the government" and where they had "nothing to fear"—i.e., from the Indigenous population.[409]

Sifton was convinced that impoverished farmers from economically and politically oppressed regions would have the strength of will—the desperation, really—needed to break the Prairie sod and endure the Prairie cold. "A stalwart peasant in a sheep-skin coat, born on the soil, whose forefathers have been farmers for ten generations, with a stout wife and a half-dozen children, is good quality," he maintained.[410] Scandinavia and Eastern Europe at the end of the nineteenth century was firmly in Stage Two of population growth—a declining death rate with a high birth rate. There was no new land left to farm, and few prospects for young men and women in the old country. They took Sifton's advice. Beginning in the 1890s, immigrants by the millions flooded across the Atlantic to Halifax's Pier 21—the Ellis Island of Canadian immigration—then headed west using the new transcontinental railroad to Manitoba and Saskatchewan and Alberta, mixing with new arrivals from America, many of them immigrants from the same parts of Europe. Sifton's gamble paid off, handsomely. Eastern Europeans not only stocked Prairie Canada but became integral to the

Canadian mosaic. As one wag observed, without Clifford Sifton we would never have had Wayne Gretzky.[411]

Lesson learned. Immigrants boosted the Canadian economy, filling the empty vastness of the land. Yes, they were alien; no, they would never join the Anglican Church. With the French and English already estranged from each other, there was no pot for these new arrivals to melt into, and so they kept many of their traditional ways, even as they adapted to life in a new land that was increasingly independent of Great Britain. More millions arrived from Europe after the First World War, and millions more after the Second, many of them displaced by the traumas of destruction and invasion. In the 1950s, Italy replaced Great Britain as the number-one source of immigrants. But even as people flooded in, editorialists lamented the lack of a strong national identity. Canada used to be French and British. Now it was French and British and—a lot of other things. But what single thing made it Canadian? "Well, at least we're not Americans," people concluded. It wasn't much to hang a nationalist hat on.

There were still deep biases: policies and even legislation kept Chinese and other Asian immigrants from coming into Canada. That began to change in the 1960s, when a new points system admitted potential immigrants based on education, job skills, proficiency in English or French, and ties to Canada. The points system ensured that anyone from anywhere could gain entry. Unlike the United States, which absorbed millions of Latino immigrants, many of them illegal, and Europe, which sourced its immigrants from nearby North Africa and the Middle East, Canada welcomed the whole world, but with the stipulation that new arrivals had to have the skills and education needed to find work quickly. Always, first and foremost, immigration was an economic policy, designed to ease labor shortages and buttress the population. In the 1990s, as the consequences of a chronically low birth rate begin to sink in, Ottawa opened the floodgates, inviting

250,000 immigrants a year to come to Canada. Between then and now, Canada has brought in the equivalent of three new Torontos, its largest city, with new arrivals from China, India, Philippines, and other nations from around the world supplanting the British and continental Europeans who had come before. Some people warned that these new Asian immigrants were too alien, would never fit in. But they fitted in just fine, in a country that was less a melting pot than a multicultural quilt. (There was luck in all of it, too: being surrounded by three oceans, and sharing your only land border with the United States, is a highly effective form of perimeter control.)

By now, Canada's failure as a nation was complete. To be a Canadian was something much fuzzier and ill-defined than to be a Norwegian or a Pole, or even an American or Australian—two settler cultures that succeeded in creating a single national identity. Canada had become a multicultural mélange: French, English, Scottish, Irish, German, Polish, Ukrainian, Icelandic, Hungarian, Italian, Greek, Portuguese—then Chinese, Indian, Filipino, Pakistani, Haitian, Honduran, Sri Lankan, Algerian, Jamaican, Moroccan, Guyanese—and on and on, each community preserving its distinct cultural ties, each community sharing a municipality, a province, a country. It's a pretty loosey-goosey way to run things, and it almost came a cropper when Quebecers voted in a 1995 referendum to remain in Canada by the very narrowest of margins.

But if nationalism helps hold a country together, it also, by definition, excludes. In defining what binds you to others in your nation—your language, your religion, your genes, your shared cultural assumptions (one kiss on the cheek; no, one kiss on each cheek; no, three kisses, starting with the left cheek; no . . .) you are distinguishing your group from every other group. This makes it harder for you to understand, much less join, other groups, and harder still for other groups to understand or join you. Danes are Danes, Japanese are

Japanese, and that's all there is to it. Even other settler countries, such as the United States or New Zealand, have such a strong national ethos that newcomers know they must either embrace that ethos or go somewhere else.

Canada, not so much. Canadians seek to accommodate each other. For critics, this "culture of accommodation"[412] makes the place formless, purposeless, ultimately meaningless—"the greatest hotel on earth," the Canadian writer Yann Martel called it.[413] He said it in praise; others used the phrase to disparage a country with clean towels but no identity.

But the very inability of Canada to gel as a nation is the secret to its success as a postnational state. People from every part of the world and from every walk of life can come to Canada, typically settle in one of its large cities, and then set to work making a new life in a welcoming new land. It has made Canada the most diverse yet peaceful and harmonious country on earth. In recent years, nativist and populist anger has risen in the United States, Britain, and continental Europe, leaving Canada something of an outpost of openness. "Irredeemably dull by reputation, less brash and bellicose than America, Canada has long seemed to outsiders to be a citadel of decency, tolerance and good sense," observed *The Economist*. But with former allies building walls against each other, "today, in its lonely defence of liberal values, Canada seems downright heroic."[414] When *Rolling Stone* put Canada's prime minister on its cover in July 2017, imploring in the headline, "Why can't Justin Trudeau be our president?" it was really asking, Why can't the United States be more like Canada? For Americans on the left, at least, that seems to be the feeling these days.

But before we burst into song, let's admit some uncomfortable truths: not everything about Canada's attitude to immigrants is as halcyon as it seems.

———

Donald Trump's inauguration as president in January 2017 spurred
fears of deportation among foreigners living in the United States.
Hundreds of them, mostly Somalis, trekked through the ice and
snow from Minneapolis to the Manitoba border seeking asylum in
Canada. When summer arrived, thousands of others, mostly Haitians,
crossed into Quebec—almost six thousand in August alone.[415] Polls
showed that Canadians were not happy with these claimants from a
country that does not normally send Canada refugees. One poll
showed that two thirds of Canadians did not consider the asylum
seekers legitimate refugees.[416] The chaos at the border—at one point,
the army had to be called in to provide temporary accommodation—
undermined confidence in Canada's immigration system.

Keith Banting researches public policy at Queen's University in
Kingston, Ontario. For years, he and his graduate students have
tracked the evolution of Canadian attitudes toward immigration
and multiculturalism. Canadians, he observes, aren't quite as tolerant as they like to think they are. "The population could roughly be
divided three ways," he argues. "One third of Canadians really don't
support multiculturalism. One third are enthusiastic multiculturalists. And one third are what you could call 'soft multiculturalists':
They support the current policies, but with reservations. And that
support could change."[417]

In fact, Canadians living outside Quebec aren't very different
from Americans in their attitudes toward immigration and integration. About six in ten Americans and Canadians oppose allowing
religious headgear for police officers and members of the military.
About four in ten oppose requiring employers to make a special
effort to hire minorities and immigrants; about two in ten oppose
allowing women to wear a hijab, the Muslim head scarf, in public.[418]

And as for inside Quebec? The uncomfortable truth is that
Quebecers are far less tolerant of multicultural accommodation

than their counterparts in the rest of Canada. Part of this has to do with the policy of *laïcité*, the French devotion to secularism that was itself a reaction to the authority of the Catholic Church. Yet many defenders of *laïcité* also defend the historical ties to Catholicism. So hijabs on the street are an abomination, but the crucifix in the National Assembly is perfectly reasonable. Such reasoning led a sovereigntist government, in 2013, to introduce legislation banning the wearing of "conspicuous" religious symbols, such as a niqab or kippa, by workers in the public service.[419] The government was defeated in an election before the bill could be passed. But in 2017, the Liberal government passed a watered-down version of the previous bill. Many intellectuals and politicians—including Justin Trudeau—refer to "interculturalism" in Quebec: the effort to integrate other cultures into the majority francophone culture while continuing to respect differences.

Multiculturalism "is a non-starter in Quebec because everybody knows there is a majority culture in Quebec," said Gérard Bouchard, a sociologist who co-chaired a government commission into the accommodation of minorities. "It is the francophone culture. Any model to manage diversity in Quebec must take into account this major fact."[420] Though Canada has never cohered as a single nation, Quebecers are proudly nationalist. The Canadian Parliament recognized as much when it passed a motion in 2006 recognizing that "the Québécois form a nation within a united Canada."

Quebecers work hard to preserve their national identity, with laws restricting the use of English and requirements that immigrant children attend French-language schools. Because the ability to speak French advantages immigrants coming into Quebec, the province has a different mix of newcomers than in the rest of Canada. While the top three source countries for Canada these days are the Philippines, India, and China, the top source countries for Quebec are France, Algeria, and China.[421] Other major source countries for Quebec, but not for the rest of Canada, include Haiti and Morocco. The patterns of colonialism dictate that many Quebec immigrants come from French West Africa. Many of these immigrants are Muslim. They also tend to be less well educated than immigrants coming into the rest of Canada. So there are tensions, both economic and social. And it probably is no coincidence that Quebec takes in a smaller share of immigrants than its population warrants. In 2015, Quebec accounted for 18 percent of immigrants despite having 23 percent of Canada's population.[422]

Quebec, in other words, grapples with the challenges of preserving its national identity while also bringing in sufficient numbers of immigrants to offset its low fertility rate, even as the rest of Canada absorbs wave after wave of new arrivals with relatively little social upheaval. But even in the rest of Canada, a significant minority of the population is uncomfortable with those newcomers and the efforts to accommodate them within a multicultural context. Canadian politicians of all stripes must protect and preserve tolerance and diversity within the Canadian mosaic. That mosaic is a far more successful and resilient structure than nationalism, of whatever variety. For when it comes to preserving and renewing a society, nationalism can be a curse.

The xenophobic Hungarian prime minister, Viktor Orbán, calls refugees a "poison." "Every single migrant poses a public security and terror risk," he maintains.[423] In fact, he has no time for immigrants of any variety. "Hungary does not need a single migrant for the economy to work, or the population to sustain itself, or for the country to have a future," he declared in 2016.[424] Really? A nation of just under ten million, Hungary is losing more than thirty thousand people a year, and aging rapidly.[425]

But Hungary is as Hungarian as Japan is Japanese. Ninety percent of the population is ethnically Hungarian, or Magyar. The Hungarian language, by the way, is one of the hardest in the world to learn. Its origins are Uralic rather than Indo-European, and so it has nothing in common with other European languages. There are thirty-five different cases, fourteen vowels, definite and indefinite verb forms, and a plethora of idioms that make sense only to Hungarians. The word for computer is *számítógép*.[426] So even if Hungary did welcome immigrants, which it doesn't, people might think twice about it, for linguistic reasons alone.

If a nation with a distinct history and culture, a distinct language, even distinct physical features (think fair-haired Scandinavians), a particular set of social norms, a certain form of government, and a common religion brings in large numbers of people who speak a different language, have a different history, culture, and set of social norms and worship a different god, integration can be difficult. The majority culture will expect the newcomers, who may look physically distinct from them, to become, as much as possible, just like them. But just like them isn't possible. So the new arrivals cluster in ghettos and *banlieues*, never really feeling that they belong, and never really being allowed to. Worse, as the numbers of new arrivals grow, the native-born may lash out in a nationalist reaction. This can even happen in a settler culture like the United States. Latinos are actually integrating into the larger American culture quite well, but not well enough to keep angry nativists from electing Donald Trump. And as we've discussed, efforts by the Quebec government to preserve the Quebec language and culture, even as it brings in large numbers of Muslim immigrants from French-speaking parts of Africa and the Caribbean, have led to tensions and misunderstanding.

Even so, those tensions are manageable, within Quebec and without. As the Syrian airlift unfolded in 2016, the *New York Times* wrote in wonder about "ordinary Canadians, trying to intervene in one of the worst problems on earth . . . book club members, hockey moms, poker buddies and grandmothers," many with little connection to the Middle East, even as "much of the rest of the world was treating refugees with suspicion or hostility."[427]

The less nationalist the state, the easier the job of absorbing immigrants. The weaker the culture, the easier the task of promoting multiculturalism. The less the sense of self, the less the sense that another is the Other. That doesn't mean anything goes: Canada's Charter of Rights and Freedoms is so robust that nations in search of precedents now use the Canadian template more than the American.[428] Canada remains a nation steeped in the democratic and parliamentary traditions of Great Britain, the free, fraternal, and equal aspirations of France, the hard-won European principle of religious and social tolerance. Every Canadian who is truly Canadian cherishes these things.

But that's why people come to Canada, and find so many of their own kind in Canada, and live happily and well, though they sigh regretfully when it becomes perfectly clear their children have no interest in learning the old language. As a cohesive, clearly defined nation, Canada may be not much to look at. As a tolerant, peaceful, multicultural and *growing* postnation, it seems to work pretty well.

THIRTEEN

WHAT LIES AHEAD

We have looked at a past when there were many births and many early deaths and a present in which fewer are being born, but those who are born live longer. Our future will contain something we have never experienced: a world growing smaller in numbers by choice. If depopulation is only a glimmer, today—a worrying statistic in some government report whose importance only the *nomenklatura* fully understand—what will it be like half a century from now, when that glimmer becomes blinding? What will the world be like for a child born today when she reaches middle age in a time of population decline? What will that world be like for her child? We believe there will be much about that world to admire. It will be cleaner, safer, quieter. The oceans will start to heal and the atmosphere cool—or at least stop heating. People may not be growing wealthier, but that might not matter so much. Power centers will shift—and centers of innovation and creativity, too. We will live in a world of cities, with less and less in between. In many parts of the world, we may live in a city that feels itself getting old.

We are not saying that declining fertility is an all-powerful, unstoppable predestination that will mold humanity's future. The old imperatives will always be at work: the will to power; the will to wealth; concern—or lack of it—for the health of the planet; the desire to create the new, to innovate, to explore; the desire to preserve the past, to slow things down, to hold on to what we've got. And always, there will be moments when one leader's decision shapes the fate of many millions, for good or ill. Our purpose has been to point out that something new must be added to the mix: the decline in national populations already underway in some parts of what used to be called the North; the decline that is soon to come in parts of the South; the end of explosive growth in the last places that are still explosively growing. Population decline will not exclusively determine our future, but it will help to shape it. We have mostly ignored this approaching reality for too long; we must ignore it no longer.

Answer this quick question: Which U.S. state do you think has the lowest per capita carbon emissions?

You might have picked California, with its aggressive cap-and-trade system to fight global warming. Hawaii would be a good guess, because its temperate climate reduces both heating and air conditioning costs. You might have considered Wyoming or Montana, because they're the least densely populated of the contiguous states. But all these guesses are wrong. The winner is New York. And the reason is New York City.[429] We know it's counterintuitive, but the more densely packed the city, the better things are for the environment, especially in the fight against global warming. Someone driving a car alone emits six times the greenhouses gases of someone riding the subway.[430] New York subways are especially good for the environment because they're so overcrowded, further reducing per capita emissions. Most major cities in the developed world rely heavily on public transit to move people around. The average Londoner spends 11.5 days each year in the Tube.[431]

As we've already seen, urbanization is a global phenomenon. Developed countries are already highly urban—two thirds of Icelanders live in Reykjavik—and developing countries are urbanizing rapidly—a quarter of the people in Egypt live in Cairo. The United Nations predicts that by 2060 two thirds of the planet's population will be living in cities or big towns.[432] Rapid urbanization in a developing country can bring all sorts of problems: inadequate infrastructure, poor health care, overcrowded schools, increased poverty, skyrocketing crime.[433] Even in advanced countries, keeping up with infrastructure needs and fighting air pollution is a never-ending battle. But overall, crowding people into cities makes it easier to deliver more services—public transportation, sewers and water, electricity—at a lower cost, while also helping the environment.

Encouraging people to abandon the countryside is also environmentally sound. Again, this seems counterintuitive. Who hasn't dreamt of getting away from the city, building a log home in the bush, maybe beside a lake, heating the house with solar panels, and living close to and in concert with nature? Many have already embraced the lifestyle. They aren't helping the environment one bit.

You still have to drive to the nearest town for groceries. The road is pretty rough, so you need a four-wheel drive. Those things drink a lot of gas. You may need a second car, if different people have different schedules. If it snows in the winter, that means a snow blower, and even if you have the discipline to shovel, a municipal snow plow still has to come out to clear your road. If you have children, a school bus will pick them up and drop them off. So wasteful. And only the big city, which is a long way away, has the specialists you need when the knee starts to act up. Back and forth, back and forth. That house sits in a clearing—probably half an acre, at least—that once was bush, and the bush wants it back. If you want to contribute to the fight against global warming, live in a city in a high-rise apartment— where radiant heat seeps through walls into other people's units, lowering heating costs—and commute by subway. In decades to come, with global warming costing governments trillions in mitigation— from building levies to repairing storm damage—the penalties imposed on rural dwellers for their flagrant waste of energy and resources may be so harsh that only the very wealthy can afford to get away from it all.

Urbanization will lend the fight against global warming and other environmental battles a new ally: trees, as marginal farmland returns to bush. Again, this process is already well underway. In settler countries, there are still people old enough to remember where the family farm used to be, before folks moved into town. Typically, that farm was settled in the mid-nineteenth century by European immigrants. The soil was often less than stellar, and the climate less than ideal, so life was hardscrabble. If you could get corn to grow, you fed a herd of dairy cattle. There would be a large vegetable garden for the family, with much of the produce pickled for winter use, and the rest stored in the cold cellar. Maybe the Depression forced the family off the land; maybe the good times that came after the war tempted them into town, where there was electricity and a supermarket. If you drive out to the old homestead today, you may be able to find what's left of the fence, but maybe not. Everything's gone back to bush.

In the next decade, the amount of farmland in the world will start to decrease.[434] Already, improvements in agricultural technology and the efficiency of corporate over family farms has seen the amount of land under cultivation start to shrink in places. Between 2007 and

2012, seven million acres of American farmland disappeared.[435] Some of that was eaten up by suburbs, but much of it was land that could no longer be farmed profitably. When population decline arrives in a few decades, even more farmland will disappear. Reforestation of marginal farmland, whether naturally or by businesses creating woodlots, is unambiguously good for the environment. Farms pollute. There's the methane from the animals, the fertilizer that leaches into the nearest stream. The bush that replaces the open field captures carbon and contributes oxygen. Endangered species have a larger habitat, improving their odds. Later in this century, with further advances in genetically modified crops, only a fraction of the land currently under cultivation will be needed. The rest will return to nature, helping the planet to cool.

The world's oceans are also under tremendous stress. Overfishing, pollution of coastal waters from agricultural and urban runoff, and a host of other human abuses are disrupting the food chain. The damage extends from bleached coral to endangered whales. The sooner we act to limit the warming of the air, the better it will be for our oceans. But ultimately, reducing the size of the human population is the best prescription for protecting the seas. Fewer mouths to eat fish.

On December 12, 2015, in Paris, all nations agreed to limit the impact of climate change through human activity to less than two degrees Celsius above pre-industrial levels. But world leaders have made similar promises, going all the way back to Kyoto in 1997, and still the planet warms. The key decisions are being made by a handful of (mostly) men in the capitals of China, the United States, and India, the three largest emitters. As China and India modernize, they rely heavily on coal-fired generators to expand their electrical grid. Building a coal-fired generating station is just about the worst thing you can do to the air. The good news is that the rapidly falling cost of solar energy—and outrage from middle-class taxpayers in smog-choked cities—is helping to wean both countries off coal. China announced the cancellation of 103 planned plants in 2017,[436] and India has lowered its annual coal use to 600 million tons. (There were fears it would reach 1.5 billion tons by 2020.)[437]

As for the United States, the second-largest emitter, here is one encouraging statistic: electricity use in that country has been flat since 2007, even though the economy has grown substantially. One reason, depressingly, might be manufacturing plants closing their doors as jobs shift overseas. But another, more encouragingly, could be off-grid electricity generation—people heating their homes with solar panels, for instance—and energy conservation.[438] For all three of these highest-emitting countries, and the rest of the world, major advances in battery storage capacity to preserve energy generated by solar and wind could lessen the need for fossil fuels overall.

Nonetheless, the world isn't expected to reach peak fossil fuel until around 2040, because of growing demand in the developing world.[439] China's coal-generated electrical capacity is still three times that of the United States, India still has plans for 370 new coal-fired generating stations on its books,[440] and in 2017 Donald Trump withdrew the United States from the Paris accord (though many state governments plan to meet their commitments anyway). The fight to contain global warming remains an uphill struggle. The good news is that population decline could play a major role in limiting carbon emissions. One recent study projected that if the UN's low-variant model played out, relative emissions would decline by 10 percent by 2055 and 35 percent by 2100.[441] The solution to producing less carbon dioxide might ultimately be producing fewer humans.

We might predict a future in which much of a shrinking humanity lives in high-rise apartment buildings in large cities, with much of the land between the cities gone back to bush. Tropical rainforests

and northern boreal forests will expand, capturing carbon and contributing oxygen. Renewable forms of energy will lessen and ultimately eliminate the need for fossil fuels. Urbanization, innovation,
and depopulation might be the best solution to halting the march
of climate change. With any luck, a baby born today—or at worst one
born a decade or two from now—will reach middle age in a cleaner,
healthier world.

But will it be a peaceful world? That's a conundrum. Much will
depend on China. At the October 2017 Communist Party Congress,
which gathers every five years, President Xi Jinping emerged as the
most powerful Chinese leader since Mao. In a landmark speech,
Xi laid out a program that by 2050 would see China equipped with
a fully modernized economy, "global combat capability," and an
authoritarian-state-directed capitalism that "offers a new option for
other countries and nations who want to speed up their development while preserving their independence."[442] China, in other
words, intends to replace the United States as the dominant economic, military, and ideological power.

And yet.

All those unhappy, unmarried young men. The old growing
poorer and more numerous every year. Growth slowing after
decades of Wild East expansion. Restive minorities in the hinter-
lands. Restive city dwellers demanding less Internet censorship.

By 2050, rather than straddling the globe, China may be gripped
by internal unrest fueled by rapid population decline. History tells
us that there are few things more dangerous than an empire in turmoil. In 1914, the German government faced street demonstrations,
a restless Reichstag, and a growing middle class that demanded
political freedoms. "As the domestic political balancing act became
more difficult, the temptation grew for Germany's rulers to unify

their country through foreign policy initiatives."[443] Such as a quick little war that would have the boys home for Christmas. Together with its tottering Austro-Hungarian ally, Germany dragged the world into the first of two cataclysmic wars, the greatest folly and tragedy of modern times.

Will the Chinese be similarly tempted? It could be something that puts Taiwan firmly in its place, or that lets everyone know the South China Sea is *mare nostrum*. A quick little war. The boys will be home by Chinese New Year.

That doesn't have to happen. China could evolve peacefully into a mature global power, managing its demographic challenges with restraint. And if the other hot spots—North Korea, Iran, and who-knows-where-next—manage to avoid provoking war, then the world could enter a new era of peace: a geriatric peace. The political scientist Mark Haas coined this term. "The world is entering an unprecedented demographic era," he wrote way back in 2007. "Never before has social aging been as pervasive and extensive an issue as it will be in coming decades."[444] Haas argued that the rapid and serious aging of the Chinese and Russian populations will make it impossible for them to overtake the United States as the world's leading economic and military power. They will be consumed by the challenge of meeting the demands of their graying societies. Thanks to robust immigration, the U.S. will age less rapidly than other great powers, further cementing its lead. Though Haas's prediction had little uptake, we think he was on to something, and we would add the more intangible factor of a world that has fewer young people—fewer hotheads looking for trouble—and more old. As African and Middle Eastern fertility rates plummet, warlords and ideologues will have fewer recruits to draw from. Slowing growth means weakening competition for scarce resources. The press of a crowded Africa against a hollowing-out Europe may ease.

One huge variable in the quest for peace will be, as always, the Middle East, the most strife-filled place on earth. Here as well, we look with hope to the beneficence of declining fertility. The most unhappy nations also have the highest fertility rate: Afghanistan (5.2), Iraq (4.0), Yemen (3.8). These clan-based cultures are intensely religious, mostly rural, and deeply unsettled. These are some of the worst places in the world for a woman to live in. But Iran's fertility rate is only 1.8, thanks to decades of efforts by the Iranian government to limit population growth. Alarmed by the success of its efforts, Tehran is now trying to encourage parents to have more children. But we know how well that works. Besides, the mullahs have so mismanaged the economy that parents can't afford to have more kids.[445]

Tunisia, the one country to emerge from the Arab Spring with a more democratic government, has a fertility rate of 2.0. Even Saudi Arabia, where women's rights are so restricted under Sharia law that only in 2017 did the House of Saud relent and allow them to drive a car, the fertility rate is only 2.1, the replacement rate. The reason is simple: In 1970, the literacy rate among Saudi women was 2 percent. But in a gesture of (relative) enlightenment, the Saudi government permitted women to attend school. Today, they account for 52 percent of university graduates. Clerics may issue fatwas against women watching soccer games (lest they be carried away by the sight of men's thighs), but we know from watching the rest of the world how this story will end—eventually.[446]

Conventional wisdom holds that the higher Palestinian fertility rate threatens to make Israelis a minority in their own country, wherever its borders might eventually be drawn. But within Israel, the fertility rate of Palestinian and Israeli women is identical: 3.1.[447] That's the highest fertility rate in the developed world—twice as high as most other countries'. The Jewish population, an island in a hostile Arab sea, feels an imperative to keep its numbers up. Arabs in Israel, by contrast, are bringing their fertility rate down as women acquire better education and more rights. The revenge of the Palestinian cradle will not overwhelm the Jews, but such high fertility rates, combined with robust immigration, threaten to leave Israelis with no room for everyone, as the population heads to around sixteen million by mid-century, twice what it is today. With no demographic victory in sight for either side, both would be wise to seek a just and lasting peace.

The Canadian scholar Bessma Momani has identified a new generation of young Arab men and women: well educated, increasingly secular, tuned in through their smartphones to global events, entrepreneurial, and impatient with the old men who run and ruin their countries. This new generation's day will come, Momani believes. "There is already a social and cultural revolution in the very thinking of the youth. There is fundamentally a change in values." [448] One romantic stat: 64 percent of Saudi youth want to marry for love, a 10 percent increase from a decade ago. "We have to stop thinking that the future will be worse than the present," she insists. "I don't believe it." Was the anticorruption campaign launched by Saudi crown prince Mohammed bin Salman in November 2017 an overture to that revolution, or just another false spring? The world watches.

One great question remains: Does the United States still have the will to lead in this century? Everything remains in its favor. Immigration, both legal and illegal, will bolster the population. Scientists, engineers, and programmers will flood into the still open American market, stimulating innovation. Undocumented workers will supply the labor for jobs too menial or difficult for robots, hoping—as all immigrants who start at the bottom hope—for a better life for their children.[449] There is absolutely no reason to believe the twenty-first century will not belong to America. Unless . . .

The great danger is that the United States will throw away the very tool that has been the secret to its greatness. Nativist, anti-immigrant sentiment plagues the republic today as it has so often in the past. How deeply will Donald Trump's America First movement take root? Will the U.S. close its borders to illegal immigrants who are vital to the construction and service sectors? Will it deprive itself of the software engineer in Shanghai who has the Next Big Thing in his head and is willing to share it with a venture capitalist in California? A United States walled off from the world will suffer an unhappy fate, and it will deserve that fate. But history suggests that the American people have more and better sense. As Churchill never said (but everyone attributes to him anyway): "Americans can always be counted on to do the right thing—after they have exhausted all other possibilities."[450]

If America does falter, another great power may rise to dominance: India. The country is modernizing and growing, despite its many internal contradictions. With its fertility rate now at replacement rate, India could enjoy decades of Goldilocks years, with a large young population generating and consuming wealth. Eventually, India's population will also begin to subside, but in the meantime the world watches in fascination as this teeming, dynamic society moves toward center stage.

With an immigration intake three times that of the United States, on a per capita basis, Canada's population should broach fifty million by 2060. Any further increase in the annual intake, which many business and thought leaders are recommending, could push that number all the way up to sixty million.[451] By then, all things being equal, Germany's population will have shrunk from the current eighty million to as low as sixty-eight million.[452] Though it's hard to imagine it, Canada's global standing could improve simply because of the size of its population. But numbers will never be the secret to this country's success. Some nations may come to embrace immigration as a solution to their aging societies. But immigration without an entrenched ethos of multiculturalism is a disastrous recipe. With Canada' openness to new arrivals and its accommodative culture, the twenty-first century beckons as the nation's golden age.

Someone born around the middle of this century can expect to live to one hundred.[453] Some biologists believe that by the end of the century, life expectancy will have reached 150.[454] That's wonderful, but a very old population is also a very expensive population. Retirement ages will have to be raised to buttress the workforce, pension plans, and tax revenues. You'll live longer, but you'll work longer too. There's money to be found by closing empty schools. Automation, artificial intelligence, and other spurs to productivity could take care of the problem of labor shortages, though robots thus far have proved to be pretty useless at purchasing refrigerators and other staples of the consumer economy. And the affluence gap between corporate executives and sought-after knowledge workers, on the one hand, and regular folk, on the other, simply has to narrow. That's not left wing. That's just safety valve.

Some analysts predict smaller families will make society richer by allowing parents to work longer hours, thus increasing their skill at the work they do and making it possible to lavish more attention and money on their only child when they finally get home.[455] We're not so sure. But we don't want to become reverse Malthusians, predicting a world of increasing poverty and social stress through population decline. Things have a way of working themselves out.

We do worry about a loss of innovation and creativity. The song not written, the cure not discovered, the technology not perfected because there are fewer alive this year than the year before—how do you quantify that? How do you measure the loss of creative energy that comes with having fewer young? On the other hand, the relentless drift from farm to city will bolster creativity. What do jazz, poststructuralism, and the graphical user interphase all have in common? None of them was developed on a farm. Besides creativity and innovation don't depend so much on numbers as on attitude. The city-state of Athens numbered only 250,000 when Plato wrote *The Republic*; England had only four million souls when Shakespeare wrote *King Lear*. What Classical Greece and Renaissance Europe both shared, however, was a sense of optimism. The world was an exciting place; new discoveries arrived almost daily, it seemed, and people looked to the future with confidence. Societies in decline also produce great art and ideas, but their masterpieces are often tinged with a sense of irony and loss. A shortage of youthful optimism could be the highest price we pay for letting our population diminish.

But not all the world will be aging in the same way. Africa will still be young, even at the end of this century. The continent will be dominated by super cities—chaotic, no doubt, and smelly and badly planned, but also vital and vibrant and bursting with new ideas. We have a hunch that the really exciting music and theater, the truly groundbreaking innovations, the revolutionary new thinking in the last decades of this century will more likely come from Lagos or Mumbai than from Paris or Tokyo.

Even the least fertile countries in Europe and Asia could, if they wanted to, stabilize their populations by accepting immigrants. But this view may be naive. Immigration without multiculturalism, as we've said, is a recipe for exclusion, ghettoization, marginalization, violence, and ultimately, the worst of fates: the collapse of the public square, the inability of different groups within a society to share space and assumptions and values together. It's all well and good to say newcomers are welcome, so long as they adapt to our ways. But for immigration to work, each side has to adapt; each side has to give. A nationalist lack of social elasticity is what keeps too many societies from properly integrating newcomers.

The settler societies of the United States, Canada, Australia, and New Zealand, which represent the most lasting legacy of the British Empire, are more open to newcomers. Yet even though their populations are almost entirely composed of immigrants or the descendants of immigrants, they are not immune to social rigidity. The legacy of slavery continues to separate white from black in the United States; the legacy of colonization continues to estrange indigenous and non-indigenous in Canada and elsewhere. But in general, the greater the sense of national or ethnic coherence, the slimmer the chances for integrating newcomers into a harmonious whole. We wonder whether Hungarians will ever stop feeling Hungarian, or the Japanese, Japanese. We wonder whether they will ever welcome strangers into their midst as equals. And yet for societies that want to stabilize their populations, maybe even grow again, there is no other way.

And even immigration will one day disappear as an option. China once exported many immigrants. Now it exports fewer, and some who left are returning home. Eventually, the Philippines and other countries will run out of surplus population as they continue their march toward urbanization, modernization, and the inevitable 2.1 and below. And their domestic economies are likely to become more prosperous as well. One thing that has struck us as we worked on this book is the way in which urbanization leads not only to better-educated women and lower fertility rates but to better governance and a more economically advanced society. There is too little space left to speculate on possible correlations between urbanization, female empowerment, and political and economic development. But still, there's reason to hope.

Of course, a time could come when, for reasons we can't foresee, people start having more babies. Yes, this seems unlikely from the current perspective. But perspectives can change. Governments could help, with subsidies for in vitro fertilization, baby bonuses, child support, parental leave programs that encourage the father to do his share, and increased state support for daycare. But such programs are expensive, and the results uncertain. Quebec's heavily subsidized daycare program is stretching the government's finances, yet the province's fertility rate, at 1.7, is only marginally higher than the national average of 1.6.[456] (The fact that Quebec favors immigrants from French-speaking countries with high fertility rates, such as Haiti and Algeria, could explain at least some of the difference.) And beyond the cost to taxpayers, the idea of governments telling women they should have more babies for the sake of the nation seems to us repugnant.

But maybe people will change on their own. Divorce rates are down in part because children felt the pain of divorce in their family, or in the families of their friends, and resolved to avoid it. Perhaps a generation of people who grew up with one or no siblings will want their children to experience the messy joys of a home with lots of kids. Big families are great: there is the rough discipline imposed by your big brother (whom you worship nonetheless), the conspiratorial bonding of sisters, the son or daughter who came last and is so spoiled. There is the noise and mess and fun of children running around in all directions. And Christmas morning? It was made for households full of kids. Have you ever met someone who grew up with lots of brothers and sisters who wishes they'd been an only child? We haven't.

And maybe women will finally achieve the full equality they deserve. Maybe a third child won't set back her career—at least no more than it sets back his career—because he throws himself into parenting every bit as much as she does. We are still a long way from this. But every year the gap narrows a little bit.

Two or three generations from now, with each generation possessing only one or two children per family—or, as often as not, none—people could be very lonely. Family reunions won't fill a living room. The swings will sit empty, rusting. No children screaming up and down the street. Some day in the future, people might say to each other: Let's have another. And another. Who cares if we're both in our fifties? Lots of people are having babies in their fifties, now, and it's perfectly safe for mother and child. Let's grow old surrounded by kids.

We have described a future of population decline, one that takes us to the end of this century. But that decline isn't inevitable for every generation to come, for every century to come, world without end, amen. There are so many possibilities. Will Europe look upon Africa with admiration and envy? Will scientists start to study the impact of global cooling? Will we live in a time of terrible war or the *Pax Indica*, of endless diminishment or of renewal?

Enough. The future will make its own way; we must make ours. We must cherish our old and encourage our young and promote equality for all. We must welcome newcomers and share our spaces with them, while preserving freedom and tolerance, which make a society worth living in. Population decline need not be a time of social decline. But we do need to understand what is happening to us and what is about to happen. All the years we've been together on this earth, we have never faced such a thing.

We will grow fewer. Just imagine.

ACKNOWLEDGMENTS

The authors are grateful to their agent, John Pearce, who enthusiastically embraced this book from the very beginning. Our editor, Douglas Pepper, kept us on the right track from start to finish; *Empty Planet* would have been a much lesser book without him. We slept well at night knowing that Tara Tovell copy-edited and proofread the manuscript. To everyone at Signal and McClelland & Stewart, our sincere thanks. If anything did creep in that shouldn't have, that's on us.

From Darrell Bricker: A project as big as this book involves many people. Those who were kind enough to share their knowledge through interviews are mentioned throughout the book. Others who helped in notable ways include Priscilla Branco, Henri Wallard, Leciane Amadio, Cal Bricker, Joseph Bricker, Clifford Young, Bobby Duffy, Gideon Skinner, Simon Atkinson, Ben Page, Mike Colledge, Becky Hunter, Amit Adarkar, Tripti Sharma, Parijat Chakraborty, David Somers, Roger Steadman, Tom Wolf, Hilda Kiritu, Rod

Phillips, Virginia Nkwanzi, Danilo Cersosimo, Mari Harris, John Wright, Mark Davis, Sharon Barnes, Michael Barnes, and Robert Grimm. I would also like to thank my colleagues around the world at Ipsos Public Affairs, many of whom also helped along the way.

Most of all I would like to thank Didier Truchot, CEO of Ipsos. Not only has he given me the opportunity to work as CEO of Ipsos Public Affairs, an incredible platform for any social researcher, he has also encouraged me (even pushed me) to be curious about the world.

From John Ibbitson: I had the good fortune to teach a graduate seminar in global population decline in the autumn of 2016 at the University of Ottawa. I am grateful to Roland Paris for extending that invitation, and to Kayanna Brown, Mathieu Cusson, Rahul Kitchlu, Mohammed Omar, and Laurence Villeneuve, whose contributions enriched this book.

My thanks to Judith Lindikens and Nathaniel Boyd for arranging a dinner party in Brussels, and to Bavo Olbrechts, Sofi Peppermans, Adrien Lucca, Estelle De Bruyn, Pieter Geenen, Helena Desiron, Thierry Homans, Daneel Bogaerts, Nele Lambrichts, and Stef Kunnecke for putting up with my bothersome questions.

To everyone at the *Globe and Mail*, from my colleagues in the Ottawa bureau to bureau chief Bob Fife, editor-in-chief David Walmsley and publisher Philip Crawley, please know that working with you is a joy and a privilege.

And last and most, to Grant, always.

NOTES

1   Jasmine Coleman, "World's 'Seventh Billion Baby' Is Born," *Guardian*, 31 October 2011. http://www.theguardian.com/world/2011/oct/31/ seven-billionth-baby-born-philippines. And "Indian Baby Picked as the World's 'Seven Billionth Person.'" *BBC News*, 31 October 2011. http://www.bbc.com/news/world-south-asia-15517259. And "World's 'Seven Billionth' Baby Born in Russia," *Forbes*, 31 October 2011. http://www.forbes.com/sites/kenrapoza/2011/10/31/worlds-seven -billionth-baby-born-in-russia/.

2   "World Welcomes 7 Billionth Baby," *Herald*, 31 October 2011. http://www.herald.co.zw/world-welcomes-7-billionth-baby

3   Joel K. Bourne Jr., *The End of Plenty: The Race to Feed a Crowded World* (New York: Norton, 2015), introduction. https://books.google.ca/books?id=XAmdBAAAQBAJ&printsec=frontcover &dq=the+end+of+plenty+the+race+to+feed+a+crowded+world&hl=en&sa =X&ved=oahUKEwjIpr6ysIXYAhUi8IMKHbPoCJ4Q6AEIJzAA#v=onepage &q=the%20end%20of%20plenty%20the%20race%20to%20feed%20a% 20crowded%20world&f=false

4   "Italy Is a 'Dying Country' Says Minister as Birth Rate Plummets,"
     Guardian, 13 February 2015. http://www.theguardian.com/world /2015
     /feb/13/italy-is-a-dying-country-says-minister-as-birth-rate-plummets

5   Robert Krulwich, "How Human Beings Almost Vanished from Earth in
     70,000 B.C.," *NPR*, 22 October 2012. http://www.npr.org/sections/krulwich
     /2012/10/22/163397584/how-human-beings-almost-vanished-from-earth
     -in-70-000-b-c

6   "The Toba Supervolconic Eruption of 74,000 Years Ago," *Access Cambridge
     Archeology* (Cambridge University, 2014). https://www.access.arch.cam.
     ac.uk/calendar/the-toba-supervolcanic-eruption-of-74-000-years-ago

7   See, for example, Nicole Boivin et al., "Human Dispersal Across Diverse
     Environments of Asia During the Upper Pleistocene," *Quaternary
     International*, 25 June 2013, 32. http://www.sciencedirect.com/science
     /article/pii/S1040618213000245

8   Sarah Gibbens, "Human Arrival in Australia Pushed Back 18,000 Years,"
     National Geographic, 20 July 2017. https://news.nationalgeographic.
     com/2017/07/australia-aboriginal-early-human-evolution-spd

9   Jared Diamond, *Guns, Germs, and Steel: The Fates of Human Societies*
     (New York: Norton, 1997), 41.

10   Ian Sample, "Could History of Humans in North America Be Rewritten by
     Broken Bones?" *Guardian*, 26 April 2017. https://www.theguardian.com
     /science/2017/apr/26/could-history-of-humans-in-north-america-be
     -rewritten-by-broken-mastodon-bones

11   Ian Morris, *Why the West Rules—For Now: The Patterns of History and
     What They Reveal About the Future* (New York: Farrar, Straus and Giroux,
     2010), 296.

12   "Historical Estimates of World Population," International Programs data-
     base, table (Washington, D.C.: United States Census Bureau, 25 July 2017).
     https://www.census.gov/population/international/data/worldpop/
     table_history.php

13   Ole J. Benedictow, "The Black Death: The Greatest Catastrophe Ever," *History
     Today*, 3 March 2005. http://www.historytoday.com/ole-j-benedictow
     /black-death-greatest-catastrophe-ever

14   Samuel K. Cohn Jr., "Epidemiology of the Black Death and Successive
     Waves of Plague," *Medical History*, Supplement 27, 2008.
     http://www.ncbi.nlm.nih.gov/pmc/articles/PMC2630035/

15   "Plague" (Atlanta: Centers for Disease Control, 14 September, 2014).
https://www.cdc.gov/plague/transmission

16   Ibid.

17   Mark Wheelis, "Biological Warfare at the 1346 Siege of Caffa," *Emerging
Infectious Diseases Journal*, Vol. 8, No. 9 (September 2002).
http://wwwnc.cdc.gov/eid/article/8/9/01-0536_article

18   Katherine Shulz Richard, "The Global Impact of the Black Death"
ThoughtCo, 3 March 2017. https://www.thoughtco.com/global-impacts-of
-the-black-death-1434480

19   G.D. Sussman, "Was the Black Death in India and China?" *Bulletin of the
History of Medicine*, Vol. 85, No. 3 (Fall 2011). http://www.ncbi.nlm.nih.gov
/pubmed/22080795

20   Benedictow, "The Black Death."

21   Ibid.

22   David Routt, "The Economic Impact of the Black Death," *EH.net
Encyclopedia*, 20 July 2008. https://eh.net/encyclopedia/the-economic
-impact-of-the-black-death

23   C.W. "Plagued by Dear Labour," *Economist*, 21 October 2013.
http://www.economist.com/blogs/freeexchange/2013/10/economic
-history-1

24   Ker Than, "Massive Population Drop Among Native Americans,
DNA Shows," *National Geographic News*, 5 December 2011.
http://news.nationalgeographic.com/news/2011/12/111205
-native-americans-europeans-population-dna-genetics-science

25   William M. Donovan, *The Native Population of the Americas in 1492*
(Madison: University of Wisconsin Press, 1992), 7.

26   Nathan Nunn and Nancy Quinn, "The Columbian Exchange: A History
of Disease, Food and Ideas," *Journal of Economic Perspectives*, Vol. 24, No. 2
(Spring 2010), p. 165. https://web.viu.ca/davies/H131/ColumbianExchange.pdf

27   *World Population to 2300* (New York: United Nations Department
of Economic and Social Affairs/Population Division, 2004), Table 2.
All historical global population numbers are drawn from this table.
http://www.un.org/esa/population/publications/longrange2/
WorldPop2300final.pdf

28   Steven Pinker, *The Better Angels of Our Nature: Why Violence Has Declined*
(New York: Penguin, 2011).

29   Alfred Crosby, *Germs, Seeds and Animals: Studies in Ecological History*
     (New York: Routledge, 1994).

30   Pamela K. Gilbert, "On Cholera in Nineteenth Century England,"
     BRANCH: Britain, Representation and Nineteenth-Century History (2013).
     http://www.branchcollective.org/?ps_articles=pamela-k-gilbert-on-cholera
     -in-nineteenth-century-england

31   Sharon Gouynup, "Cholera: Tracking the First Truly Global Disease," *National
     Geographic News,* 14 June 2004. http://news.nationalgeographic.com/news
     /2004/06/0614_040614_tvcholera.html

32   Judith Summers, *Soho: A History of London's Most Colourful Neighborhood*
     (London: Bloomsbury, 1989), 113–17. http://www.ph.ucla.edu/epi/snow
     /broadstreetpump.html

33   David Vachon, "Doctor John Snow Blames Water Pollution for Cholera
     Epidemic," *Father of Modern Epidemiology* (Los Angeles: UCLA
     Department of Epidemiology, 2005). http://www.ph.ucla.edu/epi/snow
     /fatherofepidemiology.html

34   "Population of the British Isles," *Tacitus.NU.* http://www.tacitus.nu
     /historical-atlas/population/british.htm

35   Max Roser and Esteban Ortiz-Ospina, "World Population Growth," *Our
     World in Data,* 2013/2017. http://ourworldindata.org/data/population-growth
     -vital-statistics/world-population-growth

36   Michael J. White et al., "Urbanization and Fertility: An Event-History
     Analysis of Coastal Ghana," *Demography,* Vol. 45, No. 4 (November 2008).
     http://www.ncbi.nlm.nih.gov/pmc/articles/PMC2834382

37   Elina Pradhan, "Female Education and Childbearing: A Closer Look
     at the Data," *Investing in Health* (Washington, D.C.: World Bank),
     24 November 2015. http://blogs.worldbank.org/health/female
     -education-and-childbearing-closer-look-data

38   Michael Haines, "Fertility and Mortality in the United States," *EH.net
     Encyclopedia,* 19 March 2008. https://eh.net/encyclopedia/fertility-and
     -mortality-in-the-united-states.

39   Michael J. McGuire, "John L. Leal: Hero of Public Health,"
     Safedrinkingwater.com, 25 September 2012. https://safedrinkingwaterdotcom
     .wordpress.com/2012/09/25/john-l-leal-hero-of-public-health

40   Ibid.

41   "Life Expectancy" (Canberra: Australian Institute of Health and Welfare,
     Australian Government, 7 February 2017). https://www.aihw.gov.au/reports
     /life-expectancy-death/deaths/contents/life-expectancy

42   "Fertility Rates" (Australian Bureau of Statistics, Australian Government,
     25 October 2012). http://www.abs.gov.au/ausstats/abs@.nsf/Products
     /3301.0~2011~Main+Features~Fertility+rates

43   "Harry W. Colmery Memorial Park" (Topeka: American Legion,
     Department of Kansas). http://www.ksamlegion.org/page/content
     /programs/harry-w-colmery-memorial-park

44   "Harry W. Colmery" (Indianapolis: American Legion, 2017).
     http://www.legion.org/distinguishedservicemedal/1975/harry-w-colmery

45   "Servicemen's Readjustment Act (1944)," *Ourdocuments.gov.*
     http://www.ourdocuments.gov/doc.php?flash=true&doc=76

46   World Health Organization; World Food Program; United Nations
     Educational, Scientific and Cultural Organization; United Nations
     Children Fund.

47   Max Roser, "Life Expectancy," *Our World in Data*, 2017. http://ourworld
     indata.org/data/population-growth-vital-statistics/life-expectancy

48   Max Roser and Esteban Ortiz-Ospina, "World Population Growth,"
     Our World in Data, April 2017. https://ourworldindata.org/world
     -population-growth/

49   Mike Hanlon, "World Becomes More Urban Than Rural," *Gizmag*,
     29 May 2007. http://www.gizmag.com/go/7334

50   *Soylent Green*, DVD, directed by Richard Fleischer (Los Angeles: MGM,
     1973). http://www.imdb.com/title/tt0070723/

51   *Inferno*, DVD, directed by Ron Howard (Los Angeles: Sony, 2016).

52   Donna Gunn MacRae, "Thomas Robert Malthus,"*Encyclopedia Britannica.*
     http://www.britannica.com/biography/Thomas-Robert-Malthus

53   Thomas Malthus, *An Essay on the Principle of Population as It Affects the
     Future Improvement of Society, with Remarks on the Speculations of Mr. Godwin,
     M. Condorcet, and Other Writers* (London: J. Johnson, 1798).
     http://www.econlib.org/library/Malthus/malPop1.html#Chapter%20I

54   Ibid.

55   Ibid.

56   Ibid.

57   Ibid.

58   Ron Broglio, "The Best Machine for Converting Herbage into Money," in
     Tamar Wagner and Narin Hassan, eds., *Consuming Culture in the Long
     Nineteenth Century: Narratives of Consumption 1700–1900* (Lanham: Lexington,
     2007), 35. https://books.google.ca/books?id=NAEZBjQwXBYC&pg=PA35
     &dq=weight+of+cow+1710+and+1795&hl=en&sa=X&ved=0ahUKEwiwib
     _7oInKAhUFGB4KHRmZCqUQ6AEIHDAA#v=onepage&q=weight%20of
     %20cow%201710%20and%201795&f=false

59   Elizabeth Hoyt, "'Turnip' Townsend and the Agriculture Revolution,"
     Elizabeth Hoyt. http://www.elizabethhoyt.com/extras/research
     /revolution.php

60   Tim Lambert, "A History of English Population," *Localhistories.org,* 2017.
     http://www.localhistories.org/population.html

61   Paul Ehrlich, *The Population Bomb* (Rivercity: Rivercity Press, 1968), xi.

62   Ibid., 17.

63   Ibid., xii.

64   Ibid., 25.

65   Tom Murphy, "U.N. Says MDGs Helped Lift 1 Billion People Out of Poverty,"
     Humanosphere, 8 July 2015. http://www.humanosphere.org/world-politics
     /2015/07/u-n-says-mdgs-helped-lift-1-billion-people-out-of-poverty

66   "National Air Quality: Status and Trends of Key Air Pollutants" (Washington,
     D.C.: Environmental Protection Agency, 2017). https://www.epa.gov/air-trends

67   Dan Egan, "Great Lakes Water Quality Improved, but There Are Still
     Issues, Report Says," *Milwaukee Journal-Sentinel,* 14 May 2013.
     http://www.jsonline.com/news/wisconsin/great-lakes-water-quality
     -improved-but-there-are-still-issues-report-says-i49uq79-207463461.html

68   Prabhu Pingali, "Green Revolution: Impacts, Limits and the Path Ahead,"
     Proceedings of the National Academy of Sciences of the United States of America,
     31 July 2012. http://www.ncbi.nlm.nih.gov/pmc/articles/PMC3411969

69   Tania Branagan, "China's Great Famine: The True Story," *Guardian,* 1
     January 2013. http://www.theguardian.com/world/2013/jan/01/china
     -great-famine-book-tombstone

70   Annual GDP per capita in constant dollars based on purchasing power parity.
     Ami Sedghi, "China GDP: How it has changed since 1980," *Guardian,* 23 March
     2012 (then updated). http://www.theguardian.com/news/datablog/2012
     /mar/23/china-gdp-since-1980

71 "GDP Per Capita of India," *Statistics Times* (Delhi: Ministry of Statistics and Programme Implementation [IMF], 19 June 2015). http://statisticstimes.com/economy/gdp-capita-of-india.php

72 Such as Max Roser and Esteban Ortiz-Ospina, "Global Extreme Poverty," *Our World in Data*, 2013/2017. http://ourworldindata.org/data/growth-and-distribution-of-prosperity/world-poverty

73 Clyde Haberman, "Retro Report: The Population Bomb?" *New York Times*, 31 May 2015. http://www.nytimes.com/2015/06/01/us/the-unrealized-horrors-of-population-explosion.html?_r=0

74 Donella H. Meadows et al., *The Limits to Growth: A Report on the Club of Rome's Project on the Predicament of Mankind* (New York: Universe Books, 1972), 23.

75 Ibid., 183.

76 Graham Turner and Cathy Alexander, "*The Limits to Growth* Was Right: New Research Shows We're Nearing Collapse," *Guardian*, 2 September 2014. http://www.theguardian.com/commentisfree/2014/sep/02/limits-to-growth-was-right-new-research-shows-were-nearing-collapse

77 Joel K. Bourne Jr., *The End of Plenty: The Race to Feed a Crowded World* (New York: Norton, 2015), ch. 14.

78 John Bongaarts and Rodolfo A. Bulatao, eds., *Beyond Six Billion: Forecasting the World's Population* (Washington, D.C.: National Academy Press, 2000), ch. 2. http://www.nap.edu/read/9828/chapter/4

79 *World Population Prospects 2017* (New York: United Nations Department of Economic and Social Affairs/Population Division, 2017). https://esa.un.org/unpd/wpp. All current and projected population and fertility data in this book is drawn from this source unless otherwise noted.

80 Wolfgang Lutz interview with Darrell Bricker, 15 April 2016.

81 Tedx Talks, "We Won't Be Nine Billion: Jørgen Randers at TEDx Maastricht," *YouTube*, 11 May 2014. https://www.youtube.com/watch?v=73X8R9NrX3w

82 "Don't Panic," *Economist*, 24 September 2014.

83 Gapminder Foundation, "Don't Panic: Hans Rosling Showing the Facts About Population," *YouTube*, 15 December, 2014. https://www.youtube.com/watch?v=FACK2knCo8E

84 "World Population to Peak by 2055: Report," *CNBC*, 9 September 2013. http://www.cnbc.com/id/101018722

85 "The Astounding Drop in Global Fertility Rates Between 1970 and 2014," *Brilliant Maps*, 23 June 2015. http://brilliantmaps.com/fertility-rates

86 "Margaret Sanger's the Woman Rebel—One Hundred Years Old," *Margaret Sanger Papers Project* (New York: New York University, 2014). https://sangerpapers.wordpress.com/2014/03/20/margaret-sangers-the-woman-rebel-100-years-old

87 *OECD Health Statistics 2014: How Does Spain Compare?* (Paris: OECD, 2014). http://www.oecd.org/els/health-systems/Briefing-Note-SPAIN-2014.pdf

88 Ashifa Kassam et al., "Europe Needs Many More Babies to Avert a Population Disaster," *Guardian*, 23 August 2015. https://www.theguardian.com/world/2015/aug/23/baby-crisis-europe-brink-depopulation-disaster

89 "Population Projection for Spain, 2014–2064" (Madrid: Instituto Nacional de Estadistica, 28 October 2014). http://www.ine.es/en/prensa/np870_en.pdf

90 Rebecca Flood, "Spain Appoints 'Sex Tsar' in Bid to Boost Declining Population," *Independent*, 25 February 2017. http://www.independent.co.uk/news/world/europe/spain-sex-tsar-population-crisis-baby-parents-demographic-government-a7599091.html

91 Ilan Shrira, "History's Mysteries: Why Do Birth Rates Decrease When Societies Modernize?" *Psychology Today*, 14 March 2008. https://www.psychologytoday.com/blog/the-narcissus-in-all-us/200903/history-s-mysteries-why-do-birth-rates-decrease-when-societies

92 David Gushee, "Why Is Christianity Declining?" *Religion News Service*, 6 September 2016. http://religionnews.com/2016/09/06/why-is-christianity-declining

93 Patricia Miller, "Women Are Leaving the Church, and the Reason Seems Clear," *Religion Dispatches*, 25 May 2016. http://religiondispatches.org/women-are-leaving-church-and-the-reason-seems-clear

94 Oliver Smith, "Mapped: The World's Most (and Least) Religious Countries," *Telegraph*, 16 April 2017. http://www.telegraph.co.uk/travel/maps-and-graphics/most-religious-countries-in-the-world/

95 Linda L. Malenab-Hornilla, "Overview of Urbanization in the Philippines," *Overview of the Philippines Action Plan*, 14 December 2015. http://www.urbangateway.org/icnup/sites/default/files/ICNUP%20Philippines.pdf

96 "Rankings," *2016 Gender Gap Report* (Davos: World Economic Forum, 2016). http://reports.weforum.org/global-gender-gap-report-2016/rankings/

97 Joes Torres, "Church Attendance in Philippines Declines," *UCA News*, 25 April 2017. http://www.ucanews.com/news/church-attendance-in-philippines-declines/78988

98   Danielle Erika Hill and Scott Douglas Jacobsen, "Women's Rights in the
     Philippines: An Overview," *Humanist Voices*, 11 May 2017. https://medium.com
     /humanist-voices/womens-rights-in-the-philippines-an-overview-55ab86df42a

99   "Highlights of the 2010 Census-Based Population Projections" (Quezon
     City: Philippines Statistics Authority, 9 August 2016). https://www.psa.
     gov.ph/statistics/census/projected-population

100 "Total Fertility Rate, 1960–2014," *Statistics Explained* (Luxembourg: Eurostat,
     14 March 2016). http://ec.europa.eu/eurostat/statistics-explained/index.php
     /File:Total_fertility_rate,_1960–2014_(live_births_per_woman)_YB16.png

101 Nikos Konstandaras, "Greece's Dismal Demographics," *New York Times*,
     9 December 2013. http://www.nytimes.com/2013/12/10/opinion/greeces
     -dismal-demographics.html

102 "Italy Is a 'Dying Country' Says Minister as Birth Rate Plummets," *Guardian*,
     13 February 2015. http://www.theguardian.com/world/2015/feb/13/italy-is-a
     -dying-country-says-minister-as-birth-rate-plummets

103 Zosia Wasik, "Poland's Shrinking Population Heralds Labour Shortage,"
     Financial Times, 4 September 2015. https://www.ft.com/content/3001e356
     -2fba-11e5-91ac-a5e17d9b4cff

104 Ibid.

105 Valentina Romei, "Eastern Europe Has the Largest Population Loss in Modern
     History," *Financial Times*, 27 May 2016. http://blogs.ft.com/ftdata/2016/05/27
     /eastern-europe-has-the-largest-population-loss-in-modern-history

106 Evan Hadingham, "Ancient Chinese Explorers," *Nova*, 16 January 2001.
     http://www.pbs.org/wgbh/nova/ancient/ancient-chinese-explorers.html

107 Neil Cummins, "Marital Fertility and Wealth During the Fertility
     Transition: Rural France 1750–1850," *Economic History Review*, Vol. 66,
     No. 2 (2013), pp. 449–76. http://onlinelibrary.wiley.com/doi/10.1111/j
     .1468-0289.2012.00666.x/epdf?r3_referer=wol&tracking_action
     =preview_click&show_checkout=1&purchase_referrer=www
     .overcomingbias.com&purchase_site_license=LICENSE_DENIED
     _NO_CUSTOMER

108 Jan van Baval and David S. Reher, "What We Know and What We Need to
     Know About the Baby Boom," paper prepared for the Annual Meeting
     of the Population Association of America, San Francisco, May 2012.
     http://paa2012.princeton.edu/papers/120715

109 Ibid., p. 23.

110 Jonathan Luxmoore, "With Decline in Participation, Brussels
     Archdiocese to Close Churches," *National Catholic Reporter*, 8 February
     2013. https://www.ncronline.org/news/world/decline-participation
     -brussels-archdiocese-close-churches

111 Jon Anderson, "Belgium's Crisis of Faith," *Catholic Herald*, 15 October 2015.

112 "Marriage and Divorce Statistics," *Statistics Explained* (Luxembourg:
     Eurostat, 2 June 2017). http://ec.europa.eu/eurostat/statistics-explained
     /index.php/Marriage_and_divorce_statistics#Main_statistical_findings

113 "Population Forecast for Belgium" (Denver: Pardee Center for
     International Futures, University of Denver, 2017). http://www.ifs.du.edu
     /ifs/frm_CountryProfile.aspx?Country=BE

114 Doug Saunders, "Integration: A New Strategy," *Globe and Mail*, 14 January
     2016. http://www.theglobeandmail.com/news/world/saunders-avert
     -extremism-before-it-start-by-building-better-neighbourhoods
     /article27403775

115 Rick Lyman, "Bulgarian Border Police Accused of Abusing Refugees," *New
     York Times*, 23 December 2015. http://www.nytimes.com/2015/12/24/world
     /europe/bulgarian-border-police-accused-of-abusing-refugees.html

116 Ruth Alexander, "Why Is Bulgaria's Population Falling Off a Cliff?" *BBC
     News*, 7 September 2017. http://www.bbc.com/news/world-europe-41109572

117 Alan Yuhas, "Muslim Population to Reach 10% by 2050, New Forecast
     Shows," *Guardian*, 2 April 2015. https://www.theguardian.com/world/2015
     /apr/02/muslim-population-growth-christians-religion-pew

118 Patrick Worrall, "Fact Check: Will Britain Have a Muslim Majority by
     2015?" *Channel 4*, 14 June 2013. http://blogs.channel4.com/factcheck
     /factcheck-will-britain-have-a-muslim-majority-by-2050

119 "Gunnar Myrdal, Analyst of Race Crisis, Dies," *New York Times*, 18 May 1987.
     http://www.nytimes.com/1987/05/18/obituaries/gunnar-myrdal-analyst
     -of-race-crisis-dies.html?pagewanted=all

120 Mary Johnson, "Alva and Gunnar Myrdal: The Great Happiness of 'Living to
     Be Very Old and Together,'" *People*, 11 August 1980. http://www.people.com
     /people/archive/article/0,,20077164,00.html

121 Ibid.

122 Stephen Philip Kramer, "Sweden Pushed Gender Equality to Boost Birth
     Rates," *We News*, 26 April 2014. http://womensenews.org/2014/04/sweden
     -pushed-gender-equality-boost-birth-rates

123 Kajsa Sundström, "Can Governments Influence Population Growth?" OECD
      Observer, November 2001. http://www.oecdobserver.org/news/archivestory
      .php/aid/563/Can_governments_influence_population_growth_.html

124 Youngtae Cho interview with John Ibbitson, October 2016.

125 The observation was delivered at the 2016 Canada–Korea Forum, hosted
      annually by the Centre for International Governance Innovation, Waterloo,
      Canada (27 October 2016).

126 "World's Largest Cities," worldatlas.com. http://www.worldatlas.com/city-
      pops.htm. However, defining the population of cities is no easy task. They
      can be defined by their administrative boundary (the limits of the city's
      government), their "urban agglomeration" (the contiguous urban area), or
      their "metropolitan area" (the region economically connected to and
      dependent on the city). The United Nations World Urbanization Prospects
      assesses all the world's major cities based on the urban agglomeration
      measurement, which we will use throughout this book for purposes of con-
      sistency. By that measure, Seoul has population of 9.8 million. The World's
      Cities in 2016 (New York: United Nations Department of Economic and
      Social Affairs/Population Division, 2016). http://www.un.org/en
      /development/desa/population/publications/pdf/urbanization/the
      _worlds_cities_in_2016_data_booklet.pdf

127 David Pilling, "The End of Asia's Demographic Dividend," Financial Times,
      14 March 2012. https://www.ft.com/content/bd935806-6d00-11e1-a7c7
      -00144feab49a

128 Meagan Hare, "A Brief History of the Walkman," Time, 1 July 2009.
      http://content.time.com/time/nation/article/0,8599,1907884,00.html

129 Olga Garnova, "Japan's Birthrate: Beginning of the End or Just a New
      Beginning?" Japan Times, 10 February 2016. http://www.japantimes.co.jp
      /community/2016/02/10/voices/japan-birth-rate-beginning-end-just-new
      -beginning/#.V6YoWWUz5Ec

130 "Inspectors Knock," Economist, 20 August 2016. https://www.economist.com
      /news/asia/21705375-getting-passport-not-easy-inspectors-knock

131 "Japanese Citizenship: How to Become Japanese," Just Landed.
      https://www.justlanded.com/english/Japan/Japan-Guide/Visas-Permits
      /Japanese-citizenship

132 John Creighton Campbell, "Japan's Aging Population: Perspectives of
      'Catastrophic Demography,'" Journal of Asian Studies, Vol. 67, No. 4

(November 2008). http://www.jstor.org/stable/20203491?seq=1#page
_scan_tab_contents

133   Sarah Harper, *How Population Change Will Transform Our World* (Oxford:
      Oxford University Press, 2016), 50.

134   Adam Taylor, "It's Official: Japan's Population Is Dramatically Shrinking,"
      Washington Post, 26 February 2016, https://www.washingtonpost.com
      /news/worldviews/wp/2016/02/26/its-official-japans-population-is
      -drastically-shrinking

135   "Japanese Voters Want to Plan to Handle Declining Population,"
      Economist, 5 October 2017. https://www.economist.com/news
      /asia/21730003-election-campaign-disappointing-them-japanese
      -voters-want-plan-handle-declining?fsrc=scn/tw/te/bl/ed
      /japanesevoterswantaplantohandleadecliningpopulation

136   "Age Dependency Ratio," *Data* (Washington, D.C.: World Bank, 2016).
      http://data.worldbank.org/indicator/SP.POP.DPND

137   Naoyuki Yoshino and Farhad Taghizadeh-Hesary, *Causes and Remedies for
      Japan's Long-Lasting Recession: Lessons for the People's Republic of China* (Tokyo:
      Asian Development Bank Institute, 2015). http://www.adb.org/publications
      /causes-and-remedies-japan-long-lasting-recession-lessons-china

138   Paul Yip et al., *An Analysis of the Lowest Total Fertility Rate in Hong Kong
      SAR* (Tokyo: Hitotsubashi University). http://www.ier.hit-u.ac.jp/pie
      /stage1/Japanese/seminar/workshop0612/yip.pdf . The United Nations
      estimate is 1.2.

139   Kelsey Chong, "South Korea's Troubled Millennial Generation," *BerkeleyHaas*,
      27 April 2016. http://cmr.berkeley.edu/blog/2016/4/south-korea/#fn4

140   Ibid.

141   Ibid.

142   Garnova, "Japan's Birthrate."

143   Takao Komine, "Effective Measures to Halt Birthrate Decline," *Discuss
      Japan* (*Japan Foreign Policy Forum*, Vol. 22, undated). http://www.japanpol-
      icyforum.jp/pdf/2014/no22/DJweb_22_eco_01.pdf

144   "Labor Force Participation Rate: Female," *Data* (Washington, D.C.: World
      Bank, 2016). http://data.worldbank.org/indicator/SL.TLF.CACT.FE.ZS

145   "Mother's Mean Age at First Birth," *World Factbook* (Washington, D.C.:
      Central Intelligence Agency, 2017). https://www.cia.gov/library
      /publications/the-world-factbook/fields/2256.html

146 "S. Korea's Marriage Rate Hits Record Low Level Last Year Amid Economic Slowdown," *Pulse by Maeil Business News Korea*, 7 April 7 2016. http://pulsenews.co.kr/view.php?no=256641&year=2016

147 "List of Countries by Refugee Population," *Wikipedia*, compiled from UNHCR data. https://en.wikipedia.org/wiki/List_of_countries_by_refugee_population

148 Chris Burgess, "Japan's 'No Immigration Principle' Looking as Solid as Ever," *Japan Times*, 28 June 2014. http://www.japantimes.co.jp/community/2014/06/18/voices/japans-immigration-principle-looking-solid-ever/#.WC8q33cZPBI

149 "The Upper Han," *Economist*, 19 November 2016. http://www.economist.com/news/briefing/21710264-worlds-rising-superpower-has-particular-vision-ethnicity-and-nationhood-has

150 "New Pledge of Allegiance to Reflect Growing Multiculturalism," *Chosunilbo*, 18 April 2011. http://english.chosun.com/site/data/html_dir/2011/04/18/2011041801112.html

151 "How Large Is the Job Market for English Teachers Abroad?" *International TEFL Academy*. https://www.internationalteflacademy.com/faq/bid/102201/how-large-is-the-job-market-for-english-teachers-abroad

152 Off-the-record interview with John Ibbitson.

153 Rajeshni Naidu-Ghelani, "Governments Organize Matchmaking as Asia's Birthrates Fall," CNBC, 24 October 2012. http://www.cnbc.com/id/49471704

154 MentosSingapore, "Mentos National Night," *YouTube*, 1 August 2012. https://www.youtube.com/watch?v=8jxU89x78ac

155 "South Korea's New Drive to Boost Flagging Birthrate," BBC News, 26 August 2016. http://www.bbc.com/news/blogs-news-from-elsewhere-37196870

156 "Mother's Mean Age at First Birth."

157 Sarah Jane Glynn, "Families Need More Help to Take Care of Their Children," *Fact Sheet: Child Care* (Washington, D.C.: Center for American Progress, 16 August 2012). https://www.americanprogress.org/issues/economy/news/2012/08/16/11978/fact-sheet-child-care

158 Camilla Cornell, "The Real Cost of Raising Kids," *Moneysense*, 10 August 2011. http://www.moneysense.ca/magazine-archive/the-real-cost-of-raising-kids

159 "Over a Third of Single-Parent Families Depend on Welfare," *The Local*, 6 July 2016. https://www.thelocal.de/20160706/study-more-children-facing-poverty

160 "Adolescent Fertility Rate,"(New York: United Nations Department
    of Economic and Social Affairs/Population Division, 2017).
    http://data.worldbank.org/indicator/SP.ADO.TFRT

161 "The Wage Gap Over Time" (Washington, D.C.: National Committee on
    Pay Equity, September 2016.) https://www.pay-equity.org/info-time.html

162 Mark Hugo Lopez and Ana Gonzalez-Barrera, "Women's College
    Enrollment Gains Leave Men Behind" (Washington, D.C.: Pew Research
    Center, 8 March 2014). http://www.pewresearch.org/fact-tank/2014
    /03/06/womens-college-enrollment-gains-leave-men-behind

163 "Growth in the Proportion of Female Medical Students Begins to Slow"
    (London: General Medical Council, October 2013). http://www.gmc-uk.org
    /information_for_you/23490.asp

164 "Women Still Underrepresented in STEM Fields," USA Today, 21 October
    2015. http://www.usnews.com/news/articles/2015/10/21/women-still
    -underrepresented-in-stem-fields

165 Claire Cain Miller, "The Gender Pay Gap Is Largely Because of Motherhood,"
    New York Times, 13 May 2017. https://www.nytimes.com/2017/05/13/upshot
    /the-gender-pay-gap-is-largely-because-of-motherhood.html

166 "Project on Student Debt: State by State Data 2015" (Washington, D.C.:
    Institute for College Access and Success, 2015). http://ticas.org/posd/map
    -state-data-2015

167 "Social Indicators of Marital Health and Well-Being," State of Our Unions,
    2011. http://www.stateofourunions.org/2011/social_indicators.php

168 Joyce A. Martin et al., "Births: Final Data for 2015," National Vital Statistics
    Reports, Vol. 66, No. 1 (5 January 2017). https://www.cdc.gov/nchs/data
    /nvsr/nvsr66/nvsr66_01.pdf

169 Kathryn Blaze Carleson, "Curtain Lifts on Decades of Forced Adoptions for
    Unwed Mothers in Canada," National Post, 9 March 2012. http://nationalpost
    .com/news/canada/curtain-lifts-on-decades-of-forced-adoptions-for
    -unwed-mothers-in-canada

170 "Intercountry Adoption: Statistics" (Washington, D.C.: Bureau of Consular
    Affairs, Department of State, 2017). https://travel.state.gov/content
    /adoptionsabroad/en/about-us/statistics.html

171 Emma Graney, "Looking to Adopt in Alberta? Statistics Show There Are
    Fewer Children Waiting for a Home," Edmonton Journal, 7 July 2016.
    http://edmontonjournal.com/news/insight/alberta-adoption-numbers-plunge

172 Ryan Middleton, "2015 Highest Grossing Music Festivals," *Music Times*, 19 January 2016. http://www.musictimes.com/articles/62358/20160119/2015 -highest-grossing-music-festivals-coachella-edc-outside-lands-top-list.htm

173 James Beal, "Welcome to Oldchella: The Rolling Stones, Paul McCartney, Bob Dylan and Other Legendary Rockers Take to the Stage for Mega Show," *The Sun* (U.K. edition), 10 October 2016. https://www.thesun.co.uk /tvandshowbiz/1943185/coachella-the-rolling-stones-paul-mccartney-bob -dylan-and-other-legendary-rockers-took-to-the-stage-for-mega-show

174 "Welcome to the Boomaissance; Mindshare North American Releases New Culture Vulture Trends Report," PR *Newswire*, 26 January 2017. http://www .prnewswire.com/news-releases/welcome-to-the-boomaissance-mindshare -north-america-releases-new-culture-vulture-trends-report-300397650.html

175 "Baby Boomers Will Control 70% of Disposable Income" (London: Impact Business Partners, 22 February 2016). https://impactbp.com/baby-boomers

176 Feng Wang, "China's Population Destiny: The Looming Crisis," Washington, D.C.: Brookings Institution, 30 September 2010. https://www.brookings.edu /articles/chinas-population-destiny-the-looming-crisis

177 Ibid.

178 *World Economic Outlook, April 2017: Gaining Momentum?* (Washington, D.C.: International Monetary Fund, 2016). http://www.imf.org/en/Publications /WEO/Issues/2017/04/04/world-economic-outlook-april-2017

179 "2017 World Population Data Sheet" (Washington, D.C.: Population Reference Bureau, 2017). http://www.prb.org/pdf17/2017_World_Population.pdf

180 "Median Age by Continent," *MapPorn* (Reddit, 2017). https://www.reddit.com /r/MapPorn/comments/6lgvdm/median_age_by_continent_6460x3455/

181 "Kenya," *World Factbook* (Washington, D.C.: Central Intelligence Agency, 14 November 2017). https://www.cia.gov/library/publications/the-world -factbook/geos/ke.html

182 "Kenya SPEC Barometer Survey" (Paris: Ipsos Public Affairs, 16 July 2016), data confidential.

183 "Kenya," *World Factbook*.

184 "Kenya SPEC Barometer Survey."

185 Ibid.

186 "Kenya," *World Factbook*.

187 Ibid.

188 Ibid.

189 "Kenya Demographic and Health Survey, 2014" (Nairobi: Kenya National Bureau of Statistics, 2015). https://dhsprogram.com/pubs/pdf/FR308 /FR308.pdf

190 "Kibera Facts and Information," *Kibera-UK*. http://www.kibera.org.uk/facts-info

191 Interview with Darrell Bricker. All interviews in this chapter were conducted on a confidential basis.

192 "Corruption by Country: Kenya" (Berlin: Transparency International, 2016). https://www.transparency.org/country/KEN

193 "2017 Index of Economic Freedom" (Washington, D.C.: Heritage Foundation, 2017). http://www.heritage.org/index/ranking

194 "Table of Country Scores," *Freedom in the World 2016* (Washington, D.C.: Freedom House), 2017. https://freedomhouse.org/report/freedom -world-2016/table-scores

195 Interview with Darrell Bricker.

196 Ibid.

197 "Kenya," *World Population Prospects 2017* (New York: United Nations Department of Economic and Social Affairs/Population Division, 2017). https://esa.un.org/unpd/wpp/Graphs/Probabilistic/FERT/TOT

198 Chris Wamalwa, "Education in Kenya Needs Faster Reform," *World Policy Blog*, 17 May 2017. http://www.worldpolicy.org/blog/2017/05/23/education -kenya-needs-faster-reform

199 "Education in Kenya," *World Education News and Review*, 2 June 2015. http://wenr.wes.org/2015/06/education-kenya

200 "Kenya Fact Sheet," UNESCO *Global Partnership for Girl's and Women's Education, One Year On.* (New York: UNESCO, 2012). http://www.unesco.org /eri/cp/factsheets_ed/KE_EDFactSheet.pdf

201 Mokua Ombati, "Education Gender Parity: Challenges of the Kenyan Girl," *Journal of Women's Entrepreneurship and Education*, Nos. 3–4 (2013). https://www.academia.edu/6037067/Educational_Gender_Parity _Challenges_of_the_Kenyan_Girl

202 Wolfgang Lutz, William P. Butz, Samir KC, eds., *World Population and Human Capital in the Twenty-First Century* (Vienna: Wittgenstein Centre for Demography and Global Human Capital, 2014), executive summary.

203 "Kenya Demographic and Health Survey, 2014."

204 Nana Naitashvili, "Infant Mortality and Fertility," *Population Horizons*, Summer 2014. https://www.ageing.ox.ac.uk/download/143

205 Elizabeth Mareb, "Kenyan Population Expected to Hit 81 Million as Fertility
     Rates Soar." *Daily Nation*, 6 September 2015. http://www.nation.co.ke/news
     /Kenyan-population-to-hit-81-million-as-fertility-rates-soar/-/1056/2860682
     /-/ybvkdx/-/index.html
206 Interview with Darrell Bricker.
207 Ibid.
208 Ibid.
209 "Bride Price App—The Easy Way to Calculate Dowry" *Up Nairobi*, 24 July
     2014. http://www.upnairobi.com/oldsite/dt_portfolio/bride-price-app
210 Interview with Darrell Bricker.
211 Ibid.
212 Geoffrey York, "Trump's Aid Cuts Risk Pushing Women 'into the Dark
     Ages,' Spelling Trouble for Rising World Population." *Globe and Mail*, 6
     April 2017. http://www.theglobeandmail.com/news/world/africa
     -contraception-and-population-growth/article34599155
213 *Women's Rights in Africa* (Addis Ababa: African Union Commission, 2017).
     http://www.ohchr.org/Documents/Issues/Women/WRGS
     /WomensRightsinAfrica_singlepages.pdf
214 Ibid.
215 Valerie Amos and Toyin Saraki, "Female Empowerment in Africa: The
     Critical Role of Ecucation," *Times Higher Education*, 29 April 2017.
     https://www.timeshighereducation.com/blog/female-empowerment
     -africa-critical-role-education
216 *Strategies for Girls' Education* (New York: UNICEF, 2004).
     https://www.unicef.org/sowc06/pdfs/sge_English_Version_B.pdf
217 "Overview of Gender Parity in Education," *UNESCO e-Atlas of Gender
     Inequality in Education* (Paris: UNESCO, 2017). http://www.tellmaps.com
     /uis/gender/?lang=en#!/tellmap/-1195952519
218 *The World Bank in Kenya* (Washington, D.C.: World Bank).
     http://www.worldbank.org/en/country/kenya/overview
219 "Kenya," *World Factbook*.
220 Alex Cuadros, "The Most Important Criminal Conviction in Brazil's
     History," *New Yorker*, 13 July 2017. http://www.newyorker.com/news
     /news-desk/the-most-important-criminal-conviction-in-brazils-history
221 "Brazil: Economic Forecast Summary (June 2017)" (Paris: OECD).
     http://www.oecd.org/eco/outlook/brazil-economic-forecast-summary.htm

222 George Martine and Gordon McGranahan, "Brazil's Early Urban
     Transition: What Can It Teach Urbanizing Countries?" (London:
     International Institute for Environment and Development, August 2010).
     https://www.citiesalliance.org/sites/citiesalliance.org/files/IIED_
     Brazil%27sEarlyUrbanTransition.pdf

223 "The Future of World Religions: Population Growth Projections
     2010–2050" (Washington, D.C.: Pew Research Center, 2 April 2015).
     http://www.pewforum.org/2015/04/02/religious-projections-2010-2050

224 Sarah R. Hayward and S. Philip Morgan, "Religiosity and Fertility in the
     United States: The Role of Fertility Intentions," Social Forces, Vol. 86, No. 3
     (2008). https://www.ncbi.nlm.nih.gov/pmc/articles/PMC2723861

225 Ibid.

226 "Religion in Latin America" (Washington, D.C.: Pew Research Center,
     13 November 2014). http://www.pewforum.org/2014/11/13/religion-in
     -latin-america

227 P.J. Henry and Geoffrey Wetherell, "Countries with Greater Gender Equality
     Have More Positive Attitudes and Laws Concerning Lesbians and Gay Men,"
     Sex Roles, October 2017. https://link.springer.com/article/10.1007/s11199
     -017-0744-0

228 "Brazil Poverty and Wealth," Encyclopedia of the Nations.
     http://www.nationsencyclopedia.com/economies/Americas/Brazil
     -POVERTY-AND-WEALTH.html

229 Sarah de Ste. Croix, "Brazil Strives for Economic Equality," Rio Times,
     7 February 2012. http://riotimesonline.com/brazil-news/rio-business
     /brazil-strives-for-economic-equality

230 Bill Worley, "Brazil Saw More Violent Deaths Than in Civil-War-Torn Syria,
     Report Says," Independent, 29 October 2016. http://www.independent.co.uk
     /news/world/americas/brazil-deaths-violent-crime-syria-police-brutality
     -report-brazilian-forum-for-public-security-a7386296.html

231 Eduardo Marques interview with Darrell Bricker.

232 Teresa Caldeira, City of Walls: Crime, Segregation, and Citizenship in São
     Paulo (Berkeley: University of California Press, 2001).

233 "Brazil Slum Dwellers Shun Home Ownership, Fearing Gentrification,"
     Reuters, 3 February 2017. http://www.voanews.com/a/rio-slum-favela-home
     -ownership-gentrification/3705588.html

234 Interview with Darrell Bricker, conducted on a confidential basis. See also: Dom Phillips, "How Directions on the Waze App Led to Death in Brazil's Favelas," *Washington Post*, 5 October 2015.

235 Ipsos is one of the private sector funders of the drop-in center.

236 Leticia J. Marteleto and Molly Dondero, "Maternal Age at First Birth and Adolescent Education in Brazil," *Demographic Research*, Vol. 28 (10 April 2013). http://www.demographic-research.org/volumes/vol28/28/28-28.pdf.

237 George Martine, "Brazil's Fertility Decline, 1965–95: A Fresh Look at Key Factors," *Population and Development Review*, Vol. 22, No. 1 (March 1996).

238 Eliana La Ferrara, Alberto Chong, and Suzanne Duryea, "Soap Operas and Fertility: Evidence from Brazil," *American Economic Journal: Applied Economics*, Vol. 4, No. 4 (October 2012).

239 Martine, "Brazil's Fertility Decline."

240 Cynthia Gorney, "Brazil's Girl Power," *National Geographic*, September 2011. http://ngm.nationalgeographic.com/2011/09/girl-power/gorney-text

241 Martine, "Brazil's Fertility Decline."

242 Caldeira, *City of Walls*, 41.

243 Eric Wyman, "Becoming Human: The Evolution of Walking Upright," *Smithsonian.com*, 6 August 2012. http://www.smithsonianmag.com/science-nature/becoming-human-the-evolution-of-walking-upright-13837658

244 "What Does It Mean to Be Human?" *Smithsonian Institution's Human Resources Program*. http://humanorigins.si.edu/human-characteristics/humans-change-world

245 "The Genographic Project: Map of Human Migration," *National Geographic*. https://genographic.nationalgeographic.com/human-journey

246 Margot Pepper, "More Than Half of Americans Have Never Travelled Outside the Country—and a Third Do Not Even Have Passports," *Daily Mail*, 23 May 2013. http://www.dailymail.co.uk/femail/article-2329298/More-half-Americans-NEVER-traveled-outside-country--passport.html

247 Guy Abel and Nikola Sander, "Quantifying Global International Migration Flows," *Science*, 28 March 2014. http://science.sciencemag.org/content/343/6178/1520.figures-only

248 "Irish Potato Famine: Introduction," *The History Place*, 2000. http://www.historyplace.com/worldhistory/famine/introduction.htm

249 Jim Shaughnessy, "The Great Famine Coffin Ships' Journey Across the

Atlantic." *IrishCentral*, 18 June 2015. http://www.irishcentral.com/roots
/genealogy/the-great-famine-coffin-ships-journey-across-the-atlantic.
And "Irish Potato Famine: Coffin Ships," *The History Place*, 2000.
http://www.historyplace.com/worldhistory/famine/coffin.htm

250 "John F. Kennedy and Ireland," *John F. Kennedy Presidential Library and
Museum*. https://www.jfklibrary.org/JFK/JFK-in-History/John-F-Kennedy
-and-Ireland.aspx

251 Alexandra Molnar, *History of Italian Immigration* (South Hadley: Mount
Holyoke College, 9 December 2010). https://www.mtholyoke.edu
/~molna22a/classweb/politics/Italianhistory.html

252 Max Roser and Esteban Ortiz-Espina, "Global Extreme Poverty," *Our
World in Data*, 2013/2017. http://ourworldindata.org/data/growth
-and-distribution-of-prosperity/world-poverty

253 "Global Figures at a Glance," *Global Trends 2015* (Geneva: UNHCR, 2016).
http://www.unhcr.org/figures-at-a-glance.html

254 Bernard Wasserstein, "European Refugee Movements After World War
Two," *BBC History*, 17 February 2017. http://www.bbc.co.uk/history
/worldwars/wwtwo/refugees_01.shtml

255 "Flight and Expulsion of Germans (1944–50)," *Wikipedia*. https://en.wikipedia
.org/wiki/Flight_and_expulsion_of_Germans_(1944–50)

256 "World War II China: Refugees," *Children in History*. http://histclo.com
/essay/war/ww2/cou/china/home/w2ch-ref.html

257 Rana Mitter, "Forgotten Ally? China's Unsung Role in WWII," *CNN*,
31 August 2015. http://histclo.com/essay/war/ww2/cou/china/home
/w2ch-ref.html

258 *International Migration Report 2015* (New York: United Nations
Department of Economic and Social Affairs/Population Division,
September 2016). http://www.un.org/en/development/desa/population
/migration/publications/migrationreport/docs/MigrationReport2015.pdf

259 "Country Comparison: Population," *World Factbook* (Washington, D.C.:
Central Intelligence Agency). https://www.cia.gov/library/publications
/the-world-factbook/rankorder/2119rank.html

260 Ibid.

261 *Global Trends: Forced Displacement in 2015* (Geneva: UNHCR, 20 June 2016).
http://www.unhcr.org/576408cd7.pdf

262 "Nearly Half a Million Displaced Syrians Return Home," *Al Jazeera*, 1 July 2017.

http://www.aljazeera.com/news/2017/07/million-displaced-syrians-return
-home-170701040728296.html

263 *International Migration Report 2015.*

264 Ibid.

265 Ibid.

266 Ibid

267 Ibid.

268 Ibid.

269 Anna Gonzalez-Barrera, "More Mexicans Leaving Than Coming to the
     U.S." (Washington, D.C.: Pew Research Center, 19 November 2015).
     http://www.pewhispanic.org/2015/11/19/more-mexicans-leaving-than
     -coming-to-the-u-s

270 Keith Ellison for Congress, "Keith on ABC's 'This Week' 7/26/15," *YouTube*,
     24 May 2016. https://www.youtube.com/watch?v=FHkPadFK34o

271 "Full Text: Donald Trump Announces a Presidential Bid," *Washington
     Post*, 16 June 2015. https://www.washingtonpost.com/news/post-politics
     /wp/2015/06/16/full-text-donald-trump-announces-a-presidential-bid/
     ?utm_term=.ea78b474e6a9

272 Yankee Patriot News, "Trump: 'Compete Shutdown on Muslims Entering the
     United States—Speech," *YouTube*, 8 December 2015. https://www.youtube.com
     /watch?v=YWlQ3buH9FI

273 Jeffrey Sparshott, "Immigration Does More Good Than Harm to Economy,
     Study Finds," *Wall Street Journal*, 22 September 2016. http://www.wsj.com
     /articles/immigration-does-more-good-than-harm-to-economy-study-finds
     -1474568991

274 Ibid.

275 *International Migration Report 2015.*

276 "Worldwide Displacement Hits All-Time High as War and Persecution
     Increase" (Geneva: UNHCR, 18 June 2015). http://www.unhcr.org/news
     /latest/2015/6/558193896/worldwide-displacement-hits-all-time-high-war
     -persecution-increase.html

277 "Fecund Foreigners?" *Economist*, 30 April 2016. http://www.economist.
     com/news/international/21697819-immigrants-do-less-raise-birth-rates
     -generally-believed-fecund-foreigners?frsc=dg%7Ca

278 *World Urbanization Prospects: The 2014 Revision, Highlights* (New York:
     United Nations, Department of Economic and Social Affairs, Population

Division, 2014). https://esa.un.org/unpd/wup/Publications/Files/WUP2014-Highlights.pdf

279 Ibid.

280 Ibid.

281 Howard French, "How Africa's New Urban Centers Are Shifting Its Old Colonial Boundaries," *Atlantic*, 1 July 2013. http://www.theatlantic.com/international/archive/2013/07/how-africas-new-urban-centers-are-shifting-its-old-colonial-boundaries/277425

282 *World Population Prospects, 2017 Revision* (United Nations Department of Economic and Social Affairs/Population Division, 2017). https://esa.un.org/unpd/wpp

283 "China vs. United States," *Index Mundi*, 2017. http://www.indexmundi.com/factbook/compare/china.united-states

284 Branko Milanović, "Inequality in the United States and China," *Harvard Business Review*, 17 January 2014. https://hbr.org/2014/01/inequality-in-the-united-states-and-china

285 Feng Wang, "China's Population Destiny: The Looming Crisis," *Brookings*, 30 September 2010. https://www.brookings.edu/articles/chinas-population-destiny-the-looming-crisis

286 Joan Kaufman, "China Now Has the Lowest Fertility Rate in the World," *National Interest*, 1 December 2016. http://nationalinterest.org/blog/the-buzz/china-now-has-the-lowest-fertility-rate-the-world-18570?page=2

287 Aileen Clarke and Mónica Serrano, "See How the One-Child Policy Changed China," *National Geographic*, 13 November 2015. http://news.nationalgeographic.com/2015/11/151113-datapoints-china-one-child-policy

288 Xin En Lee, "What Does the End of the One-Child Policy Mean for China?" *CKGSB Knowledge*, 6 April 2016. http://knowledge.ckgsb.edu.cn/2016/04/06/demographics/what-does-the-end-of-the-one-child-policy-mean-for-china

289 Ibid.

290 Wu Yan, "Chinese Life Expectancy Up to More Than 76 Years," *China Daily*, 27 July, 2017. http://www.chinadaily.com.cn/china/2017-07/26/content_30256796.htm

291 Ibid.

292 Ibid.

293 Wang, "China's Population Destiny."

294 Marc Weisskopf, "Is a Pregnant Woman's Chance of Giving Birth
to a Boy 50 Percent?" *Scientific American*, 15 November 2004.
https://www.scientificamerican.com/article/is-a-pregnant-womans-chan

295 Kaufman, "China Now Has the Lowest Fertility Rate in the World."

296 Simon Denyer, "Researchers May Have 'Found' Many of China's
30 Million Missing Girls," *Washington Post*, 30 November 2016.
https://www.washingtonpost.com/news/worldviews/wp/2016/11/30
/researchers-may-have-found-many-of-chinas-30-million-missing-girls/
?utm_term=.d30effid7438

297 Wang, "China's Population Destiny."

298 Kaufman, "China Now Has the Lowest Fertility Rate in the World."

299 Susan E. Short, Ma Linmao, and Yu Wentao, "Birth Planning and
Sterilization in China," *Population Studies*, Vol. 54, No. 3 (November 2000),
pp. 279–91. https://www.ncbi.nlm.nih.gov/m/pubmed/11640214

300 Douglas Todd "High Birthrate Among Immigrant Women Has
Implications for Canada," *Vancouver Sun*, 8 August 2013. http://www.
vancouversun.com/life/High+birthrate+among+immigrant+women
+implications+Canada/8766093/story.html#__federated=1

301 "China's Demographic Divisions Are Getting Deeper," *Economist*, 21
September 2017. https://www.economist.com/news/china/21729573
-no-province-has-many-babies-some-shortfalls-are-much-worse-others
-chinas-demographic

302 Yang Fan, "Low Fertility in China: How Credible Are Recent Census
Data," International Union for Scientific Study of Population, undated.
https://iussp.org/sites/default/files/event_call_for_papers/Low%20
Fertility%20in%20China-How%20Credible%20are%20Recent%20
Census%20Data-YangFan.pdf

303 Kaufman, "China Now Has the Lowest Fertility Rate in the World."

304 Katie Ngai, "China's Population Could Drop Below 1 Billion by the End
of the Century," *Shanghaiist*, 2 July 2016. http://shanghaiist.com
/2016/07/02/china_population_to_drop_below_1_billion.php

305 "China's Demographic Divisions Are Getting Deeper."

306 Nita Bhalla, "Rickshaw Drivers Take 'Respect for Women' Message to
Delhi's Streets," *Reuters*, 12 November 2014. http://in.reuters.com/article/
india-women-autorickshaws-idINKCN0IW1GN20141112

307 Interview with Darrell Bricker.

308 K. Srinivasan and K.S. James, "The Golden Cage: Stability of the
     Institution of Marriage in India," *Economic and Political Weekly*, Vol. 50,
     No. 13 (28 March 2015).

309 "India Sees Huge Spike in 'Honour' Killings," *Al Jazeera*, 7 December 2016.
     http://www.aljazeera.com/news/2016/12/india-sees-huge-spike-honour
     -killings-161207153333597.html

310 Srinivasan and James, "The Golden Cage."

311 Interview with Darrell Bricker.

312 Ibid.

313 Interview with Professor K.S. James by Darrell Bricker.

314 Geeta Panday, "Why Do Women Go to Sterilisation Camps?" *BBC News*,
     11 November 2014. http://www.bbc.com/news/world-asia-india-29999883

315 Ibid.

316 Ibid.

317 Dhananjay Mahapatral, "Half of Delhi's Population Lives in Slums," *Times
     of India*, 4 October 2012. http://timesofindia.indiatimes.com/city/delhi
     /Half-of-Delhis-population-lives-in-slums/articleshow/16664224.cms

318 "'Pakistan Would Move Toward China, Russia, as US Is Declining Power,'"
     Times of India, 6 October 2016. http://timesofindia.indiatimes.com/world
     /pakistan/Pakistan-would-move-towards-China-Russia-as-US-is-declining
     -power/articleshow/54708689.cms

319 *Global Trends 2030: Alternative Worlds* (Washington, D.C.: National
     Intelligence Council, 2012). https://globaltrends2030.files.wordpress.com
     /2012/11/global-trends-2030-november2012.pdf

320 "QS World University Rankings 2016–2017," *QS*. https://www.topuniversities
     .com/university-rankings/world-university-rankings/2016

321 Ayez Ahmed, "Is the U.S. a Declining Power?" *International News*, 14 August 2016.
     https://www.thenews.com.pk/print/142341-Is-the-US-a-declining-power

322 "Best Selling Books of All Time," *James Clear*. http://jamesclear.com
     /best-books/best-selling

323 Ely Ratner and Thomas Wright, "America's Not in Decline—It's on the Rise,"
     Washington Post, 18 October 2013. https://www.washingtonpost.com
     /opinions/americas-not-in-decline--its-on-the-rise/2013/10/18/4dde76be
     -35b1-11e3-80c6-7e6dd8d22d8f_story.html?utm_term=.894898e7b074

324 Josef Joffe, "The Canard of Decline," *American Interest*, 10 October 2013.
     http://www.the-american-interest.com/2013/10/10/the-canard-of-decline

325 "Most Say Immigrants Strengthen the Country" (Washington, D.C.: Pew
     Research Center, 8 December 2016). http://www.people-press.org/2016/12
     /08/3-political-values-government-regulation-environment-immigration
     -race-views-of-islam/#most-say-immigrants-strengthen-the-country

326 Jens Manuel Krogstad, Jeffrey S. Passel, and D'Vera Cohn, "Five Facts
     About Illegal Immigration in the U.S." (Washington, D.C.: Pew Research
     Institute, 27 April 2017). http://www.pewresearch.org/fact-tank/2017
     /04/27/5-facts-about-illegal-immigration-in-the-u-s/

327 Nan Marie Astone, Steven Martin, and H. Elizabeth Peters, "Millennial
     Childbearing and the Recession" (Washington, D.C.: Urban Institute, April
     2015). http://www.urban.org/sites/default/files/alfresco/publication-pdfs
     /2000203-Millennial-Childbearing-and-the-Recession.pdf

328 Ibid.

329 Jeffrey S. Passel and D'Vera Cohn, "Number of Babies Born to Unauthorized
     Immigrants Continues to Decline" (Washington, D.C.: Pew Research Center,
     26 October 2016). http://www.pewresearch.org/fact-tank/2016/10/26/number
     -of-babies-born-to-unauthorized-immigrants-in-u-s-continues-to-decline/

330 David Drozd, "Tables Summarizing Births and Fertility Rates by Race
     and Ethnicity of the Mother in the U.S. and Nebraska, 1989–2013" (Omaha:
     Center for Public Affairs Research, University of Nebraska at Omaha,
     January 2015). http://www.unomaha.edu/college-of-public-affairs-and
     -community-service/center-for-public-affairs-research/documents/fertility
     -rates-by-race-ethnicity-us-nebraska.pdf

331 Ibid.

332 "Teenage Pregnancy in the United States" (Washington, D.C.: Centers
     for Disease Control and Prevention, 2016). http://www.cdc.gov
     /teenpregnancy/about

333 Douglas Main, "Why the Teen Birthrate Keeps Dropping," *Newsweek*,
     20 May 2015. http://www.newsweek.com/2015/05/29/why-teen-birth
     -rate-keeps-dropping-333946.html

334 Heather Boonstra, "What Is Behind the Decline in Teen Pregnancy?"
     Guttmacher Policy Review, 3 September 2014. https://www.guttmacher.org
     /about/gpr/2014/09/what-behind-declines-teen-pregnancy-rates

335 Eileen Patten and Gretchen Livingstone, "Why Is the Teen Birth Rate Falling?"
     (Washington, D.C.: Pew Research Center, 29 April 2016). http://www
     .pewresearch.org/fact-tank/2016/04/29/why-is-the-teen-birth-rate-falling

336 "African Americans Are Increasingly Affluent, Educated and Diverse,"
     Nielson Newswire, 19 September 2015. http://www.nielsen.com/us/en
     /insights/news/2015/african-americans-are-increasingly-affluent-educated
     -and-diverse.html

337 Laura Shin, "The Racial Wealth Gap: Why a Typical White Household
     Has 16 Times the Wealth of a Black One," *Forbes,* 26 March 2015.

338 "Are We Talking Enough About the Black Middle Class?" *Pacific Standard,*
     13 April 2015. https://psmag.com/are-we-talking-enough-about-the-black
     -middle-class-13dbfed92322#.r2eacnui1

339 "African Americans Are Increasingly Affluent, Educated and Diverse."

340 *The Condition of Education 2017* (Washington, D.C.: National Center for
     Education Statistics, May 2017). https://nces.ed.gov/pubs2017/2017144.pdf

341 John Gramlich, "Hispanic Dropout Rate Hits New Low, College Enrollment
     at New High" (Washington, D.C.: Pew Research Center, 27 September 2017).
     http://www.pewresearch.org/fact-tank/2017/09/29/hispanic-dropout-rate
     -hits-new-low-college-enrollment-at-new-high/

342 Anna Gonzalez-Barrera and Jens Manuel Krogstad, "What We Know About
     Illegal Immigration from Mexico" (Washington, D.C.: Pew Research Center,
     20 November 2015). http://www.pewresearch.org/fact-tank/2015/11/20
     /what-we-know-about-illegal-immigration-from-mexico/

343 D'Vera Cohn, "Future Immigration Will Change the Face of America
     by 2065," (Washington, D.C.: Pew Research Center, 6 October 2015).
     http://www.pewresearch.org/fact-tank/2015/10/05/future-immigration
     -will-change-the-face-of-america-by-2065

344 Teresa Welsh, "Minority Babies Outnumber Whites Among U.S. Infants,"
     McClatchy, 22 June 2016. http://www.mcclatchydc.com/news/nation-world
     /article85591172.html

345 Richard Alba, "The Myth of a White Minority," *New York Times,* 11 June 2015.
     http://www.nytimes.com/2015/06/11/opinion/the-myth-of-a-white
     -minority.html?_r=0

346 Ibid.

347 "Anti-semitism," *Father Coughlin,* 2017. http://www.fathercoughlin.org
     /father-coughlin-anti-semitism.html

348 Bilal Qureshi, "From Wrong to Right: A US Apology for Japanese Internment,"
     NPR, 9 August 2013. http://www.npr.org/sections/codeswitch/2013/08/09
     /210138278/japanese-internment-redress

349 G. Edward White, "The Unacknowledged Lesson: Earl Warren
     and the Japanese Relocation Controversy," *VQR*, Autumn 1979.
     http://www.vqronline.org/essay/unacknowledged-lesson-earl
     -warren-and-japanese-relocation-controversy

350 Stuart Anderson, "Immigrants and Billion-Dollar Startups," NFAP
     Policy Brief (Washington, D.C.: National Foundation for American Policy,
     March 2016). http://nfap.com/wp-content/uploads/2016/03/Immigrants
     -and-Billion-Dollar-Startups.NFAP-Policy-Brief.March-2016.pdf

351 Giovanni Peri, "Do Immigrant Workers Depress the Wages of Native
     Workers?" IZA *World of Labor*, May 2014. https://wol.iza.org/articles
     /do-immigrant-workers-depress-the-wages-of-native-workers/long

352 Gonzalez-Barrera and Krogstad, "What We Know About Illegal Immigration
     from Mexico."

353 Mick Dodson interview with Darrell Bricker.

354 John Ibbitson, *Stephen Harper* (Toronto: McClelland & Stewart, 2015),
     248.

355 Bernie Farber, "The Terrible Legacy of Duncan Campbell Scott,"
     Huffington Post, 23 January 2017. http://www.huffingtonpost.ca/bernie
     -farber/duncan-campbell-scott-legacy_b_14289206.html

356 "Aboriginal People in Canada: Key Results from the 2016 Census"
     (Ottawa: Statistics Canada, 25 October, 2017). http://www.statcan.gc.ca
     /daily-quotidien/171025/dq171025a-eng.htm

357 David Macdonald and Daniel Wilson, *Shameful Neglect: Indigenous Child
     Poverty in Canada*, (Ottawa: Canadian Centre for Policy Alternatives, 17
     May 2016). https://www.policyalternatives.ca/publications/reports
     /shameful-neglect

358 Matthew McClearn, "Unsafe to Drink," *Globe and Mail*, 21 February 2017.
     https://www.theglobeandmail.com/news/water-treatment-plants-fail-on
     -reserves-across-canada-globe-reviewfinds/article34094364/

359 Michael Shulman and Jesse Tahirali, "Suicide Among Canada's First
     Nations: Key Numbers," CTV *News*, 11 April 2016. http://www.ctvnews.ca
     /health/suicide-among-canada-s-first-nations-key-numbers-1.2854899

360 Vivian O'Donnell and Susan Wallace, "First Nations, Métis and Inuit
     Women," *Women in Canada: A Gender-Based Statistical Report* (Ottawa:
     Statistics Canada, 30 November 2015). http://www.statcan.gc.ca/pub/89
     -503-x/2010001/article/11442-eng.htm#a14. And Paula Arriagada, "First

Nations, Métis and Inuit Women," *Women in Canada: A Gender-Based Statistical Report* (Ottawa: Statistics Canada, 23 February 2016). https://www.statcan.gc.ca/pub/89-503-x/2015001/article/14313-eng.htm

361   "More Victims Tell of Sexual Abuse on Reserves," *CTV News*, 14 December 2011. http://www.ctvnews.ca/more-victims-tell-of-sexual-abuse-on-reserves-1.740390

362   Barry Anderson and John Richards, *Students in Jeopardy: An Agenda for Improving Results in Band-Operated Schools* (Toronto: C.D. Howe Institute, January 2016). https://www.cdhowe.org/sites/default/files/attachments/research_papers/mixed/Commentary_444_0.pdf

363   *Aboriginal Demographics from the 2011 National Household Survey* (Ottawa: Aboriginal Affairs and Northern Development Canada, May 2013). https://www.aadnc-aandc.gc.ca/eng/1370438978311/1370439050610

364   "Aboriginal People in Canada: Key Results from the 2016 Census."

365   "Births and Pregnancy Outcome," *Overview of Australian and Torres Strait Islander Health Status 2016* (Perth: Australian Indigenous Health Infonet, 2017). http://www.healthinfonet.ecu.edu.au/health-facts/overviews/births-and-pregnancy-outcomes

366   *Trends in Indigenous Fertility Rates* (Canberra: Australian Bureau of Statistics, 2010). http://www.abs.gov.au/ausstats/abs@.nsf/Products/8C7C1A01E4D5F9C2CA2577CF000DF0A7?opendocument

367   Simon Collins, "New Zealand's 'Baby Blip' Officially Over as Fertility Rate Drops," *New Zealand Herald*, 18 February 2015. http://www.nzherald.co.nz/lifestyle/news/article.cfm?c_id=6&objectid=11403961

368   C. Matthew Snip, "The Size and Distribution of American Indian Population: Fertility, Mortality, Migration, and Residence," in Gary D. Sandefur, Ronald R. Rindfuss, and Barney Cohen, eds., *Changing Numbers, Changing Needs: American Indian Demography and Public Health* (Washington, D.C.: National Academies Press, 1996). http://www.ncbi.nlm.nih.gov/books/NBK233098

369   Sarah Cannon and Christine Percheski, "Fertility Change in the American Indian and Alaska Native Population, 1980–2010." *Demographic Research*, Vol. 37, Article 1, 4 July 2017. https://www.demographic-research.org/volumes/vol37/1/37-1.pdf

370   Ibid.

371   Althea Sumpter, "Geechee and Gullah Culture," *New Georgia Encyclopedia*, 27 July 2017. http://www.georgiaencyclopedia.org/articles/arts-culture/geechee-and-gullah-culture

372 Katherine Shulz Richard, "The Gullah," *ThoughtCo*, 3 March 2017.
     https://www.thoughtco.com/the-gullah-language-1434488

373 "St. Helena Island, South Carolina Demographic Data," *TownCharts*.
     http://www.towncharts.com/South-Carolina/Demographics/St-Helena
     -Island-CCD-SC-Demographics-data.html

374 Alastair Kneale, "Increase in Manx Population Needs to Be Fought
     Tooth and Nail," *Transceltic*, 31 August 2015. http://www.transceltic.com
     /blog/increase-manx-population-threat-needs-be-fought-tooth-and-nail

375 Ellan Vannin, "Isle of Man Population Falls for the First Time in 30 Years,
     According to Census," BBC, 9 March 2017. http://www.bbc.com/news
     /world-europe-isle-of-man-39205163

376 Sarah Whitehead, "How the Manx Language Came Back from the Dead,"
     Guardian, 2 April 2015. https://www.theguardian.com/education/2015/apr
     /02/how-manx-language-came-back-from-dead-isle-of-man

377 Beatrice Debut, "Kenyan Tribe of Honey Eaters Faces Extinction," *Agence
     France Presse*, 10 July 2007. http://www.terradaily.com/reports/Kenyan
     _Tribe_Of_Honey_Hunters_Fights_Extinction_999.html

378 Ibid.

379 Peter Grant, ed., *State of the World's Minorities and Indigenous Peoples 2016*
     (London: Minority Rights Group International, 2016). http://minorityrights
     .org/wp-content/uploads/2016/07/MRG-SWM-2016.pdf

380 Ibid.

381 Genesis 11: 1–9, *The Bible* (King James Version). https://www.biblegateway
     .com/passage/?search=Genesis+11%3A1-9&version=KJV

382 Rikka Fredriksson, Wilhelm Barner-Rasmussen, and Rebecca Piekkeri,
     "The Multinational Corporation and a Multilingual Institution: The Notion
     of a Corporate Common Language," *Corporate Communications*, Vol. 11,
     No. 4 (2006), pp. 406–23.

383 Steffanie Zazulak, "English: The Language of the Internet," *Pearson
     English*, 21 August 2015. https://www.english.com/blog/english-language
     -internet

384 Stephen Anderson, "How Many Languages Are There in the World?"
     (Washington, D.C.: Linguistic Society of America, 2010). http://www
     .linguisticsociety.org/content/how-many-languages-are-there-world

385 "How Many Spoken Languages," *Infoplease*. http://www.infoplease.com
     /askeds/many-spoken-languages.html

386 "Languages of the World," BBC. http://www.bbc.co.uk/languages/guide
    /languages.shtml

387 "Are Dying Languages Worth Saving?" BBC Magazine, 15 September 2010.
    http://www.bbc.com/news/magazine-11304255

388 John H. McWhorter, "What the World Will Speak in 2115," Wall Street
    Journal Europe, 9 January 2015. https://www.wsj.com/articles/what-the
    -world-will-speak-in-2115-1420234648

389 "Arctic Mosque Lands Safely in Inuvik," CBC News, 23 September 2010.
    http://www.cbc.ca/news/canada/north/arctic-mosque-lands-safely-in
    -inuvik-1.907731

390 "Immigration and Ethnocultural Diversity in Canada" (Ottawa: Statistics
    Canada, 15 September 2016). https://www12.statcan.gc.ca/nhs-enm/2011
    /as-sa/99-010-x/99-010-x2011001-eng.cfm

391 "Population and Dwelling Counts," 2016 Census (Ottawa: Statistics Canada,
    15 November 2017). http://www12.statcan.gc.ca/census-recensement
    /2016/rt-td/population-eng.cfm

392 "A Long-Term View of Canada's Demographics," Century Initiative,
    2 October 2016. http://www.centuryinitiative.ca/2016/10/02/cboc

393 "Growth of the Canadian Population 2013–2063" (Ottawa: Statistics Canada,
    30 November 2015). http://www.statcan.gc.ca/pub/91-520-x/2014001
    /section02-eng.htm

394 "Immigration and Ethnocultural Diversity in Canada" (Ottawa: Statistics
    Canada, 15 September 2016). http://www12.statcan.gc.ca/nhs-enm/2011
    /as-sa/99-010-x/99-010-x2011001-eng.cfm

395 Teresa Welsh, "Five Countries That Take in the Most Migrants," US News,
    25 September 2015. http://www.usnews.com/news/slideshows/5-countries
    -that-take-the-most-immigrants

396 "Immigration and Ethnocultural Diversity in Canada."

397 Economist Intelligence Unit, "The Safe Cities Index 2015," 2015.
    https://dkf1ato8y5dsg.cloudfront.net/uploads/5/82/eiu-safe-cities-index
    -2015-white-paper-1.pdf

398 Derek Flack, "Toronto Named Most Diverse City in the World,"
    TOBlogspot, June 2016. http://www.blogto.com/city/2016/05/toronto
    _named_most_diverse_city_in_the_world/

399 Charlotte England, "Sweden Sees Record Numbers of Asylum Seekers
    Withdraw Applications and Leave," Independent, 25 August 2016.

http://www.independent.co.uk/news/world/europe/refugee-crisis-asylum
-seekers-sweden-applications-withdrawn-record-numbers-a7209231.html

400 A confidential conversation between a Swedish journalist and John Ibbitson,
winter 2016.

401 "Migrant Crisis: Migration to Europe Explained in Seven Charts," BBC
News, 4 March 2016. http://www.bbc.com/news/world-europe-34131911

402 Allison Jones, "Justin Trudeau to Syrian Refugees: 'Welcome Home.'"
Canadian Press, 11 December 2015. http://www.macleans.ca/news/canada
/justin-trudeau-to-syrian-refugees-welcome-home

403 Philip Connor, "USA Admits Record Number of Muslim Refugees in 2016,"
(Washington, D.C.: Pew Research Center, 5 October 2016). http://www
.pewresearch.org/fact-tank/2016/10/05/u-s-admits-record-number-of-muslim
-refugees-in-2016

404 Kathryn Blaze Carlson, "'None Is Too Many': Memorial for Jews Turned
Away from Canada in 1939," *National Post*, 17 January 2011. http://news
.nationalpost.com/news/none-is-too-many-memorial-for-jews-turned
-away-from-canada

405 John Ibbitson, "Poll Says Canadians Oppose Trudeau's Refugee Plan.
What Will History Say?" *Globe and Mail*, 24 November 2015. http://www
.theglobeandmail.com/news/politics/politics-notebook-poll-says-canadians
-oppose-trudeaus-refugee-plan-what-will-history-say/article27449197/

406 The authors made a similar argument in Darrell Bricker and John Ibbitson,
*The Big Shift: The Seismic Change in Canadian Politics, Business, and Culture
and What It Means for Our Future* (Toronto: HarperCollins, 2013).

407 Ramsey Cook, "Godwyn Smith," *Dictionary of Canadian Biography* (Toronto
and Montreal: University of Toronto and Laval University Press, 2017).
http://www.biographi.ca/en/bio/smith_goldwin_13E.html

408 "Sir Clifford Sifton," *Canadian Encyclopedia* (Toronto: Historica Canada, 2017).
http://www.thecanadianencyclopedia.ca/en/article/sir-clifford-sifton

409 "Prairie Immigration and the 'Last Best West,'" *Critical Thinking Consortium*.
https://tc2.ca/sourcedocs/history-docs/topics/immigration/the-last-best
-west.html

410 Erica Gagnon, "Settling the West: Immigration to the Prairies from 1867 to
1914" (Halifax: Canadian Museum of Immigration at Pier 21, 2016).
https://www.pier21.ca/research/immigration-history/settling-the-west
-immigration-to-the-prairies-from-1867-to-1914

411 Mohammed Omar, University of Ottawa graduate student, 2016, offered
     in class.

412 John Ibbitson, *The Polite Revolution: Perfecting the Canadian Dream*
     (Toronto: McClelland & Stewart, 2006).

413 Leah McLaren, "Canadian Martel Wins Booker," *Globe and Mail*, 23 October
     2002. http://www.theglobeandmail.com/life/canadian-martel-wins-booker
     /article757348

414 "Liberty Moves North," *Economist*, 29 October 2016. http://www.economist
     .com/news/leaders/21709305-it-uniquely-fortunate-many-waysbut-canada
     -still-holds-lessons-other-western

415 Allan Woods, "Canada Not Ready for Second Wave of Asylum Seekers,
     Union Head Warns," *Toronto Star*, 19 September 2017. https://www.thestar
     .com/news/canada/2017/09/19/5712-asylum-seekers-crossed-canada-us
     -border-in-august.html

416 Rebecca Joseph, "More Than Half of Canadians Think Ottawa Isn't in
     Control of Refugee Issue in Quebec: Ipsos Poll," *Global News*, 16 August
     2017. https://globalnews.ca/news/3673174/refugee-quebec-army-poll

417 John Ibbitson, "Immigration, Intolerance and the 'Populist Paradox," *Globe
     and Mail*, 18 June 2017. https://www.theglobeandmail.com/news/politics
     /immigration-intolerance-and-the-populist-paradox/article35355350

418 *Multiculturalism Policy Index* (Kingston: Queen's University). http://www
     .queensu.ca/mcp

419 Ingrid Perritz and Les Perreaux, "Quebec Reveals Religious Symbols to
     Be Banned from Public Sector," *Globe and Mail*, 10 September 2013.
     https://www.theglobeandmail.com/news/politics/quebec-unveils-plan
     -for-controversial-charter-of-values/article14214307

420 Jonathan Montpetit, "Quebec Group Pushes 'Interculturalism' in Place
     of Multiculturalism" *Globe and Mail*, 7 March 2011. https://www
     .theglobeandmail.com/news/politics/quebec-group-pushes-interculturalism
     -in-place-of-multiculturalism/article569581

421 "Quebec Immigration by Country," *Canadian Magazine of Immigration*,
     7 September 2016. http://canadaimmigrants.com/quebec-immigration
     -by-country

422 "Canada: Immigrants by Province—2016," *Canadian Magazine of
     Immigration*, 20 April 2017. http://canadaimmigrants.com/canada-immigrants
     -by-province-2016

423 Cynthia Kroat, "Viktor Orbán: Migrants Are 'a Poison,'" *Politico*, 27 July
     2016. http://www.politico.eu/article/viktor-orban-migrants-are-a-poison
     -hungarian-prime-minister-europe-refugee-crisis

424 Ibid.

425 "Hungary Population," *CountryMeters*, http://countrymeters.info/en/Hungary

426 "Hungarian: One of the Most Difficult Languages for Foreigners to Learn,"
     One Hour Translation. https://www.onehourtranslation.com/translation
     /blog/hungarian-one-most-difficult-language-foreigners-learn

427 Jodi Kantor and Catrin Einhorn, "Refugees Welcome," *New York Times*,
     23 December 2016. http://www.nytimes.com/interactive/2016/world
     /americas/canada-syrian-refugees.html

428 John Ibbitson, "Charter That Reshaped Canada Becomes a Model to the
     World," *Globe and Mail*, 16 April 2012, A1.

429 "Energy-Related Carbon Dioxide Emissions at the State Level 2000–2013"
     (Washington, D.C.: Energy Information Administration, 17 January 2017).
     http://www.eia.gov/environment/emissions/state/analysis

430 "An Average MTA Trip Saves Over 10 Pounds of Greenhouse Gas
     Emissions," (New York: Metropolitan Transportation Authority, January
     2012). http://web.mta.info/sustainability/pdf/2012Report.pdf

431 Linda Rodriguez McRobbie, "15 Fast Facts About the London Tube," Mental
     Floss, 1 May 2018. http://mentalfloss.com/article/33491/18-facts-and-figures
     -london-tubes-150th-birthday

432 *World Urbanization Prospects: The 2014 Revision, Highlights* (New York:
     United Nations, Department of Economic and Social Affairs, Population
     Division, 2014). https://esa.un.org/unpd/Wup/Publications/Files
     /WUP2014-Highlights.pdf

433 "The Risks of Rapid Urbanization in Developing Countries," (Zurich:
     Zurich Insurance Group, 15 January 2015). https://www.zurich.com
     /en/knowledge/articles/2015/01/the-risks-of-rapid-urbanization
     -in-developing-countries

434 Max Roser, "Land Use in Agriculture," *Our World in Data*, 2016.
     https://ourworldindata.org/land-use-in-agriculture

435 "U.S. Farms and Farmers," *2012 U.S. Census on Agriculture* (Washington,
     D.C.: United States Department of Agriculture, 2014).
     https://www.agcensus.usda.gov/Publications/2012/Preliminary
     _Report/Highlights.pdf

436 Michael Forsythe, "China Cancels 103 Coal Plants, Mindful of Smog
     and Wasted Capacity," *New York Times*, 18 January 2017.
     https://www.nytimes.com/2017/01/18/world/asia/china-coal-power
     -plants-pollution.html

437 Geeta Anand, "India, Once a Coal Giant, Is Fast Turning Green," *New York
     Times*, 2 June 2017. https://www.nytimes.com/2017/06/02/world/asia
     /india-coal-green-energy-climate.html

438 Justin Fox, "The De-Electrification of the U.S. Economy," *Bloomberg*,
     12 April 2017. https://www.bloomberg.com/view/articles/2017-04-12
     /the-de-electrification-of-the-u-s-economy

439 Gregory Brew, "The Secret Behind Better Oil Major Earnings," *OilPrice.com*,
     4 August 2017. http://oilprice.com/Energy/Oil-Prices/The-Secret-Behind
     -Better-Oil-Major-Earnings.html

440 "India's Coal Plant Plans Conflict with Climate Commitments," *Phys.Org*
     (Washington, D.C.: American Geophysical Union, 25 April 2017). https://
     phys.org/news/2017-04-india-coal-conflict-climate-commitments.html#jCp

441 Gregory Casey and Oded Galor, "Is Faster Economic Growth Compatible
     with Reductions in Carbon Emissions? The Role of Diminished
     Population Growth," *IOP Science Environmental Research Letters*, Vol. 12,
     No. 1 (5 January 2017). http://iopscience.iop.org/article/10.1088/1748-9326
     /12/1/014003

442 Rush Doshi, "Xi Jinping Just Made It Clear Where China's Foreign Policy Is
     Headed," *Washington Post*, 25 October 2017. https://www.washingtonpost.com
     /news/monkey-cage/wp/2017/10/25/xi-jinping-just-made-it-clear-where
     -chinas-foreign-policy-is-headed/?utm_term=.198413186a9

443 David Stevenson, *Cataclysm: The First World War as Political Tragedy*
     (New York: Basic Books, 2004), 15.

444 Mark L. Haas, "A Geriatric Peace? The Future of U.S. Power in a World
     of Aging Populations," *International Security*, Vol. 32, No. 1 (Summer 2007),
     pp. 112–47. http://www.belfercenter.org/sites/default/files/legacy/files
     /is3201_pp112-147.pdf

445 "Iran Attempts to Reverse Falling Birth Rate," *Associated Press*, 6 January 2014.
     http://www.telegraph.co.uk/news/worldnews/middleeast/iran/10554866
     /Iran-attempts-to-reverse-falling-birth-rate.html

446 Sarah Drury, "Education: The Key to Women's Empowerment in
     Saudi Arabia?" (Washington, D.C.: Middle East Institute, 30 July 2015).

http://www.mei.edu/content/article/education-key-women's
-empowerment-saudi-arabia

447 "Decline in Fertility Rate Among Palestinians, Says Statistics Bureau,"
     WAFA, 29 December 2016. http://english.wafa.ps/page.aspx?id
     =gedjk6a51964762047agedjk6

448 Bessma Momani, *Arab Dawn: Arab Youth and the Demographic Dividend They
     Will Bring* (Toronto: University of Toronto Press, 2015). Quote derived from
     a summary of the book presented by the author at an event sponsored by the
     Brookings Institution, 28 December 2015. https://www.brookings.edu/events
     /arab-dawn-arab-youth-and-the-demographic-dividend-they-will-bring/

449 Haas, "A Geriatric Peace? The Future of U.S. Power in a World of Aging
     Populations."

450 *Quote Investigator*. http://quoteinvestigator.com/2012/11/11/exhaust
     -alternatives

451 National Population Projections Team (report prepared by Nora Bohnert,
     Jonathan Chagnon, and Patrice Dion) *Population Projections for Canada (2013 to
     2063), Provinces and Territories (2013 to 2038)* (Ottawa: Statistics Canada, 2015).
     http://www.statcan.gc.ca/pub/91-520-x/91-520-x2014001-eng.pdf

452 *New Projection of Germany's Population by 2060* (Berlin: Federal Statistics
     Office, 2015).

453 John Bingham, "Average Life Expectancy Heading for 100," *Telegraph*,
     15 January 2015. http://www.telegraph.co.uk/news/politics/11348561
     /Average-life-expectancy-heading-for-100.html

454 "Biologist Believes Average Life Span Will Reach 150 by End of Century,"
     Toronto Star, 7 September 2015. https://www.thestar.com/life/health
     _wellness/2015/09/07/biologist-predicts-average-life-span-will-reach
     -150-by-end-of-century.html

455 Casey and Galor, "Is Faster Economic Growth Compatible with Reductions
     in Carbon Emissions?"

456 "Birth and Total Fertility Rate, by Province and Territory" (Ottawa:
     Statistics Canada, 26 October 2016). http://www.statcan.gc.ca/tables
     -tableaux/sum-som/l01/cst01/hlth85b-eng.htm

INDEX

A NOTE ABOUT THE TYPE

The text of *Empty Planet* has been set in Arno Pro, an old-style serif typeface designed by Adobe Principal Designer Robert Slimbach in 2007. Named for the Arno River that runs through Florence, Slimbach's font family also alludes to the Italian Renaissance in form by recalling late 15th century Venetian and Aldine faces. A multi-purpose and highly readable type well-suited for book design, Arno Pro is characterized by a constant stroke weight, a small x-height, and italics inspired by the *cancellaresca* of calligrapher and printer Ludovico degli Arrighi.